*I could hear everything, together with the hum of my hotel neon.
I never felt sadder in my life. LA is the loneliest and most
brutal of American cities... LA is a jungle.*
Jack Kerouac

Those who delight in dwelling on the macabre often embellish her history, elevating her role to budding movie starlet or making oblique references to her bit-part roles. But there were no bit parts, for the Black Dahlia was never a starlet. Like many thousands of young women who have haunted the streets of Hollywood before and since, she was never more than a pathetic shadow player at the fringes of a culture frantically fluttering around Hollywood's glowing lamp like a painted colony of doomed moths.
Marvin J. Wolf and Katherine Mader

She had been a pitiful wanderer, ricocheting from one cheap job to another and from one cheap man to another in a sad search for a good husband and a home and happiness. Not bad. Not good. Just lost and trying to find a way out. Every big city has hundreds just like her.
Jim Richardson, Los Angeles Examiner

Betty always wanted to be an actress. She was ambitious and beautiful, and full of life, but she had her moments of despondency. She was gay and carefree one minute, then blue and in the depth of despair the next... She was a good girl. I can't imagine who did this dreadful thing. I'm anxious to do anything to help in tracking down the fiend.
Phoebe Short, mother of the Black Dahlia

Elizabeth Short was always on the move, and she hadn't established any close relationships that we could pin down. Nobody seemed to know her very well, but they all remembered what she looked like. She made a vivid impression, but was very secretive about her private life. She was a loner.
Detective Vince Carter

FALLEN ANGEL

The Tragic True Story of the Black Dahlia

TROY TAYLOR

Dedicated to the memory of Beth Short -- the girl that found the fame in death that she so desperately wanted in life.

Special Thanks to:
Jill Hand -- Editor
April Slaughter -- Cover Design & Advice
Rene Kruse and Rachael Horath
Elyse Horath and Thomas Reihner
Del & Sandy Sapko -- for the awesome Black Dahlia tattoo on my back
Orrin Taylor
& Helayna Taylor

Original Cover Artwork Designed by
© Copyright 2013 by April Slaughter & Troy Taylor
Back Cover Author's Photo by Janet Morris

This Book is Published By:
Whitechapel Press
A Division of Apartment #42 Productions
Decatur, Illinois / 1-888-GHOSTLY
Visit us on the internet at http://www.whitechapelpress.com

First Edition -- June 2013
ISBN: 1-892523-84-1

Printed in the United States of America

NOTE FROM THE AUTHOR:

This is a book filled with lies -- but not lies of my own making.
The Black Dahlia case was filled with more lies than the reader can possibly imagine. The police lied. The district attorney lied. The witnesses lied. The coroner lied. Reporters lied. Authors who wrote about the case lied. And Beth herself lied compulsively. With that said, I have done the best that I could do to sort through the myriad of bizarre tales, false leads, outlandish theories and wild stories.
Any mistakes that you find within these pages are my own.
Someone probably lied to me.

HOLLYWOOD'S BILTMORE HOTEL

The lobby of Hollywood's Biltmore Hotel is crowded on a warm and sunny afternoon in early spring. A man crosses the room and taps on the call key for an elevator. As the door opens, he steps inside and presses the button for the eighth floor. As he does so, he notices that the button for the sixth floor is already illuminated. With a glance to his left, he realizes that he is not alone in the elevator. A dark-haired young woman stands in the corner and as he looks at her, she offers a faint smile.

The man smiles back at her and then looks up as the numerals above the door light up with the passage of each floor. He glances at the woman's reflection in the polished steel of the doors. Even in this blurred view, she is stunning. Her dark, nearly black hair is swept back and up in the outdated style of the 1940s, although it is very becoming on her. Her skin is pale against her jet-black dress. The shiny material clings to her every curve. She makes no sound other than the soft rustle of her dress.

Finally, the elevator reaches the sixth floor and with a soft chime, the doors slide open. The man steps aside to let her pass and notices that she is not moving. She continues to stand in the corner, seemingly unaware that the elevator has reached her floor. He finally speaks up, and his voice seems to startle the girl. He says, "This is the sixth floor."

She steps forward and moves past him off the elevator. As she does, the man trembles involuntarily. A wave of ice cold air seems to envelop him as the girl departs. Gooseflesh appears on his arms as he watches the shapely young woman walk past the doors. Then, just as she steps out onto the sixth floor, she turns back to look at him. She does not speak, but there is no mistaking the look of urgency in her blue eyes. She is begging him for help, the man realizes, but it's almost too late. The elevator doors have started to close, cutting off the young woman as she tries to re-enter the elevator. The man frantically pushes the button that will open the door and just before they close completely, they slowly start to slide open again.

But the girl in black is gone!

Confused, he leans out into the lobby of the sixth floor. He looks quickly in both directions, but the small lobby and the hallways in either direction are empty and deserted. Where could she have gone so quickly? He calls out, and his voice echoes in the stillness of the corridor. The young woman had vanished, as if she had never existed at all.

Two days later, the man is browsing in a local bookshop and happens to pick up a book about Hollywood's unsolved mysteries. As he flips through it, he is startled to see a face that he recognizes. It's the girl from the elevator! He examines the photograph and is convinced that it is the same young woman. But then he realizes such a thing is impossible. Scanning through the text, he sees that the girl died years before. How could she have been at the Biltmore Hotel just two days ago?

How indeed? Could this young woman who was killed in 1947 still be lingering at the last place that she was seen alive? Is she still looking for help - from the other side?

The young man didn't know it, but many others have recognized the beautiful girl in black. These other men also encountered her in the lobby, the elevators and the corridors of the Biltmore. The face they all recognized belonged to a lovely young woman named Elizabeth Short. In death, she would come to be known by a more colorful nickname: the Black Dahlia. Her tragic murder forever left a mark on the history of Tinseltown. She came in search of stardom but only found it in death, becoming lost in the netherworld that is the dark side of Hollywood.

1. A BRIGHT & GUILTY PLACE

Los Angeles, the fabled City of Angels, is home to the rich and famous, to palm trees, sandy beaches, orange groves, Disneyland and most of all, to that wonderful place of the American Dream known as Hollywood.

Like many people, I have always been fascinated by the glamour, the glitter and the decadence of old Hollywood. I have walked the Hollywood streets, and have searched for the names of my favorite celebrities along the Walk of Fame. I have stared in awe at the elaborate facade of the Chinese Theater and have pressed my palms into the cement handprints of film greats like Humphrey Bogart. I have always been intrigued by tales of the private lives of movie stars and by the secret inner workings of the great film studios.

But like Hollywood itself, its legends have a dark side. Around the time that I got interested in ghosts and hauntings I became interested in the less glamorous side of Hollywood. I learned that the bright photographs of its sunny streets hid whispers of crime and corruption and that its lavish homes and splendid architecture hid tales of spirits that did not rest in peace. There are many unsolved mysteries connected to Hollywood, as well as tales of scandal, depravity, murder, and, of course, ghosts.

The lure of Tinseltown has been a part of the American Dream since the first silent film makers came west to the small town of Los Angeles in the early 1900s. What began as a scheme by moviemaker Mack Sennett to make some extra money with a low-cost housing development called Hollywoodland became a movie colony for artists, writers and actors who came west to make it big.

Today, Hollywood remains not so much a place as a state of mind. In fact, it has not even been incorporated as a city since 1910, when in joined Los Angeles to share its water supply. It has a strange allure for those of us who have an interest in history, hauntings, and American crime, and for those who have lived their lives against the backdrop of the mythical silver screen. The history of the region is a dark journey through sordid tales of crime, corruption, murder and, of course, Hollywood-style scandal.

But there are few stories as lurid, terrifying and haunting as the story of the Black Dahlia.

Elizabeth Short was not the only victim to suffer a horrific death during the golden age of Hollywood. Crime thrived in the region, with the first narcotics being sold to the silent film stars, but real violence arrived with the start of Prohibition in the 1920s. As with just about everywhere else in the

country, the demand for illegal liquor was high in Los Angeles and there were dozens of bootleggers who were happy to bribe the cops to get the kegs and bottles into the right hands. With the booze came gambling and prostitutes, racetracks and boxing gyms - all of which served as a magnet for local gangsters.

And Hollywood could always be counted on for more than its share of corruption and scandal. The film industry, which was the largest business in the area by the 1920s, provided more than enough money for both excess and debauchery. A series of scandals rocked Hollywood in the early 1920s: the alleged rape and murder of Virginia Rappe by America's beloved funny man, Fatty Arbuckle, the drug-related death of Wallace Reid, the murder of director William Desmond Taylor and others. All of this gave America a front row seat to the secret activities of the movie colony and its shining stars. There was no doubt about it, with orgies, drugs, illegal hooch, and murder Hollywood had officially arrived!

LA was the scene of several sensational crimes by the late 1920s. They would be the first of many to come. In 1927, the kidnapping and dismemberment of 12-year-old Marion Parker shocked the nation. Especially chilling was the fact that the kidnapper had stuffed her dead body with rags and wired her eyes open to make her appear alive so that he could collect a $1,500 ransom from her father. In 1929, a gun battle between Jack Hawkins and Zeke Hayes and the LA police took place within the courthouse elevator.

The two men had long records, which included the alleged torture death of a San Francisco cop. When they were discovered in southern California, they found themselves set up for LA sheriff-style revenge.

These bloody crimes were just a foreshadowing of things to come.

Los Angeles continued to expand in the 1930s. Newcomers arrived on a daily basis. There were "Okies" looking for work who had been driven from their homes on the Great Plains by dust storms and economic disaster. There were scavengers looking for a quick buck and of course, dream-seekers who came to California hoping for their big break. Hollywood continued to serve as a beacon for would-be starlets and dreamers, but death and scandal sometimes shadowed even the brightest aspects of Tinseltown.

This was definitely the case with the death of actress Thelma Todd, who was brutally murdered in 1935. Though plenty of suspects and theories have been floated over the years, her murder remains unsolved. Combining the elements of gangsters, gambling, and a beautiful corpse, it was purely a Hollywood-style killing.

Another sensational case was the bizarre "Rattlesnake Murderer," which may have inspired James Cain's noir novel *Double Indemnity*. In this real-life story, Robert James was a man who loved women, kinky sex, and taking out insurance policies. He had already left a couple of dead wives behind him when he settled in Southern California. He opened a downtown barbershop and developed a noisy (according to neighbors), violent habit of lovemaking with his newly insured wife. When cash started running low, he killed her by thrusting her foot into a box that contained two rattlesnakes.

Despite a wave of reform that swept through the city in the late 1930s, as World War II loomed closer, reports of overseas fighting began to replace newspaper headlines about sensational crime. But the war began to expose other problems in LA, namely the inroads made by gangsters and the black market. Soon, readers were introduced to the king of the Los Angeles underworld, Mickey Cohen. He was the most recognizable of the city's gangsters, dressing the part in flashy suits and hanging out in all the right places. Connected to almost every type of vice in the city, he was constantly in the newspapers and was trailed by both the LAPD and the sheriff's department, who busted him for small infractions that inevitably revealed larger crimes. Rival mobsters made several attempts on Cohen's life, but it would be the FBI who would get him in the end. He was eventually imprisoned on charges of tax evasion. Apparently, Cohen failed to pay attention when Al Capone was tried and convicted on the very same charges.

Los Angeles and Hollywood changed after World War II. The end of the war saw the collapse of the black market and a decrease in crime. The postwar rise of Las Vegas emptied many of the nightspots of their big-name talent. Some of the larger venues closed down and smaller, "hip joints" became popular. The smaller clubs prospered and were joined by a few larger places like Ciro's, Mocambo, and the Crescendo on Sunset Boulevard.

In unincorporated parts of Los Angeles County, strip clubs, burlesque theaters, and gambling parlors added to the tawdry nature of the region. In the late 1940s, the Monterey Club, the Normandy, the Horseshoe, and several other lesser spots, provided a small, Vegas-style area where illicit activity was allowed to operate in obscurity.

Other nearby locations also offered assorted criminal activity. Palm Springs catered to both Hollywood stars and LA gangsters. The Dunes, a private gambling club run by former Detroit mobsters, was one of the swankiest places in town. Up in the mountains, film star Noah Beery ran a guest resort that offered untaxed, illegal booze in an isolated location that kept out the authorities. In nearby counties, those who went looking could find cockfights, dog racing, nudist colonies, and just about any other sort of vice imaginable. Small beach communities up and down the coast were favorite places to rendezvous for those trying to avoid cops and photographers.

Even though LA lost a lot of its crime after the war, the sex trade continued to operate uninhibited. In the late 1940s, Brenda Allen, one of the city's most notorious madams, faced a series of raids on her bordello. The case turned into a full-blown scandal when it was learned that a member of the vice squad was in Allen's pocket and that a lot of money had changed hands to keep her house of ill repute open. The scandal became more titillating when it was learned that scores of movie stars and film studio executives were listed in Allen's "black book." The case turned seamy and complicated and in the end, Allen was jailed, the chief of police resigned and a number of vice cops were demoted. As for the celebrities and movie executives who were caught using hookers - no one cared.

Several sordid and unsolved murders made headlines in the late 1940s. In June of 1947, a bullet to the head ended the life of Benjamin "Bugsy" Siegel, Hollywood's most notorious gangster. He had been killed in the Beverly Hills home of his girlfriend, Virginia Hill. There was much speculation as to who had "whacked" Siegel but it was considered to be a mob hit. Apparently, Bugsy had been skimming money from the construction of the Flamingo Hotel, the lavish gambling hot spot that would put Las Vegas on the map. Like most mob hits, Bugsy's murder has never been solved.

Also that same year was the murder of Jeanne French, a forty-five-year-old former socialite who had been one of the first nurses to fly aboard medical planes during World War II. Her battered, nude body was found in a vacant lot in the Mar Vista section of LA. The case was quickly coined the "Red Lipstick" murder due to the fact that her killer had used scarlet lipstick to write an obscene message on her torso. The search for the killer ended with no solutions and the crime remains unsolved.

But the most mysterious - and most gruesome crime - was the January 1947 murder of Elizabeth Short. Her dismembered body was discovered in a vacant lot in LA and would go on to become one of the most famous murders in the city's history. Dubbed the "Black Dahlia" by the local press, Short was the epitome of the small town girl who came to Hollywood to seek stardom. Her final months were traced back through the darker side of Hollywood and her mysterious and haunting murder remains unsolved to this day.

She found the fame in death that she never found in life.

2. SEVERED

The night of January 14, 1947 was a cold one in Los Angeles. A fruit frost warning had been broadcast on the late news and few people were out on the streets. There were only those who worked late, or those who were coming home from the movies or dinner and of course, the night people: the insomniacs, the homeless and the drunk. Downtown at the Hearst newspaper building, workers were preparing the presses for the midnight run of the *Examiner* - casting the lead plates, mounting the giant paper rolls, filling the ink tanks and setting up the rollers.

In the early morning hours - a few hours after midnight - of January 15, a young man in his early teens named Bobby Jones was walking his bicycle through a vacant lot near Thirty-Ninth Street and Norton Avenue in the Leimert Park neighborhood. He had gotten up before dawn to fold and prepare the newspapers for delivery on his route along Crenshaw Avenue. In those days, Leimert Park was a middle class neighborhood on the fringe of the more fashionable Adams District of downtown LA. The construction of new homes had been stopped by the war and the area north of Thirty-Ninth Street was home only to vacant lots and driveways that led to nothing but weeds and brush. The sidewalks, the fire hydrants and the driveways were there, but the houses had never been built.

Although it was dark when Bobby steered his bicycle through the weeds, he noticed a dark sedan with its lights off idling near the sidewalk. There were no streetlights nearby and he could not see the occupants of the car. There was no movement, save for the fluttering of exhaust smoke rising from the tail pipe into the chilly pre-dawn air. Assuming that the occupants were a passionate couple looking for privacy, Bobby steered his bike in the other direction and thought little of what he had seen.

Later, when he learned that whoever had been in that car had left something terrible in the nearby vacant lot, he tried to picture the faces behind the darkened windshield, but he could never envision them. He would only recall the dim flight reflecting on the windshield - and he would never forget it.

The sun rose that morning just before 7:00 a.m. but it did not burn fiercely enough to get rid of the foggy overcast for several hours. At about 10:30, a young Leimert Park housewife named Betty Bersinger was on her way to the shoe repair shop to pick up a pair of her husband's shoes. She brought along her three-year-old daughter, Anne, pushing her in a stroller down the sidewalk that bordered the vacant lots on Norton Avenue, halfway between Thirty-Ninth Street and Coliseum Avenue. As she walked, she caught a glimpse of something white lying in the weeds. She was not surprised; it wasn't uncommon for people to toss garbage there. This time, it looked as though someone had discarded a broken department store mannequin. The dummy had been shattered at the waist and the two halves lay separated from one another, with the bottom half lying twisted into a macabre pose. Who would throw such a thing into an empty lot?

Betty shook her head and walked on, but then found her glance pulled back to the ghostly, white mannequin. She looked again and saw what appeared to be red marks on the mannequin's face. She then realized to her horror that this was no department store dummy at all - the red marks were blood and the broken dummy was actually the severed body of a woman! With a sharp intake of breath, she covered her daughter's eyes to shield her from the gruesome sight. She ran to a nearby house, where she telephoned the police and tried to give a coherent report of what she had seen.

Just minutes after Betty Bersinger made her frantic call to the police, *Los Angeles Examiner* reporter Will Fowler and photographer Felix Paegel were returning downtown to the Hearst building from a story they had covered earlier that morning at the Beverly Hills Hotel. They heard a call go out over the police band for officers to report to an empty lot on Norton Avenue. It ended, "Proceed to investigate - Code Two."

"Code Two" meant that patrol cars in the vicinity should proceed to the scene as quickly as possible, but without lights and sirens. According to the call, there was a drunk woman at the scene, indecently exposed. Fowler and Paegel were only blocks away, so they decided to drive by and see what was going on. The two newspapermen turned out to be the first ones on the scene. Paegel was driving and as they passed the rows of vacant lots, looking for the drunk, naked woman, they glimpsed something lying in the weeds near the sidewalk. Fowler looked more closely and suddenly exclaimed that it was a woman who had been cut in half!

Fowler later recalled that horrifying moment, "It took a few minutes to get used to looking at this mutilated woman lying there like a discarded marionette that had been separated from itself - the torso was about a foot away from the legs and pelvis. Both halves were facing upward. Her arms were extended over her head. Her eyes were still half-open. There was no blood on the grass and her body was as white as marble."

Fowler had seen plenty of gruesome murder scenes in his career, but nothing like this. The dead woman's mouth had been cut from ear to ear and she looked like she had been badly beaten. While Fowler was studying the body, Paegel took out his Speed Graphic and began snapping photos. Within minutes, a police car pulled up to the curb and two officers - William Fitzgerald and Sgt. Frank Perkins - stepped out.

Fowler held out his press ID and explained who he was, but the two policemen weren't even listening. They were too shocked by the sight of the

The body of Beth Short as she was first seen by Betty Bersinger in the vacant lot. Police officers and reporters soon descended on the scene.

severed woman in front of them. Perkins immediately ordered Fitzgerald to get on the radio and call the watch commander to the scene. Returning to the patrol car, Fitzgerald grabbed the microphone and asked to speak to Lt. Paul Freestone, the watch commander on duty at the University Station on Jefferson Avenue.

In the days before cell phones, reporters always carried extra change in their pockets to phone in the news, so while the police were preoccupied with examining the body and calling for assistance, Fowler hurried to the nearest payphone. He dropped in a nickel and called his editor, Jim Richardson, at the *Examiner* city desk. Richardson refused to believe Fowler's description of the murder victim, but Fowler insisted that she really had been cut in half. Sensing a front-page story, Richardson told him to hurry in and start writing.

The city room was already buzzing about the murder when Fowler and Paegel arrived. Fowler began typing out the initial copy while Paegel's negatives were quickly processed. When the first 11 x 17 prints of the victim's severed body came out of the photo lab, Richardson called everyone on the city desk together and made all of them take a look. This is what they would be working on today, he told them. They were going to beat the afternoon papers with an extra edition.

By the time Fowler returned to Leimert Park, Norton Avenue was crowded with reporters and photographers. Uniformed officers were having trouble keeping back the crowd of curiosity-seekers. Reporters from the *Los Angeles Times*, the *Hollywood Citizen News* and the *Daily News* were there and Fowler spotted Agness "Aggie" Underwood, one of the few women journalists to break the gender barrier and become one of Hearst's top reporters. Aggie was the police beat reporter for the Hearst evening paper, the *Los Angeles Herald-Express*, and had a reputation for being hard as nails. But she was stunned by her first look at the murder victim. Although she had seen plenty of dead bodies in her career, when she saw the mutilated body in the weeds she staggered backwards off the edge of the curb and abruptly sat down.

Aggie had recovered her composure by the time Fowler returned to the scene. She had no idea that he had been there earlier and teased him about letting the *Times* beat him to the site. It wasn't until the *Examiner EXTRA* edition with Fowler's story and Paegel's photos beat the *Herald-Express* onto the street that Aggie realized Fowler had been there much earlier.

William Randolph Fowler was named after newspaper magnate William Randolph Hearst. His father, Gene Fowler, was a noted author and journalist. Will's father had worked for Hearst in the 1920s, when he was the managing editor of the *New York Daily American*. The family moved to California in 1935, when Gene Fowler became a prominent screenwriter at 20th Century Fox. Graduating from Beverly Hills High School in 1940, Will served in the coast guard during the war, before joining the *Examiner* in 1945 at the age of twenty-two. As a young man, he hung around with notable family friends like John Barrymore and prominent author and screenwriter, Ben Hecht, who had been a crime reporter in Chicago. W.C. Fields was his godfather. Will Fowler would become one of the main reporters covering the Black Dahlia story.

When Officer Fitzgerald informed Watch Commander Paul Freestone that they had discovered a severed corpse, Freestone sent Homicide Detective Jesse Haskins to the scene. After looking over the body, Lt. Haskins noted that the corpse was cold and alabaster white. The dead woman appeared to have been posed. She was lying on her back with her arms raised over her shoulders and her legs spread in an obscene imitation of seductiveness. Cuts and abrasions covered her body and her mouth had been slashed so savagely that her smile extended grotesquely from ear to ear. There were rope marks on her wrists, ankles and neck and investigators later surmised that she had been tied down and tortured for several days. She had been

Detectives and reporters flocked to the crime scene

sliced cleanly in two, just above the waist. Her body had been drained of blood and appeared to have been soaked in water. There was little or no blood on the grass. It was clear that she had been killed somewhere else and dumped in the vacant lot during the night.

With just one viewing of the scene, Haskins knew that this was unlike any murder he had ever encountered before. It was far beyond his experience and he was relieved when he received a call from Captain Jack Donahoe, chief of homicide in the Central Division, informing him that detectives Harry Hansen and Finis Brown from Central would be taking over the case. Detective Sgt. Hansen had been with the LAPD since 1926 and was the senior officer supervising most of the homicide investigations in Central's metropolitan district. Hansen was investigating a crime in downtown Los Angeles with Finis Brown when he received the call that morning from Captain Donahoe. He was instructed to go to Thirty-Ninth and Norton as quickly as possible.

By the time the detectives got to the scene, it was swarming with reporters, photographers and curiosity seekers. Hansen was furious that bystanders -- and even careless police personnel -- were trampling the crime scene. Hansen was the author of the police handbook on the protection of crime scene evidence and what he saw at the weed-covered lot on Norton

Avenue violated all the rules. Reporters had been allowed to roam the area, possibly obliterating tire tracks and footprints, and they had littered the scene with cigarette butts and burned flash bulbs. No one had bothered to block off the street, allowing spectators to wander about freely. Evidence was being destroyed, Hansen knew, and he immediately ordered the uniformed officers to clear the scene.

Detectives Finis Brown (left) and Harry Hansen (right) at the Black Dahlia crime scene.

Hansen told one of the officers to call Ray Pinker, head of the LAPD Crime Lab. "Get him over here," he ordered, as he knelt down at the edge of the sidewalk and studied the victim. Hansen was known for his scientific objectivity when investigating a murder case, but in more than twenty years of police work, he had never seen a victim so brutally mutilated. Finis Brown, his partner and close friend, later stated that Hansen's stoic nature was shaken by what he saw. Hansen also noted the rope marks on the girl's neck, wrists and ankles and the bruises on her face and forehead. Both cheeks had been slashed open. Her breasts were partially mutilated and her arms were bruised and bent at right angles over her head. There were knife marks in her pubic area and on her upper legs. When she was bisected at the waist, some of her organs had been removed. The body, Hansen and Brown knew

A horrifying police photograph of Elizabeth Short's body along the sidewalk of the lot.

immediately, had been deliberately placed on display near a public sidewalk. The killer wanted her to be discovered, and he wanted her discoverers to be shocked and horrified.

Based on the damp grass under the body, Hansen concluded that the remains had been placed in the lot sometimes between midnight and dawn. On the grass not far from the torso was an empty cement sack that appeared to have watery bloodstains on it. A bloodstain was also found on the sidewalk near the body and a man's bloody heel print was found near the victim's head. Not knowing for sure what they were dealing with, Hansen ordered the body to be covered until Ray Pinker arrived.

LAPD photo showing empty 50 lb. cement sacks, believed to be used by the suspect to transfer body parts from his car to curbside.

LAPD crime scene photo depicting Beth's severely mutilated body. It severed at the waist and completely drained of blood. Her face had been slashed from the corners of her mouth toward her ears,. Short also had multiple cuts on her thigh and breasts, where entire portions of flesh had been removed. One gash on her thigh was later discovered to mark the removal of a rose tattoo.

Pinker arrived shortly before noon. He was annoyed to find reporters were walking through the crime scene and told Will Fowler to move away. "I'm sorry," Fowler responded with gallows humor, "But you know how these suicides upset me."

Pinker examined the body and made the determination that the victim had been dead for ten hours - possibly longer. Pinker found that there was postmortem lividity on the front side of both parts of the body, indicating that she had been placed face down for some period of time after death. The multiple bruises, wounds and lacerations made it impossible to determine the exact cause of death; that would have to wait for an autopsy. Pinker discovered some bristle-like fragments on the victim's face and in her pubic region that he believed had come from a scrub brush. He also noted a four-

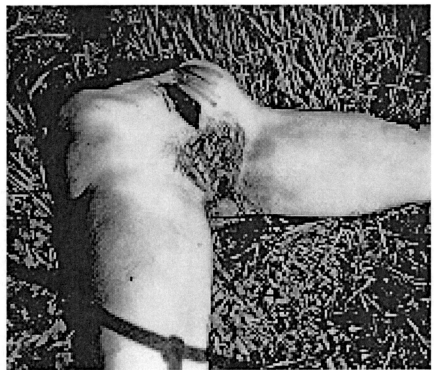

LAPD crime scene photo showing massive lacerations to Beth Short's vagina and gash in her lower abdomen — from which organs had been removed.

inch incision in the lower abdomen and that a portion of flesh that had been removed from the left leg above the knee. Pinker and Hansen surmised that the lower section of the body had probably been moved from a vehicle on the empty cement sack that was found near the body. Contours of the sack indicated that it might have been carried by more than one person.

Investigators knocking on doors in the surrounding area found a witness who corroborated newsboy Bobby Jones' story of seeing a black sedan idling at the curb early in the morning near where the body was found. Robert Meyer said that he saw a 1936 or 1937 Ford sedan drive up and park at the site in the hours before dawn. He told police that it stayed there for three or four minutes before driving away. He had seen nothing that made him suspicious, but admitted that the tall weeds in the vacant lot largely blocked his view.

Meyer believed that it was around 6:30 a.m. when he saw the Ford sedan, but Bobby Jones stated that he had seen the car around 4:00 a.m. Either one of them was wrong, or the vehicle was at the site two times that morning. Investigators found a man's wristwatch in the weeds near the body. It appeared to have been dropped there recently since it was not weathered. Could the killer have lost it when dumping the body at 4:00 a.m. and then returned to the scene at 6:30 to look for it? The police looked for fingerprints on the stainless steel backing of the watch, but apparently found nothing, since no further mention of it was ever included in the case files.

When Ray Pinker concluded his examination of the crime scene, he turned to Hansen and said, "This is the worst crime that I've ever seen committed on a woman."

No one who was there that morning - from Betty Bersinger to the reporters, the detectives, the crime lab investigators, the uniformed officers and the spectators - would ever forget what they had seen and none of them would ever be the same again. They seemed to sense that it was one of the worst murders that would ever occur in Los Angeles and they would be haunted by it for the rest of their lives.

3. JANE DOE #1

Hours passed and it was nearly 2:00 p.m. before a hearse arrived to take the body to the Los Angeles County Morgue, located in the basement of the Hall of Justice in downtown L.A. There, the remains were unloaded, wheeled up a ramp and tagged "Jane Doe #1."

The *Examiner's EXTRA* edition hit the streets at 3:00 p.m., beating all of its competing papers to the newsstands with the murder story by at least an hour. It was sold out by 5:30 p.m. and a second run of the *EXTRA* was sold out by 10:30. One of Paegel's photos of Jane Doe #1 was printed on the front page, but staff artists retouched her face, removing the gruesome slashes on each side of her mouth. A blanket was airbrushed in to cover not only her nudity, but also the fact that her body had been cut in half. It would be decades before uncensored photographs of the victim were published and the full horror of the killer's butchery was revealed.

The *Los Angeles Examiner's* headline story had a staccato quality that reflected the brutal elements of the murder:

Slain by a fiend, the body of a teenage girl was found in a vacant lot here yesterday.
The nude body was severed at the waist.
The girl had been killed elsewhere and her body taken to the lot and left in plain view, not three feet from the sidewalk.
Death came to the girl, police scientists said, after hours of torture.

The headlines had the savage punch of a radio news broadcast, hammering at readers in clipped, harsh syllables. Back in those days, few people had televisions. The one Los Angeles television station, KTLA, was only on air for three hours in the evening. The news belonged to the radio waves and the newspapers.

The evening *Herald-Express* referred to the murder as the diabolical act of a "werewolf fiend." In its final edition, the *Daily News* ran a four-column photo of the crime scene with an arrow pointing to the body under the headline - YOUNG L.A. GIRL SLAIN; BODY SLASHED IN TWO. The *Los Angeles Times* put the story on the front page of the morning edition on January 16. The headline was less lurid, but the article vividly described the victim's mutilations.

It was the Hearst papers that gave the story the biggest coverage. The *Los Angeles Examiner* and the *Herald-Express* outdid themselves in

Do You Know This Girl?

This is a photograph of an unidentified 'teen-aged girl found slain in a vacant lot on Norton avenue near Coliseum avenue. Picture was taken in death, but with marks of violence removed.

This artist's sketch was published in newspapers as the police (and reporters) tried to track down her identity. It wasn't a photo — the photographs were too horrible to print.

sensationalizing the already sensational and exploiting the murder in every way possible, living up to the attention-grabbing reputation that the Hearst papers were famous for. Their blood-soaked coverage sent shockwaves through the city and all of Southern California.

As if the basic facts in the case weren't horrible enough.

The body of Jane Doe #1 was moved to the LA County Morgue, but this did little to help with her identification. The body had been mutilated to such a degree that photos that were taken at the morgue could not produce a

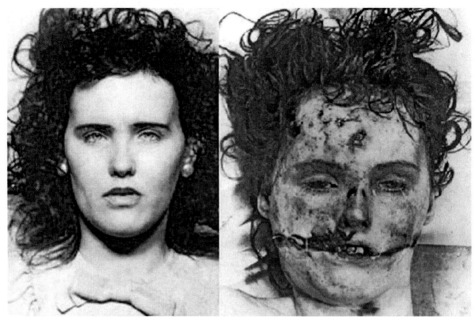

A "before and after" photograph of Beth Short and the body that had been dubbed as "Jane Doe #1" at the morgue, showing the extensive damage that had been done to her face by beatings and the knife cut to her mouth and cheeks.

true likeness - and they were too horrific to print in newspapers to ask for help from the public.

According to Finis Brown, the extent of the disfigurement had led Harry Hansen to believe that there had been a deliberate attempt to conceal the girl's identity. The knife slash through the mouth - from ear to ear - made her face unrecognizable and her fingerprints had been partially obliterated as the result of the body being immersed in water for an extended amount of time. As a result, the whorls and ridges of the fingertips had become grooved and shrunken. Nevertheless, Ray Pinker's crime lab team inked the fingers and did their best to transfer the prints to a fingerprint card.

Capt. Donahoe of homicide ordered Brown to keep him informed about every aspect of the case and when Donahoe learned that *Examiner* staff artist Howard Burke had been allowed into the morgue to make a sketch of the victim for identification purposes, he became furious. Brown explained that there were no usable photos of the girl, so they hoped that a sketch might be recognized by someone. Donahue was mollified by this, basically because the investigators had no other choice.

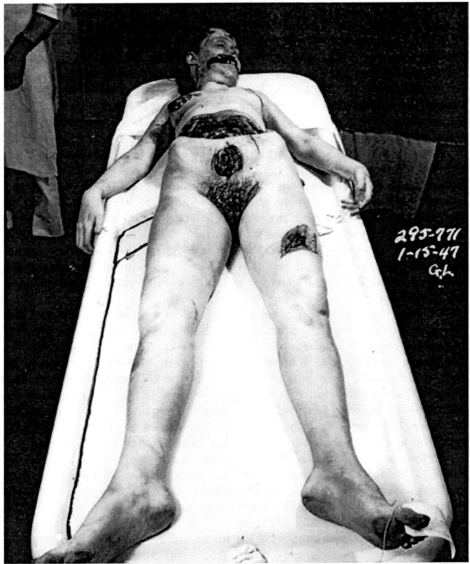

295-771
1-15-47
Gh.

Beth Short's body at the LA County morgue. She had been bound by her wrists and ankles and had sustained a heavy blow to her head. Official cause of death was attributed to blood loss from the incisions to her mouth coupled with shock as a result of a concussion.

The relationship between police officers and newspaper reporters was far different in the 1940s than it is today. Back then, they were less adversarial and recognized the need to cooperate with one another in a criminal investigation. In 1947, there were five daily newspapers in Los Angeles and all were fierce competitors - especially during a juicy murder story that captured the attention of the public. The force of highly motivated investigative reporters out on the streets trying to dig up scraps of information in time for deadline was much larger and more aggressive than the investigators of the LAPD. Thanks to this, there was a cooperative tradeoff of information between the police and the press - as well as a cooperative silence regarding information that the LAPD wanted to keep under wraps.

According to Will Fowler, when the *Examiner* learned that the crime lab had sent the fingerprint card of Jane Doe #1 to Washington, D.C., editor Jim Richardson had managing editor Warden Woolard call Capt. Donahoe and request that the LAPD give the *Examiner* a copy of the prints. Thanks to winter storms that had closed the airports in Washington, it would take days for the FBI to be able to examine the prints. Woolard suggested sending the prints to the FBI via the Hearst electronic Soundphoto service, a new system for transmitting photographs instantly to Hearst editorial offices around the country. Nothing like that had ever been done before, but Woolard believed that it would work.

Knowing that the investigation was going to be stymied by the fact that the victim was unidentified, Donahoe felt there was no harm in cooperating and sent a copy of Jane Doe #1's prints to the *Examiner* newsroom. For the first time in the history of criminal investigation, at 4:00 a.m. on January 16, 1947, a fingerprint card was transmitted to the FBI via Soundphoto. Ray Richards, head of the Hearst Newspapers Washington Bureau, received the prints from the machine and had them immediately taken to the FBI fingerprint file room. Unfortunately, though, the FBI fingerprint experts were initially unable to work with the Soundphoto prints because they lacked clarity.

Undaunted, the *Examiner* photo lab made a new photocopy, blew up the prints to a larger size and transmitted enlarged negatives rather than positives. This proved to be a success. Within an hour, FBI experts were able to identify Jane Doe #1 as Elizabeth Short, age twenty-two, born in Hyde Park, Massachusetts, on July 29, 1924.

Elizabeth Short had been arrested on September 23, 1943 with a group of soldiers and other young girls who were drinking and causing a disturbance near Camp Cooke (now Vandenberg Air Force Base), an army base north of Santa Barbara, California. Because she was a minor and unaccompanied by a parent or guardian, she'd been taken into custody, booked and fingerprinted. Her prints were still on file with the FBI and clearly matched those of Jane Doe #1.

By late morning on Thursday, January 16, the *Examiner* knew the victim's identity and broke the story in the morning edition of Friday, January 17. Thanks to their fingerprint coup, the *Examiner* had managed to scoop their

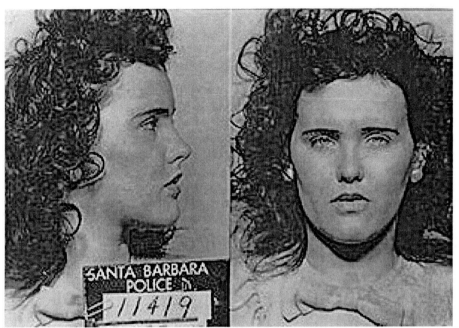

Elizabeth Short mugshot from her arrest in Santa Barbara a few years before her death. She was 19 years old and arrested for underage drinking.

rivals. By the time that the other newspapers in town learned Elizabeth Short's identity, *Examiner* reporters were already digging into her life. Will Fowler later said, "Richardson's crew worked so effectively with the clues we were digging up on our own that we were able to start making deals with LAPD homicide. This made Capt. Donahoe fume, but he had to go along."

Jim Richardson had a reputation for sharing William Randolph Hearst's penchant for sensational news, and he worked relentlessly to beat the competition with the latest scoop. He was merciless and even his own reporters disliked him. He was a genius when it came to gathering news but the demands on his staff were so great that many broke under the pressure. He was described as "inhuman" from the moment he walked into the city room in the morning, until after deadline, when the next day's edition was locked in. But if he managed to win the "scoop war," the staff could actually breathe easy for one day. They were definitely breathing easy in January 16 - but the pressure was on to find out everything they could about Elizabeth Short.

4. THE AUTOPSY

On January 16, at 10:30 a.m. - approximately the same time that Jane Doe #1 was identified as Elizabeth Short - her autopsy began in the dank basement of the Los Angeles Hall of Justice.

Over time, the LA County Coroner's Office has become one of the most famous in the world. The morgue has played host to the final remains of some of Hollywood's biggest celebrities and infamous characters, including Marilyn Monroe, William Desmond Taylor, Thelma Todd, gangster Ben "Bugsy" Siegel, George Reeves, Robert Kennedy, Sharon Tate, Janis Joplin, and many others. But it had a humble start in the earliest days of the city. In 1850, when California joined the Union, "El Pueblo de la Reina de Los Angeles" (The Town of the Queen of the Angels) averaged one murder each day, making the four thousand-person, tumbleweed town one of the wildest in the West.

The newly written California constitution divided the state into eighteen counties, requiring each to set up a coroner's office staffed by a single investigator who reported to the county clerk. To determine a cause of death back then, the coroner relied on his deductive skills, but if a case proved to be particularly complex, he would hold an inquest where, in a courtroom setting, a coroner and jury heard witnesses and defendants testify. The coroner then presented a report of the jury's findings to the country clerk.

By the 1920s, the county's population had swollen to over one million, and the eight-man Coroner's Office investigated about twenty-five hundred cases each year. The Depression fueled suicides, including many connected to what became known as "Suicide Bridge." The Colorado Street Bridge, which spans the Arroyo Seco in Pasadena, was the site of ninety-five suicides from 1919 to 1937.

To meet the increasing caseload, the county opened a central Coroner's Office in the basement of the Hall of Justice downtown and expanded the staff to include autopsy surgeons, inquest deputies, deputy coroners, and embalming technicians. Inquests and investigations remained the coroner's main tools to determine cause of death, but as forensic medicine advanced, autopsies grew in importance. By the 1940s, with the county population approaching three million, the Coroner's Office saw its caseload top more than five thousand per year.

And such was the state of the office when the body of Elizabeth Short found its way to the autopsy table. Her autopsy was to be conducted by Dr.

The LA County Coroner's Office

Frederick Newbarr, the chief autopsy surgeon for the County of Los Angeles. Dr. Victor Cefalu was assigned to be his assistant.

Dr. Newbarr concluded that the immediate cause of death was hemorrhage and shock due to the deep knife lacerations of the face and repeated heavy blows by a metal object to the face and right side of the head. Newbarr stated, "There were deep ridges on her ankles, thighs, wrists, and neck, indicating that she had been tied with rope or wire. The victim's mouth had been slit at each side to the ears while she was still alive. The excruciating pain of this would bring on shock... The blows to the face and head and the brain concussion came from blows from an iron instrument with a blunt edge." He believed that this had occurred after the cutting of the face. The bruises and marks around the cuts only occurred when the circulation of blood was unimpaired. But all of the other mutilations of the corpse were carried out after she was dead. One of the deep lacerations on the left thigh eventually proved to be where the killer sliced off a tattoo, which would have aided in the identification process. Dr. Newbarr was quoted in the press as saying that he believed the victim was "killed and mutilated while tied in a bath tub."

What was clear to Newbarr - and the investigators who studied the corpse where it was found - was that the deep cuts on the face were not done by the same instrument that was used to slice the body in half. The slashed mouth exhibited the ragged cuts of a knife, while the mutilation and bisection of the body was carried out methodically with a surgical instrument, apparently by someone who was familiar with surgical procedures. There were two different cutting instruments, two different cutting methods - one instrument used before death and one after. The fact that the body had been bisected by someone with advanced surgical knowledge was not disclosed at the time and the withholding of this vital information led to a misconception of the crime by both the press and the public that has been perpetuated for decades.

The slashed mouth and the blows to the head were characteristic of a rage murder, while the meticulous bisection of the corpse with surgical instruments showed a more methodical pathology, suggesting that more than one person many have been involved in the murder and the disposition of the body. There was no indication that the victim had been raped and an examination turned up no sign of sperm or recent sexual intercourse.

Autopsy reports are ordinarily a part of the public record, however, Elizabeth Short's autopsy report was not made available to the public. The original explanation for the sealed report was Capt. Donahoe's claim that it contained certain information that would be known only to the killer and that detectives would use this as a "control question" when establishing the credibility of a prime suspect. Although many former LAPD homicide detectives, including Harry Hansen, long ago conceded that the murderer was deceased, up until the end of the twentieth century, the LA County Coroner's Office continued to refuse the release of Elizabeth Short's autopsy report, stating that it was being sealed because the case was unsolved. Yet, there is no other cold case homicide on record in Los Angeles for which the autopsy report was not made public. In 2003, the Coroner's Office claimed that the report had been lost, even though duplicate copies of all autopsy reports were put on microfiche in the 1970s. What was the secret that was known only to Capt. Jack Donahoe, Medical Examiner Newbarr, Finis Brown, Harry Hansen and the killer?

Over the years, various rumors regarding this secret have been spread. When *Examiner* editor Jim Richardson approached Donahoe in an attempt to get a copy of the autopsy report, Donahoe told him why the report and its secret could not be released. Will Fowler recalled that Donahoe privately informed Richardson of the secret on the condition that it would never be printed in the newspaper. Fowler said that Donahoe had told Richardson that the killer had inserted an earlobe, as well as the tattooed flesh cut the victim's thigh, into her vagina. However, photos indicate that her earlobes were intact, and if the tattoo was cut from the body to avoid identification, it was unlikely that her killer would have left it with the corpse. According to Fowler, Richardson knew that Donahoe didn't tell him the truth. Nevertheless, this unpublished information was circulated as hearsay in the *Examiner* newsroom at the time. Similar rumors regarding the mysterious autopsy secret continued for years.

Police detectives had counted on the postmortem to provide some answers in the case, but the autopsy seemed to pose more questions than answers. In Hansen's experience, the method of Elizabeth Short's murder had never occurred before - the slashing of the mouth, the blows to the head, the mutilation and bisection of the body, the draining of blood, the attempt to prevent identification, the immersion in water, the transport of the remains on an empty sack found near the body, and the placement and display of the corpse near the sidewalk of a public street. This strange *modus operandi* told a terrible story in a convoluted language of the deranged.

There had been many brutal unsolved slayings of young women in the past, but no similar method could be found in the homicide files of the LAPD, nor would anything like it ever occur again during the remaining twenty-three years that Harry Hansen was on the force. The stark image of Elizabeth Short's mutilated body, lying in the weeds of the vacant lot, would stay with Detective Hansen for the rest of his life.

5. THE NEWS THAT'S FIT TO PRINT

When the *Los Angeles Examiner* identified the victim as Elizabeth Short, Jim Richardson sent Will Fowler to Santa Barbara to find out more about her 1943 arrest. He soon learned that following her arrest for underage drinking, Elizabeth Short had been sent back home to her mother, Phoebe Short, who lived in Medford, Massachusetts, a Boston suburb. Included in the arrest record were mug shots that were taken when she was booked. Fowler later recalled being struck by Elizabeth's eyes, which had a vacant look in the photograph but yet "reflected a sort of inquisitive innocence." He noted, "Her skin looked as though it had the quality of alabaster. Her dark, curly hair loosely draping this inculpable stare suggested she might have been a beautiful woman."

The *Examiner's* headline story for January 17 included the Santa Barbara police photos and an interview with a Santa Barbara policewoman named Mary H. Unkefer, the juvenile officer who had been called into the case when Elizabeth Short was arrested and it was learned she was a minor. Unkefer recalled that Elizabeth Short was living in a bungalow court with a young woman named Vera Green. There had been four soldiers from Camp Cooke in their bungalow when they were arrested. The neighbors had complained about a wild party and it was obvious to the responding officers that the soldiers were staying there for the weekend and that a good deal of drinking was going on. Vera Green initially claimed that one of the soldiers was her husband, but it was later learned that her husband was serving in the army overseas. While Elizabeth was waiting action on juvenile probation, Mary Unkefer allowed her to stay in her home. She recalled, "She was a very nice girl and was most neat about her person and clothes." When she was released by the courts, Unkefer put her on a bus for Massachusetts and gave her $10 for expense money.

Unkefer also mentioned the rose tattoo that the killer had removed from Short's left thigh. She said the girl liked to sit with her skirt hiked up sideways so that it would show. She also made another comment about Short's hair: "She had the blackest hair that I ever saw." At the time of her death, Elizabeth's hair was hennaed, but the dark roots were starting to grow in. Henna is a reddish dye made from a tropical plant. It was a popular hair dye in the 1940s. But everyone who knew Elizabeth Short prior to her disappearance could only recall her having jet-black hair. Will Fowler recalled that the corpse in the vacant lot had "reddish-brown" hair and the Jane Doe description at the morgue noted that the hair was "hennaed." If the *Examiner* article was correct in stating that her original hair color was starting to grow back in, then it can be assumed that her hair was dyed at least a week or two prior to her death, which would indicate that she tried to change her appearance shortly before she was murdered. It was also observed that her eyebrows had been lightened, as well.

When Will Fowler returned to the *Examiner* offices with copies of the photographs and arrest record, Richardson assigned Wayne Sutton to locate Elizabeth Short's mother. Sutton managed to obtain Phoebe Short's telephone number from Medford information and - for reasons that cannot be explained in human terms - Richardson told Sutton not to break the news about her daughter's murder until he had gotten as much background information from her as possible. Richardson said to tell Mrs. Short that Elizabeth had won a beauty contest in Santa Barbara. Once he got background material, then he could tell her that her daughter had been murdered. Richardson listened in on an extension as Sutton made the horribly cruel telephone call.

Sutton later recalled that Mrs. Short was overjoyed to hear the good news about her daughter and went on and on about Betty's (as she was known to the family) special beauty and charm. She told him about other beauty contests that she had won, including one in Medford. Stricken by what he was doing, Sutton glared at Richardson, cupped his hand over the phone and swore at him. Richardson was unfazed and ordered him to keep going.

Phoebe told Sutton that many men found Betty to be attractive and commented on a letter that she had recently received from her daughter, dated January 8, 1947. It had been written while Betty was visiting friends in San Diego and she told her mother that she was returning to Los Angeles with a man whom Betty referred to as "Red." Richardson urged Sutton to get the return address from her and once he had it, Richardson instructed him to tell her the truth about what had happened to her daughter.

After breaking the tragic news, Sutton recalled that Mrs. Short stayed on the line, insisting it had to be some sort of mistake, and that it was not really her daughter that he was talking about. When it was clear it was no mistake, she demanded to know "exactly what happened." Sutton tried to enlist her cooperation, telling her that the *Examiner* would pay her for her airfare and hotel if she would fly to Los Angeles for the inquest, which was scheduled for Wednesday, January 22. To Richardson's delight, she agreed to the offer, in hopes that she might be able to help in some way. But Richardson's real plan was to keep Mrs. Short in seclusion and away from

Beth Short's mother, Phoebe

the police and rival reporters long enough to get more information out of her.

In the meantime, Richardson had another scoop - and an address in San Diego where she had been staying only a week before her body was discovered. He also knew that she had been traveling with a man she referred to as "Red." Sutton later wrote that Richardson had no intention of sharing the San Diego lead with Capt. Donahoe - at least not until the *Examiner* could track down Red. By the time that Sutton hung up the phone, Richardson had already assigned two reporters, Tom Devlin and George O'Day, to immediately head south to San Diego.

Reading about the cruel telephone call made to Phoebe Short in 1947, most of us shudder in sympathy, but back then, deception and insensitivity was just part of the newspaper business - especially at the Hearst papers. They had a reputation that dated all of the way back to Hearst's start in New York at the *Journal*. He began battling it out with Joseph Pulitzer's *New York World*, which was at the top of the heap in the city as an innovative and cartoon-friendly newspaper. In 1895, the *World* launched the seminal *Hogan's Alley* comic strip, featuring a barefoot character whose oversized yellow shirt earned him the nickname of the "Yellow Kid." In the *New York Journal*, William Randolph Hearst created his own yellow kid cartoon, a blatant knock-off that stoked the feud between him and Pulitzer. Their subsequent attempts to out-sensationalize each other in print birthed the term "yellow journalism." This was most obvious in their coverage of murders. Screenwriter and novelist Ben Hecht, who had worked as a crime reporter for Hearst in Chicago, famously quipped, "A Hearst newspaper is like a screaming woman running down the street with her throat cut."

While the Hearst papers were known for their quick nickel approach to the news, LA's *Daily News* was more liberal. Originally founded in 1923 by Cornelius Vanderbilt, Jr. as a penny paper, the *Daily News* was taken over by Manchester Boddy in 1932. The paper endorsed Franklin D. Roosevelt and the New Deal and for decades, was the only liberal voice among the Los Angeles newspapers. The *Daily News* did not have the large staff of the *Los Angeles Times* or the Hearst papers. While the *Examiner* had a dozen reporters working the Black Dahlia story, the *Daily News* could only spare two, so the city desk was starving for copy. Roy Ringer was a new office employee at the *Daily News* when the Black Dahlia story broke and he later recalled that the *News* was getting hammered by Richardson and the *Examiner* scoops. Because Ringer was new on the job and unknown to competing reporters, the city desk sent him over to the *Examiner* on a spy mission. Ringer walked casually into the nearby *Examiner* building and entered the composing room, where he spotted the Dahlia story proofs hanging on spikes for the copy boys. He began stealing one of these proofs every day and racing back to the *Daily News* city desk, where the Dahlia story would be re-written. Often, it would be out on the streets before the *Examiner*. On the fourth day of his enterprising newsgathering, he felt a hand clamp down on his shoulder - it was Richardson. "Nice try," he was told and he was kicked out of the building and told not to come back.

The *Los Angeles Times* was the more conservative of the city's papers and did not engage in the lurid sensationalism of the Hearst papers, nor did it care to lead an active investigation into the murder of Elizabeth Short. The *Times* had been owned and operated by the Chandler family since the 1880s and under the rule of patriarch Harry Chandler, they literally ran the city - making appointments to the Chamber of Commerce and nominating and overseeing the election of mayors and appointments of police chiefs, sheriffs and city commissioners. During the first half of the twentieth century, the Chandlers were the political and social voice of Southern California and they spoke through the *Los Angeles Times*. Candidates for political office in LA knew that the support of Harry Chandler and the *Times* was required if they hoped to win. No mayor could be elected if he was not a Chandler choice. As insurance, Chandler always made sure that he had a majority vote of fifteen city councilmen in his pocket. A city council majority could always override an uncooperative mayor.

While the mayor's office and city council were Chandler's main power hold on the city, full control of Los Angeles depended on domination of the police department. Chandler accomplished this through a five-man police commission and it was Chandler's man - the mayor - who appointed the police commissioners. Chandler only needed three men on his side for a majority, but he usually controlled all three. This meant that Chandler controlled the LAPD.

At the time of the Black Dahlia case, the police chief was Clemence B. Horrall, a Chandler choice who had been appointed by the Chandler-controlled commission. It was common knowledge that the upper echelons of the police department and mayor's office were receiving payoffs from underworld figures like Mickey Cohen, Jack Dragna and Ben Siegel, but Chandler was not concerned, as long as it was discreet. Both William Randolph Hearst and Harry Chandler had relied on the so-called "Red Squad" within the LAPD to break the labor strikes that often plagued the newspapers, movie studios and the city's industries. The Red Squad often recruited mob goons to threaten, intimidate, beat and kidnap troublesome labor leaders. Through Chandler and his hand-picked men in the police department, the leading businessmen and film studio moguls of Los Angeles could get just about anything taken care of, accomplished and swept under the rug.

As additional control of the city police department, Chandler circumvented the city charter provisions and had Mayor Fletcher Bowron appoint an assistant police chief. Prior to 1939, there had never been an assistant chief in Los Angeles, but at the behest of Harry Chandler, Bowron appointed Chandler aide Joe Reed as assistant chief to Clemence B. Horrall. Reed was placed in power over the heads of police inspectors and deputy chiefs who should have been next in line for the new position. Reed was Chandler's chief operative within the department, reporting back to Chandler as a liaison with the chief's office.

With the death of Harry Chandler in 1944, his son, Norman, became the heir to his father's wealth and power. A slick, handsome man of forty-three when his father died, Norman enjoyed the good life and the benefits of the family fortune, but he lacked his father's drive and ruthless ambition. Norman became the publisher of the *Los Angeles Times* in 1945, but the newspaper

Editor Jim Richardson from the Examiner. The photo came from the cover of his book his life in the newspaper business.

that he published in the late 1940s and early 1950s was merely the ultra-capitalist voice for the property holdings and political interests of the Chandlers and their influential friends and supporters.

When the Black Dahlia case broke, the editors at the *Times* would have preferred to keep the hideous, sordid story on the back pages. However, they were compelled to give it front page headlines for a while to compete with the sensationalistic Hearst coverage. Primarily printing Donahoe's press releases, the *Times* had few investigative reporters working on the case, and much of what appeared in the morning *Times* was simply a rehash of what had appeared in Hearst's *Evening Herald-Express* or the previous day's *Examiner*.

Perhaps as a jab at the other, more attention-grabbing papers, on January 17, the *Times* publicly took credit for identifying the murder victim as Elizabeth Short with an announcement on page one that stated that "Capt. Jack Donahoe, given the identification by the *Times*, launched an immediate investigation to trace the movements of the girl before she fell prey to the perverted sadism of a person who apparently tortured her before she died."

However, many local residents were aware that the identification story had already appeared in the *Examiner* on the previous day, and Richardson had his revenge by running an interview with FBI chief J. Edgar Hoover that congratulated the *Examiner* for assisting the FBI in the "spectacular identification achieved under extraordinary circumstance."

While Richardson, in his particularly ruthless way, was far ahead of the competition with the Elizabeth Short story, Aggie Underwood at the *Herald-Express* had a reputation as a formidable crime reporter and she was working her own leads. Aggie had covered most of the major murder cases in Los Angeles since 1936 and had a remarkable memory, able to recall names, places and dates that often led her to one good story after another. Her exhaustive research made her agree with Harry Hansen when he said that there had never been a case in LA that was quite like the murder of Elizabeth Short.

It was Aggie who was responsible for discovering that Elizabeth Short was known in the shady dives of Hollywood and Long Beach as the "Black Dahlia." Like all the other pretty girls who came to Hollywood before and since, Elizabeth Short (who preferred the name Beth, Aggie learned) arrived hoping to make it big in the movie business. She was smart enough to know that looks weren't everything and that to break into films, she had to know the right people. So she spent most of her time trying to make new acquaintances that she could use to her advantage. Part of her plan involved making the rounds of the right nightspots and clubs. It was in such places, she was convinced, that she would come to the attention of important people in the film industry. Beth's pretty face and shapely figure got her noticed. She had done some modeling before coming to Hollywood and men couldn't keep their eyes off her. She created a dramatic impression by dressing completely in black, which emphasized her pale beauty.

In recalling how this discovery came about, Aggie stated, "The 'Black Dahlia' tag which the case assumed was dug out one day when we were all combing blind alleys and I was checking with Ray Giese, homicide detective-lieutenant, for any strange facts that might have been overlooked. Later in the squad room, he said, 'This is something you might like, Aggie, I've found out they called her the 'Black Dahlia' around a drugstore where she hung out down in Long Beach.'"

Aggie sent *Herald* reporter Bevo Means out to Long Beach to check out the detective's tip and he discovered that around the bars and clubs of Long Beach and Hollywood, she had been dubbed the Black Dahlia because of her jet-black hair and the slinky black dresses that she wore. The moniker came from the Alan Ladd movie, *The Blue Dahlia*, which was a popular film-noir movie starring Alan Ladd and Veronica Lake. It was changed to the "Black Dahlia" to fit Beth's stunning look.

Reporter Aggie Underwood learned that Beth had acquired the nickname "Black Dahlia" in the bars, nightclubs and hangouts of LA and Hollywood. Dressed all in black, she became a mysterious and evocative figure.

The Black Dahlia name first appeared in the *Herald-Express* on Friday, January 17 and all of the Los Angeles headline-hungry papers quickly seized on it. From that point on, Elizabeth Short was known as the Black Dahlia. Although not many people today recognize the name Elizabeth Short, even a passing reference to the Black Dahlia conjures up the image of LA in the 1940s: palm-lined streets filled with Hudsons and Studebakers, smoky nightclubs and a beautiful angel in black who was hunted down and murdered by some faceless fiend.

6. THE "BLACK DAHLIA"

With so many things happening at once - in the morgue, on the streets, in the detective bureaus and especially in the newspapers - detectives were often forced to follow leads that were dredged up first in the newspapers. According to an *Examiner* story, Beth Short had moved to California in 1943 to live with her father, who was working at the Mare Island Naval Base in the San Francisco area. Reportedly, she only stayed with her father for a month of two before they had a falling out that led to her departure. It was said that Beth had started dating a number of servicemen and her father, Cleo Short, complained about her frequent dates and how she often stayed out all night and slept late in the morning instead of cooking and keeping house for him. A church-going Baptist, Short admonished her for living a sinful life - although Cleo Short was certainly not someone who should have been pointing fingers at how other people lived their lives.

Short was tracked down soon after the newspaper story about Beth living with him appeared in the *Examiner*. Harry Hansen and Finis Brown found him living in an apartment at 1020 South Kingsley Drive in Los Angeles - less than two miles from where his daughter's body was discovered. Short was aware that the recently discovered Jane Doe #1 had been identified as his daughter, but the detectives found him to be strangely cold and indifferent about her murder. He told Hansen and Brown, "I broke off with the mother and the family several years ago. My wife wanted it that way. When I left the family, I provided a trust fund for their support. Five years ago, though, Elizabeth wrote to me. So I sent her money. She came out here, and she lived at my house when I was living in Vallejo."

But things did not go well. Short complained, "She wouldn't stay home. In 1943 I told her to go her way. I'd go mine. After that she headed south and worked at Camp Cooke, and then she was arrested in Santa Barbara for juvenile delinquency."

Even though the police characterized Short as "uncooperative," Hansen and Brown eventually concluded that he had no relevance to their investigation. But Short was not exactly forthright regarding the circumstances of his estrangement from his family or the events that occurred when his daughter came to live with him in California.

In 1930, Cleo Short had abandoned his wife, Phoebe, and their five daughters. His car was found on the Charleston Bridge near Boston and the police believed that he had jumped from the bridge in a fit of depression

A young Elizabeth Short

over his failing business. It would be years before Phoebe and the children would learn that Cleo was alive and well and living in California.

During the boom years of the 1920s, Cleo Short made a prosperous living building miniature golf courses in the Boston area, but after the stock market crash in 1929 and the start of the Great Depression, his company hit hard times. No longer able to support his family, he chose to abandon them instead - leaving Phoebe to deal with the foreclosure of his business, angry creditors and the problem of paying rent and feeding and clothing their children. There was no trust fund, as Short had claimed, and life was very difficult for Phoebe and the children.

Elizabeth (Betty as she was known to the family) was the third of five girls born within eight years to Cleo and Phoebe. Her youngest sister, Muriel, was only two when Cleo disappeared and she had no memory of him, but her older sisters did. Betty was eight years old when her father vanished and, according to her mother, it was the beginning of her emotional problems. Phoebe later said, "She was happy one moment - sad the next. I guess she was what you would call a manic-depressive."

43

Unable to pay rent, Phoebe moved the girls from their large, pleasant house on Evans Street in Medford to a third-floor, walk-up flat, where all five girls had to share a bedroom. Depending on Mother's Aid and welfare, Phoebe found occasional work as a bookkeeper and a clerk in a bakery. To escape from the drudgery of everyday life, she often took the children to the movies. Muriel later recalled that Betty loved the movies more than any of her sisters, and always liked to make something special out of their trips, dressing up "as if she was somebody important." Betty especially loved seeing movies in Boston's ornate movie palaces with their huge lobbies, gilded ceilings and crystal chandeliers. It was around this time that she began talking about going to Hollywood to become a movie star.

Betty began having asthma attacks shortly after the family moved to the walk-up flat. Muriel remembered that sometimes the attacks were so bad that their mother would have to call the doctor in the middle of the night to give Betty an adrenalin shot. In February 1939, she was sent to Boston Hospital for an operation to clear her lungs. The doctors told Phoebe that it would be better for Betty to be in a milder climate during the winter months; so in 1940, when Betty was sixteen, Phoebe arranged for her to stay with "friends" in Miami Beach over the winter. She got a part-time job at a beach resort and wrote home happily to report that she didn't have an asthma attack or a cold during the entire winter.

Very little is known about Betty's time in Miami. The family never revealed where she stayed, what she did or who her acquaintances had been. There were only some photos in Betty's memory book of unidentified friends and servicemen she met. Finis Brown went to Miami in the course of the murder investigation to trace her activities, but his report was filed away and never released to the public.

After her sophomore year, Betty dropped out of high school and began spending more than just the winter months in Miami. She was in Florida when the Japanese bombed Pearl Harbor, and she began dating servicemen stationed in the Miami area and obtained occasional modeling jobs. She returned to Medford in the spring of 1942 and worked as an usherette at the Tremont, one of her favorite Boston movie theaters, where she replaced a young man who had been drafted.

When Betty returned to Medford, she was no longer the sweet, innocent girl who had left a short time before. Many old friends, as well as her sisters, noted that she now wore heavy makeup and dressed provocatively in dark stockings, suede pumps and a leopard coat and hat. She spent a lot of her time hanging around a popular cafeteria owned by a man named Donald Griffin. Although Griffin was older than Betty, rumors circulated in Medford that the two of them were having an affair.

A dozen years after Cleo had vanished and was presumed dead, Phoebe received a letter from him. She was shocked to learn that he was alive and working in the shipyards in northern California. In the letter, he tried to explain that he left because he was unable to face his financial problems, but hoped Phoebe would forgive him and allow him to return to the family. Phoebe angrily replied that she no longer considered him to be her husband. As far as she was concerned, he was still dead. She would never forgive him.

However, when Betty learned that her father was living in California, she was overjoyed and began writing to him about her dreams of moving to the West Coast and finding work there. Cleo wrote back and suggested that Betty could stay with him in Vallejo until she could find a job. If she wanted to do that, he would send her money for train fare. Phoebe had mixed feelings about the arrangement, but Betty was ecstatic. All she talked about before leaving for California was getting to Hollywood. She wanted to be a movie star and she was determined to make it in show business. On a cold day in December 1942, Betty boarded a train in Boston and departed for sunny California.

When Betty arrived in Vallejo, though, she found that the skies above the San Francisco Bay area were often obscured by fog and the climate was not as sunny as she had imagined it. Worse, it was much farther from Hollywood than she had thought it was. She tried to persuade her father to take her to Los Angeles to visit, but Short thought her Hollywood dreams were foolish. According to his statements in the press, they had their falling out a short time later, in January 1943, and Betty headed south to Camp Cooke.

However, according to files that were released much later by the Los Angeles District Attorney's Office, Short didn't tell the whole story. In 1949, Harry Hansen told grand jury investigator Lt. Frank B. Jemison that when he and Finis Brown first went to question Short they found him in a drunken stupor, with empty wine bottles all over the place. He said, "He was very uncooperative, especially in view of the fact that, after all, his daughter had just been murdered."

Hansen noted that they returned the next day when Short was sober so that they could question him. They found that he had been living off and on with a Mrs. Patricia Yanke on Nebraska Street in Vallejo, where Betty had traveled to visit her father in December 1942. Mrs. Yanke revealed to investigators that Cleo's daughter had stayed at the Nebraska Street house for only a few days before Betty, Cleo and Mrs. Yanke traveled south to Los Angeles, where they stayed for three weeks in January 1943. According to neighbors that were interviewed, Cleo was an alcoholic and was drunk most of the time, and he and his daughter had many arguments about money and his drinking. While in Los Angeles, Betty met "Chuck," a sergeant in the Sixth Armored Division stationed at Camp Cooke, north of Santa Barbara. On

Photograph from the newspapers when Beth was living at Camp Cooke. She was very popular with the soldiers at the base and was once named "Camp Cutie of the Week."

January 29, 1943, following an argument about her father's drunkenness, Betty left word that she had gone north to Camp Cooke with the sergeant.

When Short spoke to the police and the press in 1947, alcohol might have impaired his memory of the visit to Los Angeles with his daughter in January 1943 and the circumstances of Betty's departure. More likely, though, he was following his usual method of blaming others for his problems and refusing to take responsibility for his actions. Just as he blamed the economy for his

46

abandonment of his family, he blamed Betty for leaving, going to Camp Cooke, and eventually, for being murdered.

Although Short had relocated to LA in 1945, he insisted that he had not seen or spoken to Betty in the four years since she had left for Camp Cooke. Nevertheless, in Harry Hansen's statement to the grand jury investigator, he made it clear that at one time Short had been a suspect in the Black Dahlia murder. Short had been working as a refrigeration repairman in a store in Hollywood on Santa Monica Boulevard when the murder took place. The detectives were satisfied, after going to the store, seeing his employment records and time sheets, and checking in the bars where he drank, that he could be eliminated as a suspect.

When it was discovered that Betty (who had started using the name Beth) had been working at the Camp Cooke Post Exchange when she was arrested in 1943, reporters interviewed several Camp Cooke employees that had known her. One of them, Inez Keeling, remembered that Beth had a "childlike charm and beauty. She was one of the loveliest girls I had ever seen." Popular with the soldiers at the camp, Beth was voted "Cutie of the Week," and an item in the camp newspaper cited her as "the main reason for the steady increase of business at PX #1."

Investigators learned that she had been living at Camp Cooke with "Chuck," the soldier she had met in LA, but that Chuck had threatened and beaten her. Beth filed a complaint with his commanding officer and she tried to attach Chuck's paycheck and obtain damages. But the damages were denied and the sergeant was shipped overseas. Beth then moved from the army base to Vera Green's bungalow apartment in Santa Barbara, where the incident took place that led to her arrest on September 23, 1943 - and of course, the subsequent fingerprinting and mug shots that led to the identification of her body.

While Jim Richardson was waiting in the *Examiner* city room for word from the reporters that he had sent to Santa Barbara and San Diego, he was working to uncover everything that he could about Elizabeth Short's life in Hollywood.

Will Fowler later recalled that the *Examiner* received a tip that Beth had been living in an apartment near Hollywood Boulevard shortly before she suddenly left the city in December 1946. Richardson sent out a team of reporters to work the Hollywood bars and nightclubs for leads. They quickly learned that Beth had been a familiar figure in a number of Hollywood cocktail lounges and had been living at the Chancellor Apartments at 1842 North Cherokee Avenue, which was just north of Hollywood Boulevard.

Reporters found Beth's name still on the mailbox of apartment 501. There were five other girls sharing the apartment, which was on the top floor overlooking the street. The building was managed by Glenn Wolfe, a suspected narcotics dealer who recruited girls for the mob-owned brothels in the city. The landlady, Mrs. Juanita Ringo, told the *Examiner* that Beth had moved into the apartment on November 13, 1946, just two months before her murder, and she left so abruptly that it seemed that she was afraid of something or someone. Mrs. Ringo said, "She looked tired and worried. I felt sorry for her, even when she got behind on the weekly rent. When I went up for rent last December 5, she didn't have it. I don't think she had a job. That night, she got the money somewhere, but she suddenly left the next morning."

One of the girls who shared Beth's apartment, Sherryl Maylond, told reporters that Beth "loved to roam Hollywood Boulevard" and that "she'd be out with a different man every night." Linda Rohr, another roommate, who worked at Max Factor in Hollywood, said that Beth seemed worried and afraid. On the morning she left, she was very upset and anxious. She told Linda, "I've got to hurry. I've got to get out of here!" Linda recalled that Beth told her that she was leaving town to visit her sister in Berkeley. But her older sister, Ginnie, who had moved to Berkeley after marrying university professor Adrian West, told detectives that she hadn't heard from Beth in some time and had no knowledge of an impending visit. But Beth didn't go north - she headed south to San Diego.

When reporter Wayne Sutton talked to Beth's mother on the telephone, he learned about a letter that she had written home from San Diego on January 8. Beth was a faithful correspondent, writing home at least once or twice a week. After getting the return address, Richardson sent *Examiner* reporters Tom Devlin and George O'Day to San Diego to see where Beth had been staying and possibly learn the identity of the man that she had referred to as "Red." The address where Beth had mailed the letter from was 2750 Camino Padero and the reporters discovered the house was the residence of Elvera French, her twenty-one-year-old daughter, Dorothy, and her twelve-year-old son, Corey.

Dorothy worked as a cashier at the Aztec Theatre in downtown San Diego on Fifth Street, not far from the Greyhound bus station. On the night of December 9, 1946, the Aztec was playing *The Jolson Story* and Dorothy recalled that she was preparing to close up after the last show when she noticed a young woman who had fallen asleep in one of the seats. Dorothy woke her up and the girl apologized, telling her that she had just arrived on the bus from Hollywood. She said she was broke, and had no place to sleep. As they walked out to the street, she told Dorothy that her name was Beth Short. She said that she'd been an usherette at a theater in Boston, and she wondered if there were any temporary jobs available at the Aztec.

Dorothy recalled, "I suggested she talk to the manager the next day. There was something sorrowful about her - she seemed lost and a stranger to the area, and I felt I wanted to help her. I wasn't sure how. She apparently

Dorothy and Elvera French

had no place to stay. I suggested she come home with me and get a good night's sleep, if that would help. She said she was thankful for my generosity."

The girls took the local bus to Pacific Beach and got off at the intersection of Balboa and Pacific Coast Highway. They walked up the hill to the housing project where Dorothy lived. Dorothy's mother, Elvera, was still awake and was having a snack in the kitchen. Introducing the unexpected guest, Dorothy explained that Beth had no place to stay. Elvera remembered later that Beth was pale and didn't look well. She brought her a pillow and blanket and suggested that she sleep on the couch.

The next morning, Dorothy's brother went to the Greyhound station and brought back the suitcases that Beth had left in the checkroom. He recalled that they were so heavy that he was sure "they were filled with rocks" - until

Matt Gordon, a decorated airman who flew with the famed Flying Tigers in the India – China Theater of Operations during the war. He was also the alleged fiance of Beth Short

Beth opened them and he saw that they were jammed with fancy clothes and undergarments.

The Frenchs soon got to know their new houseguest. Elvera's husband had been killed during World War II and Beth told her that she, too, was a war widow, and that her husband, Major Matt Gordon, had been killed in a plane crash in India while flying for the Army Air Forces. Elvera told reporters, "She mentioned that she had a baby boy by him, but that the baby had died. She showed me a newspaper clipping she'd been keeping in her purse. She said it told about her and the major."

Beth's sad story got plenty of sympathy from Elvera and Dorothy. Initially, they believed that she always wore black because she was in mourning for her dead husband and baby. But her frequent late night dates and frivolous lifestyle seemed to prove that was not the case. It wasn't until the news about Beth's murder appeared in the newspapers that they learned that she had never been married and had never given birth to a child. But was Beth really a chronic liar, or were her strange stories part of some mental condition that she suffered from? I believe that she may have told herself the same lies so many times that she had actually started to believe them. The tragic young woman wanted what the majority of women her age wanted back then: to be married to a handsome man - perhaps a serviceman - and start a family with him. In her mind, she'd had those things and lost them, sending her on the destructive course that led to her death.

Beth told the Frenchs that she had been working in Hollywood as a movie extra and was expecting some money to be sent to her at the local Western Union office. She was hoping to get a job in San Diego, and if she could stay with them for a day or two, she'd be happy to pay for the inconvenience. Dorothy told her that she was welcome to stay free of charge. After all, a lot of people were having a hard time, especially with the housing shortage after the war. Elvera told her not to worry about putting them out. Whatever Beth needed, they'd be happy to help her. But the "day or two" soon became a week, and the week turned into a month. The expected money wire never seemed to come and instead of getting up in the morning to look for a job, Beth stayed out late - often until two or three in the morning - and would sleep until noon. She claimed her late night dates were "with prospective employers."

Elvera worked at the San Diego Naval Hospital and when she came home for lunch, she often found Beth still asleep on the sofa, with her clothes strewn about the living room and her exotic lingerie draped over the furniture. Elvera recalled, "There was a strong, sweet-smelling, flowery scent in the house from her perfume. It was as though she had sprinkled perfume everywhere. She hadn't, of course; it was just her way of using it. Her clothes were quite expensive, especially the lingerie. They were brand new black silk stockings. I could tell they weren't nylon - but silk."

Silk stockings were a luxury item that were almost impossible to find during the war and were still expensive and hard to come by in 1946. How her houseguest had acquired them when she claimed to be short of funds was a mystery to Elvera. Because Beth usually slept until noon, Elvera found herself tiptoeing around the house, trying to make as little noise as possible as she made breakfast and got ready for work. Soon, she began wondering why she was doing it when Beth should have been out looking for a job instead of sleeping in. It wasn't long before Elvera lost her patience and began slamming the door when she left. As the days went on, she had a number of arguments with Dorothy about the merits of continuing to provide Beth with room and board. She had overstayed her welcome, Elvera believed, but Dorothy persuaded her mother to "be patient just a little while longer." Elvera and Dorothy both sensed that Beth was in some sort of predicament, as though she was hiding out. She had been chewing her fingernails down to the quick and at times she seemed despondent and fearful, perhaps, the women theorized, because she had been in some kind of trouble before she left Hollywood. Her moods swung back and forth, from overly cheerful to almost inconsolable. Their worry for her was the probably the main reason that Elvera didn't kick her out.

Dorothy and Elvera also recalled that Beth had bad teeth. Her smile was marred by cavities but she didn't have the money to see a dentist. Instead, she kept a supply of wax candles and used the melted wax to disguise her dental problems before going out on a date or to a "job interview."

To keep expenses down, the Frenchs did not have a telephone. When Beth needed to make calls, she went next door to a neighbor's house, or she walked down the hill to a payphone at the corner drugstore. She frequently talked about jobs that she was pursuing and told the Frenchs that she hoped to find work with Western Airlines or perhaps at the Naval Air Station. She told Dorothy that the manager at the Aztec was considering giving her a job as an usherette. One afternoon, she had an appointment with the theater manager and Beth told Dorothy she would meet her afterwards, but she never showed up. She had dinner with Dorothy's boss instead and stayed out most of the night. The next day, Dorothy noticed that she had long red scratches on her upper arms. Beth explained that she had gone to the theater manager's house for dinner. He'd had too much to drink and had starting grabbing her and had scratched her arms. Dorothy recalled that Beth never got a job at the theater, but despite the manager's behavior, she dated him again, along with other men she met in the brief time that she stayed with the Frenchs.

Elvera and Dorothy noted that the "sad soul" who had seemed "so lost and a stranger to the area" was quite adept at gathering a large entourage of male acquaintances. One of the acquaintances was Red - the mystery man who eventually drove Beth back to Los Angeles.

When the *Examiner* reporters questioned Elvera and Dorothy about Red's identity, they recalled that one day in mid-December, Elizabeth had brought an "old acquaintance" home that she had bumped into near the Western Airlines office in downtown San Diego. Beth called him "Red," and said that he was an ex-Marine Corps flyer. She had told them that Red was now flying for Western Airlines and was helping her get a job there as a stenographer. According to Elvera, Beth went out with Red every night between December 16 and 21, and then he suddenly left town. Of course, that didn't stop Beth. She dated other men until Red returned during the first week in January, when she announced that he was driving her back to LA. Elvera and Dorothy both described him as a tall, red-haired, freckle-faced man in his middle twenties. They thought that perhaps his first name was Bob, but they didn't know for sure.

Dorothy did say that when Beth decided to leave San Diego, she seemed disturbed and agitated. Dorothy attributed her behavior to an incident that occurred on January 6. She said that two days before Beth packed up and moved out, "Some people came to our door and knocked. There was a man and a woman, and another man was waiting in a car parked on the street in front of the house. Beth became very frightened - she seemed to get panicky and didn't want to see the people or answer the door. They finally went back to the car and drove away. Even our neighbor thought all of this was very suspicious."

After they saw how frightened Beth became by the visitors, the Frenchs tried to ask her who they were, but she refused to discuss it. Elvera believed that it was just after this incident that Beth contacted Red, who subsequently sent a telegram indicating that he would be in San Diego the following afternoon. When they checked at the San Diego Western Union office, reporters found that Red had sent the telegram from Huntington Park, a Los Angeles suburb, on January 7 - eight days before Beth's mutilated body was found.

The *Examiner* reporters phoned in the story and Richardson knew that he had his scoop - Red may have been the last person to see Beth alive. After knowing that his exclusive was secure, Richardson telephoned Capt. Donahoe to tell him about Red and about Beth's stay in San Diego. Donahoe agreed that Red was the new prime suspect in the murder and Richardson set the headline for the *Examiner* for Saturday, January 18.

The cops soon took over the chase from the newspapermen. When Harry Hansen checked on the telegram that was sent to Beth from Huntington Park, he found that the sender had declined to give his full name and address. Detective Brown contacted Western Airlines in San Diego and was told that none of its employees in the area matched the description of Red that had been given by Dorothy and Elvera French. After interviewing the Frenchs, Hansen and Brown questioned the neighbors. Forest Faith, who lived across the street from the French home, recalled seeing the mysterious man and woman who had frightened Beth when they knocked at the Frenchs' door several days before Beth skipped town. He had also gotten a glimpse of Red when he picked Beth up in the late afternoon of January 8. Faith said that he saw a "tall fellow with red hair" park near his home at about 6:00 p.m. The man put Beth's bags into his car and she didn't seem to be afraid of him. Faith told the detectives, "They were laughing and joking together." Faith gave Hansen and Brown a detailed description of the car and the detectives put out an all-points bulletin for Red, the number-one suspect in the Black Dahlia murder:

Suspect described as white male, American, approximately 25 years, 6 feet, 175 pounds, red hair, blue eyes and light complexion.

He is known as "Red" or "Bob."

Car is described as being possibly a 1940 Studebaker coupe, cream or light tan in color, bearing California license number with one digit preceding letter "V."

If car is located hold for fingerprints and all occupants, and notify Sergeants F.A. Brown or Harry Hansen, homicide division.

But by the time that the all-points police bulletin had been broadcast, Richardson at the *Examiner* had already found Red - the suspected "Werewolf Killer of the Black Dahlia."

7. "RED" -- SUSPECT #1

If Red have driven Beth back to LA, and they had left late in the day, as described by the witness who lived across the street from the French home, Richardson believed that they might have stopped off somewhere along the way. He told reporters Devlin and O'Day to check out every likely stopping place along the Pacific Coast Highway. This tedious task would mean talking to gas station attendants, café waitresses, motel clerks - anyone who might give them a lead to identify Red.

The tiresome job dragged on for miles and hours, with no one recalling a tall, red-haired man accompanied by a dark-haired beauty. Then, they rolled into the Mecca Motel, a "hot sheet" joint, located about twelve miles north of Pacific Beach. The clerk remembered the couple the reporters described, but not in January - they had registered back in mid-December. The clerk recalled, "Yes, the man was tall, freckle-faced, had red hair and was in his mid-twenties and he was with a striking young woman with jet-black hair."

The Mecca Hotel in 1947

The reporters asked him if he was sure the man had red hair and he replied that he was.

Looking over the register for mid-December, Devlin discovered that the couple had checked in on December 16 and he was amazed to see that they did not use the standard "Mr. and Mrs. Smith." Beth's name was on the register, right along with the name of the man with whom she'd shared the room. Next to her name was Red's full name and address - "Robert Morris Manley, 8010 Mountain View Avenue, Huntington Park, California."

Back in those days, cooperative ace reporters were given Los Angeles County Sheriff courtesy badges to help them out in scrapes with the law and of course, to gain entry into closed crime scenes. Without actually claiming that he was a cop, Will Fowler flashed his badge when Robert "Red" Manley's wife, Harriet, answered the door at their home on Mountain View Avenue. Fowler recalled that she was an attractive blonde and was holding a baby in her arms. When Harriet learned that her husband was being sought by the police, she became nervous, but she cooperated with Fowler. She told him that she had just heard from her husband, who had called her from San Francisco. He was a salesman for a hardware company that manufactured pipe clamps, and he was traveling with his boss, J.W. Palmer, on a business trip to the Bay area. Red had told his wife that he would be arriving home the next day, Sunday, January 19, after he stopped off at Palmer's house in Eagle Rock to pick up his car.

Under the impression that Fowler was a police investigator, Harriet confided in him that she had known Red for several years before they were married. They had now been married about fifteen months and had recently had their first child, a baby boy. She told him that she knew in her heart that her husband "couldn't have done anything wrong." Fowler chose not to tell Harriet that her husband was the number-one suspect in the murder of Elizabeth Short. Instead, he cautioned her not to talk to anyone else about her husband - especially any snooping reporters that might show up at her door.

Coming up with the name, address and whereabouts of the lead suspect in the Dahlia case was another extraordinary coup for Richardson and the *Examiner*. When he contacted Capt. Donahoe and told him of the discovery, LAPD detectives questioned Harriet Manley and staked out J.W. Palmer's house in Eagle Rock. They waited several hours for Manley to show up. When Palmer's car finally turned into the driveway, Robert "Red" Manley stepped out wearing a heavy, gray overcoat and a broad-brimmed hat that partially concealed his bright red hair. He stood briefly speaking to Palmer for a few moments and then started toward a tan Studebaker that was parked at the curb. As he reached for the door handle, police detectives rushed from their car with guns drawn, and closed in on him. Spotting the

Robert "Red" Manley, interrogated by the police.

detectives, Manley quickly raised his hands in the air. He immediately called out, "I know why you're here, but I didn't do it!"

Of course, *Examiner* reporters and photographers were on the scene, and flashbulbs exploded as Manley was photographed being handcuffed and placed in the detective's car. He was driven to Hollenbeck Station, where Hansen, Brown and Capt. Donahoe were waiting. Donahoe wasted no time in informing the press that he was confident that the police had apprehended Beth's killer.

But Harry Hansen had his doubts.

Before the enactment of the Miranda Act in 1966 (which requires law enforcement officials to warn suspects that they have the right to remain silent and the right to an attorney to represent them before speaking to the police) police did not have to inform detainees about their rights. In most cases, suspects were grilled mercilessly and at great length without the benefit of any kind of legal representation. And this was exactly what happened to Robert Manley that Sunday night at the Hollenbeck Station. Before he was booked, he was permitted to make one phone call, which he made to his wife. She hurried to her husband's side. Manley stood at a distance and looked at Harriet in silence for a long moment before rushing forward to embrace her. They kissed and hugged and openly wept and were allowed five minutes together before Manley's booking and interrogation began.

Manley was questioned by Hansen and Brown all Sunday night and was subjected to two lie detector tests before becoming incoherent and collapsing from fatigue. He admitted that he knew Elizabeth Short and acknowledged that he had driven her from San Diego to Los Angeles on January 9, but he adamantly maintained that he did not see her after that time and had nothing to with her murder. He had last seen her at the Biltmore Hotel in LA and only became aware that she was the victim of a gruesome murder when he read about it in the newspaper. He told the detectives, "When I saw the newspaper in San Francisco with Beth's picture on the front page, I read the story, and I got sick to my stomach."

According to Manley, he called his wife that night, but never mentioned the story because he didn't want her to know that he knew Beth. On Saturday afternoon, when he was out making business calls with his boss, his wife had called him and said that the police had been at the house and were asking about his connections to Elizabeth Short. He had told his boss that he was "in a heck of a mess and I don't know what to do."

Manley was maintaining his innocence, but the deck was stacked against him. Reporters knew a good story when they heard one and even if he didn't kill her, Red and Beth evidently had some sort of sordid relationship - which always sold papers. Photographers for the *Examiner* and the *Herald-Express* used the standard Hearst "horror-lighting" in the photos that were taken of Manley when he was undergoing the lie detector tests. It was achieved by placing the flashgun near the floor and shooting it upward, which cast weird, elongated shadows across the suspect's face, making even the most mild-mannered person look like a maniac. It was an old favorite for photographing high publicity murder suspects and the photos that appeared in the Hearst papers left little doubt in the reader's mind that Manley was the fiend who killed the Black Dahlia.

While the exact text of Manley's interview with the police was locked away in LAPD files, Capt. Donahoe did allow Aggie Underwood of the *Herald-Express* to conduct an interview with the suspect. As the *Examiner's* headlines about Red Manley's capture landed on thousands of Los Angeles front porches on Monday, January 20, Underwood was escorted by Harry Hansen to Manley's cell for an exclusive interview. Knowing that the exhausted young man had been through a grueling night of interrogation, Aggie decided to use a sympathetic, motherly approach to getting Manley to tell his story. When she sat down with him, she told him, "Look fella, you're in a hell of a spot. If you're as innocent as you say you are, tell the whole story; and if you haven't anything to hide, people can't help knowing that you're telling the truth. That way, you'll get it over with all at once, and it won't be kicking around to cause you any more trouble."

Hansen chimed in, knowing that Aggie's gentle approach just might be able to get more out of him than brutal police tactics could. He said, "She's right. Tell her everything that happened. I've known this lady for a long time - on a lot of cases - and I can tell you that she won't betray your trust."

Aggie got Manley started with a few casual queries and then he began to open up and tell his story, which ran in the *Herald-Express* that evening under the spicy headline "Kisses in Motel Bared." According to the story Manley told Aggie, a few kisses were all that transpired between him and Beth. But according to Sgt. Vincent Carter of administrative vice, who was at the station when Manley was questioned, the sanitized version that he told Aggie was not the same story that he told detectives Hansen and Brown the night before. Desperately trying to save his marriage, Manley denied to Underwood that he had slept with Beth, but he admitted privately to the detectives under questioning that he had indeed had sex with her. The language that he used when talking to Underwood could have come straight out of a 1940s movie about a repentant husband who almost slipped but who caught himself in the nick of time. She quoted him as saying, "I knew Beth Short - sure. I saw her twice. I even kissed her a couple of times. But that was it. And, believe me, knowing her has taught me to walk the straight and narrow. If ever a guy found himself in a mess - I'm it."

Manley explained that he had met Beth about ten days before Christmas 1946, when his company sent him to San Diego to make sales calls. In a tale that must have strained readers' credibility, he said that he picked Beth up on a street corner and offered her a ride home as an experiment to test his love for his wife. Manley said he and Harriet were undergoing an "adjustment period" after their first child was born and he thought that picking up a gorgeous young woman would help him decide if he still loved his wife or not.

Beth was standing on the corner across the street from the Western Airlines office, where she told Manley she worked. She allowed him to drive her to the Frenchs' house in Pacific Beach and when they arrived, Manley asked her if she would go to dinner with him. She said she would, but was worried about how she would tell the people she was staying with who he was. She decided that she would tell him that they worked together at Western Airlines.

Beth Short lived in a world of lies - lies that she spun for everyone around her and likely for herself. She told Manley that she worked at the airline because it was convenient; she plucked it out of the air like so many of the other lies that she told. Her lie was compounded when she told Dorothy and Elvera French that Red was an old friend she had bumped into downtown. He was a former pilot in the Marines who now flew for Western Airlines, she said. But the truth was that Red had never been a pilot, least of all in the Marines, and had no connection to Western Airlines at all. During the war, he had played the saxophone in an Army band before being given a Section 8 - an early discharge from service due to psychiatric problems. The military found him to be high-strung and nervous under the pressure and the routine restrictions of Army service.

Beth told the Frenchs that she and Red were going out to dinner to talk about old times and it was understood that he would be returning that evening to pick her up. Manley told Aggie that after he dropped Beth off, he drove down to the highway and got a motel room. He explained, "I registered for myself, went to the corner and got a beer. Because I was a stranger in town, I asked the people where I bought the beer where would be a good place to get dinner and maybe dance. They told me the Hacienda Club, out on University Avenue in Mission Valley.

Manley then said he went back to his room and with time to think, he started worrying about his wife. They had not been married long and he had never "stepped out" on her before - but on second thought, he hated to waste a sure thing. He said, "I cleaned up a little bit and picked up Miss Short at seven o'clock and we left and tried to find..."

At this point, Manley hesitated in his story. He corrected himself and said, "No --- we started to drive to the Club, and it took us two and a half hours to find it... Boy, it's sure easy to get lost in San Diego!"

Before he corrected himself, Manley was likely about to say that they left and went back to his motel. Even though he told Aggie that he had left Beth at the Frenchs' house and then found a room up the coast and registered "for myself," the *Examiner* reporters discovered that Manley and Beth had registered together at the Mecca Motel on the day in question - December 16. The "two and a half hours" supposedly spent looking for the Hacienda Club were more likely spent at the motel where both had registered before going to the club, which was only a fifteen-minute drive from the French house.

Manley told Aggie that they had a few drinks and danced when they finally got to the club and by then, it was midnight. They went to a drive-in, had a sandwich, and then he took Beth home. Manley denied taking her to his motel room. He said that they sat and talked in his car for a little while and that he kissed her a few times, but that was all. "She was kind of cold, I would say," he added.

Manley said that he told Beth he was married, and she had told him that she had once been married to a "Major Matt somebody... who had been killed in the war." Manley said that he walked her to the door and asked her if he could see her again the next time that he was in San Diego. Beth said yes, but told him that she didn't really like the city and might not be there long.

Manley returned to his room with a guilty conscience, he said, and made the rest of his San Diego calls the next day. On his way home, he stopped at the French house in Pacific Beach and asked to see Beth, but was told that she was at work. Since Beth never worked while staying there, though, she was probably either out somewhere or still asleep.

In his public statement, Manley made it sound like he had only seen Beth one time on December 16, before returning to Los Angeles. But according to the Frenchs, Beth was "out with Red every night from the 16th through the 21st."

After returning home, Manley never mentioned meeting Beth to his wife - but then he never forgot about Beth either. He said that when he found out that he would be returning to San Diego, he sent Beth a wire on January 7 and told her that he would be arriving the next day. She was waiting for him when he arrived at the French house and asked him if he would drive her down the road to make a telephone call. En route, however, she changed her mind and asked Manley to take her back to Los Angeles with him. He agreed, but told her that he could not leave until the next day.

According to Dorothy and Elvera French, when Beth became frightened after the strangers knocked on their door on the night of January 6, she was anxious to leave San Diego as soon as possible. Even though Manley had a business appointment and couldn't drive to LA until Wednesday, January 9, she packed her things on Tuesday and moved out that afternoon - the day she had written her mother and mentioned that she was driving to Los Angeles with Red.

As noted by the neighbor across the street, Manley parked his tan Studebaker in front of the French home in the late afternoon of January 8. They loaded Beth's bags and started up the Pacific Coast Highway. After Manley became tired, he said, they stopped at a motel. Manley's statement gave the impression that they traveled some distance before finding a motel, but according to the neighbor, Forrest Faith, he had picked up Beth around 6:00 p.m. They checked into a motel, not later as Manley claimed - but about fifteen minutes from the French house. It's my opinion that Manley was looking for "payment" for his chauffeur service back to Los Angeles.

But, of course, he denied that to Aggie Underwood. He said that they left the motel cabin and went to have dinner. On the way, Beth wanted to stop at the U.S. Grant, a large hotel in San Diego, but the place was quiet and so they went back to the Hacienda Club again. They danced and had several drinks and Manley described Beth as "gay and happy and seemed to be having a swell time." They left around midnight, picked up hamburgers from a drive-in and returned to their motel cabin.

He told Aggie, "When we got in she said she was cold, and she grabbed an overcoat and put it around her. She said she wanted a fire, so I built it. We ate the sandwiches and there was no affection between us. We talked for a while and she said she didn't feel good - said she was very cold and pulled up a chair in front of the fire, and I threw a couple of blankets over her."

Manley said that Beth dozed off in front of the fire, so he got undressed and went to bed. He went on, "When I woke up the next morning, she was

Red Manley with his wife, Harriet, in the middle of him being suspected as the Black Dahlia's killer. Manley was eventually cleared, but his marriage was doomed.

propped up on the other side of the bed, awake. She said she's had chills all night long. I hopped up and told her I had to make some calls in San Diego that morning. I did, then at 12:20 - 12 noon was checkout time at the motel - I went back and picked her up.

Manley said that Beth was smartly dressed when he returned. She was wearing a black, collarless suit, a fluffy white silk blouse, and white gloves accented by a large, black handbag and a pair of black suede high-heeled shoes. On the way to LA, they stopped for a sandwich at a roadside diner and got gas in Laguna Beach.

In his interview with Aggie, Manley failed to mention an occurrence that he had apparently revealed to Hansen and Brown. This information was discovered in 2003 in the LA District Attorney's office files and was originally given as part of Manley's testimony to investigator Frank B. Jemison during the 1949 grand jury investigation into the Black Dahlia case. Apparently, while they were driving up the Pacific Coast Highway, Beth seemed very anxious about people in the other cars that they saw along the road. Most specifically, she would turn around in her seat to study the occupants of any cars that Manley passed on the highway. Manley was struck by this odd habit and asked her about it. Beth brushed off his concern but he remembered it, even more than two years after it happened.

In his interview with Aggie Underwood, Manley said that it was in Laguna Beach that Beth told him that she had to make a telephone call to someone in Los Angeles. He waited in the car until she returned. Manley stated that he had no idea who she called, but thought it may have been her sister, Ginnie, whom Beth said she was supposed to meet in LA. Manley recalled, "I asked her where she was going to meet her and she said, 'The Biltmore Hotel'... When we got into Los Angeles, she wanted me to take her to the Greyhound bus station so she could check her bags before she met her sister. I drove her to the bus station and carried her bags in. I had to go out and move my car, but told her that I would drive around and pick her up and take her to the Biltmore."

The Greyhound station was on Sixth and Los Angeles Street - just four blocks from the Biltmore, a fashionable hotel on Olive between Fifth and Sixth Streets. It had been built in 1929 by Harry Chandler and a group of prominent Los Angeles businessmen.

Manley remembered what happened when they got to the hotel. He told Aggie, "When we got to the Biltmore she said she had to go to the restroom and asked me if I would check at the desk on whether her sister had arrived. I checked information and they had no Mrs. West registered. She said her sister was short and blonde. (Ginnie, Beth's sister, had dark brown hair and she later denied to the police that she had any plans to meet her sister at the Biltmore). I went up to a couple of short, blonde women in the lobby and asked whether they were Mrs. West - but they weren't. I was getting late and I told her that I had to leave. I had to get home. I was worried about my wife. Miss Short said she had to wait there, and I left her there."

As Manley walked to the Olive Street door, he glanced back to wave at Beth, but she had already turned and was talking to the clerk at the tobacco stand and getting change for the telephone. She was still standing there when Robert "Red" Manley walked out of the Biltmore at approximately 6:30 p.m. on Wednesday, January 9, 1947.

He swore to Aggie, "That was the last time I ever saw Miss Short. I'll take truth serum, or anything they want to give me. And I'll swear on a stack of bibles, and tell my minister, too - that was the last time I saw Beth Short. I did not kill her!"

When questioned by detectives, Biltmore employees recalled noticing Beth as she stood in the lobby. A ladies room attendant remembered seeing her at the mirror, where she had lit a paraffin candle and applied the melted wax to her teeth. Bellboy Captain Harold Studholme told the police that he saw her make several telephone calls and then wait in a chair near the bell

The Biltmore Hotel, where Beth Short was dropped off by Red Manley – and last seen alive by someone other than her killer.

station for some time before crossing the lobby and walking out onto the sidewalk from the Olive Street door at about 10:00 p.m. - more than three hours after her arrival. The doorman remembered greeting her as she stood at the edge of the sidewalk, but had no idea where she went after that.

One week later, Elizabeth Short's mutilated body was found among the weeds in a vacant lot. How she had gotten there - and where she had been for the past seven days - was unknown.

8. BROKEN DREAMS

Even though Capt. Donahoe was happy to tell the press that they had apprehended Beth's killer, Harry Hansen was convinced that "Red" Manley had nothing to do with the Black Dahlia murder. Manley's wife, Harriet, along with several other witnesses, established his whereabouts on the critical days in question - January 14 and January 15. He had repeatedly passed polygraph examinations, no bloodstains were found in his car, which did not match the description of the 1936 or 1937 black Ford sedan that was seen parked at the site where the body was discovered. Manley was guilty of cheating on his wife and acting like a fool, but he wasn't guilty of murder. Regardless, though, the newspapers had a field day with their lone suspect and Donahoe let the press hammer him for as long as they wanted before he announced Manley's release and probable innocence, admitting that there was no real evidence against him.

After an exhaustive search, police investigators and *Examiner* reporters succeeded in finding the luggage that Manley claimed Beth had checked at the Greyhounds station on January 9. The reporters were the first to grab it, but it was quickly confiscated by Capt. Donahoe. At that point, there was only the one mug shot of Beth Short to use for art and the press had to resort to artist's renderings, along with the usual X-marks-the-spot diagrams to illustrate the crime. Richardson begged Donahoe to allow photographs to be taken of the contents of Beth's luggage, but Donahoe refused. He said that the contents were "dynamite" and needed to be held in evidence. To this day, the complete contents of Elizabeth Short's luggage, checked at the bus station on January 9, have never been disclosed to the press or the public.

But Richardson wasn't about to give up. Dorothy and Elvera French had mentioned that Beth spoke of a trunk that she owned that was full of personal possessions and "memory books" that had been lost in transit when she traveled from Chicago to Los Angeles in July 1946. Richardson ordered reporters Will Fowler and Baker Conrad to find the missing trunk.

The two reporters immediately began searching frantically through Railway Express offices, freight depots and train and bus stations before finding Beth's lost luggage in the storeroom of a Railway Express agency in downtown Los Angeles. Fowler recalled that the luggage turned out to be a suitcase and some bags, not a trunk as Beth had said, but they did find the

The baggage receipt for Beth's luggage at the Greyhound Station

missing "memory books" inside. Thanks to the *Examiner*, the Black Dahlia case became one of the best-illustrated crime stories in newspaper history.

Before this cache of information hit the headlines, though, Richardson gleefully called Capt. Donahoe and said, "You're welcome to the luggage we found, Donahoe, but I want it understood that the story is ours exclusively." Richardson laid down the condition that LAPD detectives would have to come to the *Examiner* offices, where the luggage was going to be opened and examined. Will Fowler later remembered that Donahoe "blew a fuse," but unfortunately, he had no choice but to go along with Richardson's demand. If he didn't, he was warned, he'd have to read about the contents of Beth Short's luggage and the progress of the case in the *Examiner*.

When the luggage was opened in the newspaper's conference room, detectives and reporters scrutinized Beth's scrapbooks, which were found to contain dozens of photographs of Beth in Miami posing with a number of different servicemen. There was an unsigned telegram sent to Beth from Washington, D.C., that read, "A promise is a promise to a person of the world." There were also a number of love letters that were tied together with a red ribbon. They made for mournful reading, spilling the hopes and dreams of a young woman who had been through a number of disappointing wartime

A newspaper photo of a detective holding one of Beth's memory books

romances and had drifted into a desperate existence on the shady side of Hollywood - while still dreaming of love, marriage and a family.

In a letter that she wrote to Major Matt Gordon in January 1945, she gushed, "I have just received your most recent letter and clippings. And darling, I can't begin to tell you how happy and proud I am... I'm so much in love with you, Matt, that I live for your return and your beautiful letters, so please write when can and be careful, Matt for me. I'm so afraid! I love you with all my heart."

In a letter to her mother, Beth had written that she had become engaged to Major Gordon, and that they planned to marry when he returned from overseas. However, while Beth was writing love letters to Gordon, she was also writing love letters to other servicemen she was attracted to, including a Stephen Wolak, whom she also said she hoped to marry. But Wolak, in a very kind tone, wrote back to Beth, "When you mentioned marriage in your letter, Beth, I got to wondering about myself. Seems like you have to be in love with a person before it's a safe bet. Infatuation is sometimes mistakenly accepted for true love, which can never be."

And yet, Beth continued to dream. Found among her love letters was correspondence between Beth and a Lt. Joseph Gordon Fickling, an army pilot she had met in September 1944, shortly before he was sent overseas.

Although she also expressed her hopes of marrying Lt. Fickling, he had written to her, "Time and again, I've suggested that you forget about me as I've believed it's the only thing for you to do to be happy."

But Beth kept insisting they could work things out. In an unmailed letter that she wrote to Lt. Fickling from San Diego, dated December 13, 1946, she told him, "Frankly, darling, if everyone waited to have everything all smooth before they decide to marry, none of them would ever be together... I'll never love any man as I do you. And I should think that you would stop and wonder whether or not another woman will love you so much."

All of Beth's letters were filled with longing, but none of them as much as those written to Major Matt Gordon, whom she had met during one of her visits to Florida. She lied to herself, but perhaps deep down she understood their relationship was merely a brief wartime encounter. All of Beth's letters expressed hopes of marriage, but there was no indication in any of Gordon's correspondence that marriage was his intention. And of course, Beth's dreams of becoming Mrs. Gordon were dashed when he died in a plane crash in India in November 1945. But in Beth's fevered imagination, they had actually been married. She told Dorothy and Elvera French that she was a widow, and had lost Matt's child. In Beth's mind, her hopes had transformed into a tragic romantic fantasy that even she had started to believe.

As Jim Richardson noted, "She had been a pitiful wanderer, ricocheting from one cheap job to another and from one cheap man to another in a sad search for a good husband and a home and happiness. Not bad. Not good. Just lost and trying to find a way out. Every big city has hundreds just like her."

And I would agree with that - but I'd be willing to bet that Los Angeles had more than its share.

The inquest was scheduled for Wednesday, January 22, at 10:30 a.m. Richardson had arranged for Phoebe Short to fly into Los Angeles from Boston on Saturday, January 18. She met briefly with Will Fowler before making a connecting flight to Berkeley to spend a few days with her daughter and son-in-law, Ginnie and Adrian West. She gave a brief statement to Fowler at the airport, "Betty always wanted to be an actress. She was ambitious and beautiful, and full of life, but she had her moments of despondency. She was gay and carefree one minute, then blue and in the depth of despair the next... She was a good girl. She wrote often - at least once a week. It was only two weeks ago that I received a letter from San Diego. I can't imagine who did this dreadful thing. I'm anxious to do anything to help in tracking down the fiend."

Before she left him, she told him that she would be returning from Berkeley on Wednesday to attend the inquest. She touched his hand and said, "I have suffered deeply, but the worst is yet to come."

When Phoebe returned to Los Angeles, she was accompanied by Ginnie and her husband, Adrian. They were met at the airport by *Examiner* reporters, who drove them to the coroner's office at the Hall of Justice. Visual identification of the remains had to be made for the official record, prior to the inquest. True to form, Cleo Short had refused to identify the body, leaving Beth's mother and sister to carry out the painful task. When they arrived, Harry Hansen and Finis Brown escorted them to the morgue's viewing window, where they would be shown the body on the other side of the glass.

Phoebe gasped as the coroner's aide pulled back the sheet and she got the first look at her daughter's mutilated face. There was a moment of silence before Ginnie choked out, "I can't tell, Mama, I don't know."

Phoebe told Hansen that her daughter had a birthmark on her shoulder that she could recognize. When the sheet was lowered, both women began to sob. There was no question - it was Betty.

Phoebe Short had been brave and resolute from the day she received the terrible telephone call from the *Examiner* office, but at the sight of her daughter's slashed and mutilated remains, she completely fell apart. She began to sob uncontrollably and collapsed into the arms of Harry Hansen, who had a tough time maintaining his own composure. He led Phoebe to a nearby chair and sat down beside her, trying to reassure her that he was going to do everything in his power to find the monster that had killed her daughter. Phoebe wondered aloud why the newspapers and the police had painted such a bad picture of her little girl. She kept repeating over and over through her tears, "She was a good girl, she was a good girl..."

After Phoebe and Ginnie were given time to recover, they were escorted to the coroner's hearing room in the Hall of Justice, where the inquest into what was officially called Case #7569 was scheduled to take place. The nine inquest jurors were presided over by Coroner Ben H. Brown. Called to testify were Detectives Jess Haskins, Harry Hansen, Dr. Frederic Newbarr, Phoebe Short and Robert Manley. Manley came to the hearing accompanied by his wife, Harriet, and his father, William.

The testimony in the inquest into what was probably the most bizarre murder in Los Angeles history was rather perfunctory and without any real surprises. In an ordinary homicide case, a full copy of the autopsy report is presented to the jury and read and elaborated on by the medical examiner on the witness stand. In the Black Dahlia case, though, the jury was not given a copy of the report, which had been sealed. A transcript of the inquest reveals that, as Dr. Newbarr read the report, Coroner Brown interrupted when he approached the most significant part of the autopsy - the description of the organs that had been removed by the killer. He stopped him by saying,

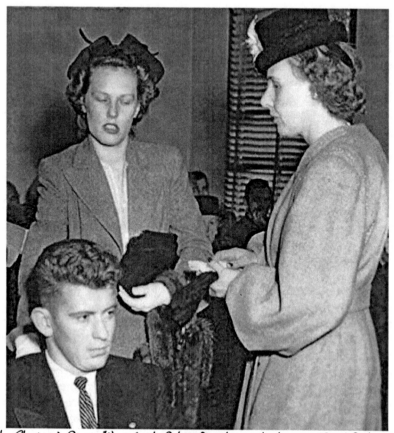

Phoebe Short and Ginnie West (with Robert Manley in the foreground) at Beth's inquest.

"Doctor, I don't believe it will be necessary for you to read all of this. It is rather long, and I don't think we need to read it all here. The essential findings with regard to the cause of death have already been expressed, and that is the concussion of the brain and the lacerations of the face."

If Dr. Newbarr had been allowed to continue, the secret sealed in the autopsy report would have become public and, as some believe, the startling motive in the murder of Elizabeth Short would have become evident to the jurors. But those facts would remain hidden for more than fifty years.

At the conclusion of the forty-five-minute inquest, the coroner's jury confirmed the death in Case #7569 to be a homicide. Death had come as the result of hemorrhage and shock due to deep knife lacerations to the face, blows by a blunt metal object and concussions to the brain by "person or persons unknown."

When the hearing concluded, the witnesses filed out of the coroner's chambers and *Examiner* reporters escorted Phoebe, Ginnie and her husband out the back door to avoid the rival press. No longer a suspect, Robert "Red" Manley walked out the front door as a free man. He likely believed the Black Dahlia nightmare was now behind him, but he soon found himself mixed up in it again. Soon after the murder was reported in the papers, Robert Hyman, the proprietor of a café on South Crenshaw, reported that someone had put a relatively new pair of high heel shoes and a large handbag in the incinerator behind the café - which was just twenty blocks away from the Black Dahlia dump site. Suspecting that they might be connected to the murder, he removed the items from the incinerator and placed them on top of a trashcan while he called the police. But by the time the police arrived, a garbage truck had made its rounds and removed the shoes and handbag, along with the trash.

After Beth's purse was discovered at the city dump, Robert Manley was brought into headquarters to try and identify the purse, based on what she had been carrying when he drove her from San Diego to Los Angeles

After a search of the city dump, the shoes and handbag were recovered by the police and Robert Manley was picked up by detectives and brought in to see if the items had belonged to Beth Short. As in a lineup, the items were mixed in with twenty other handbags and pairs of shoes. Without hesitation, Manley picked out a pair of black suede pumps, which he said that Beth had been wearing when he drove her to Los Angeles. He remembered them because they had double heel caps. He had taken Beth to a shoe repair shop in San Diego so that she could have them put on. Manley also identified a black plastic handbag as the one she was carrying when he last saw her in the lobby of the Biltmore Hotel on January 9. Although the purse had been emptied, Manley pointed out that faint traces of Beth's distinctive perfume were still noticeable inside.

Robert Manley was no longer a suspect in the murder, but his involvement in the case continued to haunt him. His affair with Beth Short ultimately turned his life into a nightmare. His photograph had been published with his sordid story in newspapers across the country and the notoriety resulting from his brief fling with a pretty girl ended up costing him his marriage, his job, and his sanity. About a month after police questioned him, he had a nervous breakdown for which he received shock treatments. In 1954, he was diagnosed as a paranoid schizophrenic and committed to a mental institution. He was in and out of mental institutions for many years and died in a nursing home in 1986.

After the inquest, Beth's remains were released to the Pierce Brothers Mortuary. Phoebe decided to have her daughter buried at the Mountain View Cemetery in Oakland, near the home of Ginnie and Adrian West. On Saturday, January 25, 1947, Beth was laid to rest after a brief service with only her mother, Ginnie and Adrian in attendance.

But there seemed to be little chance that she would rest in peace.

The Black Dahlia's killer was still at large and the detectives no longer had a solid suspect - or even a single clue as to where to look for one.

9. THE DARK SIDE OF HOLLYWOOD

One of the many complications of the Black Dahlia case was the press coverage that it received. It was a mixed blessing. On one hand, if not for the newspapers, the dogged reporters and the hard-bitten editor Jim Richardson, the police would not have uncovered the clues that they did manage to dig up in the case - or at least not as quickly as they did. But on the other hand, the sensational, and often lurid, coverage that the murder received brought the crackpots out of the woodwork and every one of them was eager to confess to the killing.

After the LAPD released Robert Manley, scores of people came forward to confess to the murder and to bask in the limelight of notoriety, illuminated by the press photographers' flash bulbs. The homicide division received more than fifty confessions within the first weeks of the investigation, and the newspapers splashed the choicer ones on their front pages, along with large photos. The reporters fought tooth and nail for all of the gory details before finally dismissing each one of them as a hoax. There were the habitual confessors, known to the LAPD as "confessing Sams," and there were the homeless drunks who just wanted a meal and a bed for the night; but there were also some confessors who were fairly convincing and forced the LAPD to use hundreds of man-hours investigating their claims.

One young man, Daniel Voorhees, said that he "couldn't stand it any longer" and had to confess to the murder of Beth Short. Although he was quite vivid in the way he described how he had cut her body in half, he claimed that he had first met Beth in "Los Angeles on Fourth and Hill Street in 1941." However, Beth wasn't in California in 1941, nor did Voorhees have any knowledge of the secret that had been withheld in the autopsy report. According to Harry Hansen, the odds that a phony suspect or false confessor could have guessed the secret were one in a million.

Another confessor was an Army corporal named Joseph Dumais, who was stationed at Fort Dix, New Jersey. He grabbed headlines after he gave a fifty-page handwritten confession to his commanding officer, who stated that he was "definitely convinced of Dumais' guilt." Dumais claimed that he had been "bar-hopping with Elizabeth Short in Los Angeles on January 9th or 10th" when he blacked out and later had "flashbacks" of committing the gruesome murder. But the "flashbacks" did not include knowledge of the secret information, and Finis Brown dug up witnesses who placed Dumais in New Jersey on the dates in question. Brown later recalled, "None of the confessors ever came close to answering the key question that Harry had put together from the confidential files."

While the police were being inundated with false confessions, they also received numerous "tips" and "leads" from imaginative "witnesses" who had gotten caught up in the sensational Black Dahlia headlines. Many claimed that they had spotted Beth during the week she had seemingly vanished from the Biltmore Hotel. Among them were Mr. and Mrs. William Johnson, who managed the Hirsh Hotel at 300 East Washington Boulevard. Perhaps irritated that the Biltmore was getting more publicity than their hotel (although why anyone would want such publicity is a puzzle), the Johnsons claimed that Beth and a man had checked into their hotel under the name Mr. and Mrs. Barnes on January 12. Hansen and Brown quickly discounted the tip, along with many other false leads that involved Beth and her "jet-black hair" after January 9. The detectives knew that Beth's hair had been hennaed to a lighter color prior to her return to Los Angeles. This was overlooked by the phony tipsters and saved the LAPD from taking many excursions down dead-end trails. Eventually, the Johnsons admitted that they were "mistaken."

At the height of the case, more than four hundred investigators and officers of the LAPD and the sheriff's department were assigned to look for the Dahlia's killer. They knocked on doors all over the Leimert Park area, questioned known sex offenders and searched storm drains, basements and attics. They tried to discover where Beth had been murdered and where she had been between the evening of January 9 and January 14. Although a number of witnesses came forward insisting that they had seen Beth in Hollywood, in downtown Los Angeles, or in San Diego between those dates, Hansen and Brown concluded that there was no viable lead as to where she had been during that week. They believed that she had been abducted and held captive at a secluded location until she was murdered and her body was moved to the empty lot on Norton Avenue.

Finis Brown stated, "No matter how questionable each lead appeared on the surface, we had to track it down, and in this case, each lead seemed to open into something else, and it went on and on, and none of them were giving a clue to the missing week, or to the murder itself."

Investigators learned that prior to Beth's return to LA with Red Manley on January 9, she had been a resident of the city on three separate occasions. Her brief initial visit with Cleo Short and Mrs. Yanke in January 1943 ended when she traveled to Camp Cooke. She was later arrested in Santa Barbara and sent back to her mother in Massachusetts.

After spending a few weeks in Medford, Beth returned to Miami for the winter season of 1943-1944. She stayed at the El Mar Hotel, which was not far from Miami Beach and the Victory Canteen, a place popular with servicemen and where volunteers provided food, drinks and music for the

Beth, before her return to Los Angeles

troops. At the time, Miami was a winter playground for the rich and famous, especially since the war in Europe had cut off their access to resorts in Italy and the south of France. Miami employment records obtained by Finis Brown showed that Beth worked as a waitress for several months at the Rosedale Delicatessen, one of the first in the city to serve Jewish-style fare. She then became a part-time waitress at a popular restaurant on the ground floor of the Vanderbilt Hotel called Mammy's, whose slogan was *Where the Stars Come out at Night and Play until Dawn*. In letters to her family, Beth said that she was also "modeling" for a Miami man named "Duffy" Sawyer.

Beth traveled to Los Angeles for the second time in August 1944. She stayed briefly at the Clinton Hotel in downtown LA, where she shared a room with a slim, dark-haired girl named Lucille Varela. The Clinton was operated by Nate Bass, who owned a number of bars in the downtown area that were tied in to the mob. He was referred to as "Mr. Main Street" by the vice squad working out of Central. According to vice squad officer Sgt. Charles Stoker, Bass was known to run ads in southern states and cities like Miami offering girls employment in the movies or as models in Hollywood. Stoker said, "Girls who answered these advertisements would be screened as potential "B-Girls," and some were sent to a hotel in Hollywood, where efforts were made to induce them into a life of prostitution."

Beth's roommate at the Clinton, Lucille Varela, was another Hollywood hopeful - one of the hundreds who arrived each month with dreams of becoming a movie star. It was difficult for these girls to work nine-to-five jobs and still manage to make the casting rounds at the studios. While waiting for their big break, Lucille and girls like her worked the downtown and Hollywood bars in the evening as B-Girls. These girls were not prostitutes. B-Girls received money from the bars where they worked by pushing drinks on thirsty, and lusty, male customers. B-Girls made sure that these men's thirsts were quenched, if not their lust. A professional B-Girl would push drinks, but she never slept with the bar patrons. The rule of the game was to get the cash without delivering the merchandise, and on some occasions, unsuspecting men were slipped a "Mickey" and woke up without their wallets.

Beth was a perfect candidate for the B-Girl game - she was gorgeous, had a flirtatious personality and she dressed the part. While trying to break into the movies, Lucille and Beth made the B-Girl rounds, pushing drinks at Hollywood bars where the bartenders passed along just enough cash to get them from day to day. It was a dangerous game and it often ended up taking the girls to places where they never intended to go - to an even seedier side of Hollywood than what they saw on the grimy surface. Many of the LA bars were run by the mob and many of the B-Girls ended up being recruited as prostitutes.

Mob madam Brenda Allen ran a high-class call-girl ring from her spacious apartment at Casa Fedora on South Fedora Street in the Wilshire Division. Catering to movie moguls, actors and the city's elite, she was always on the lookout for new recruits with special talents. In a call-girl setup organized through Mickey Cohen and Ben "Bugsy" Siegel, Allen had connections with major studios that wanted to keep visiting stars, moguls and moneymen happy. She advertised her services in the Players Directory, which was published by the Academy of Motion Picture Arts and Sciences as a handy guide for Hollywood producers and casting directors seeking "talent."

High-priced call girls and fancy bordellos were always a part of Hollywood history. One of the first Hollywood madams was Pearl Morton, who was a notorious purveyor of girls in the movie colony. During the 1920s and 1930s, Lee Francis was the city's premier madam and she boasted an influential clientele of important businessmen and, of course, important

Famous Hollywood madam, Brenda Allen

people in the movie business. Francis had at least four bordellos under her management and she always kept a fresh supply of chilled imported champagne and Russian caviar at every house. That way, whenever the vice squad showed up for one of their scheduled "raids" - and finding no one in the house to arrest - she could make sure the lawmen were served some high-class refreshments.

Lee's brothels each had its own swimming pool, tennis court, full-service restaurant, fully-stocked bar, and, of course, dozens of girls to choose from. The brothels were not used only for sexual purposes, but also as a sort of club where men could relax, play cards, or go for an afternoon swim when they were supposed to be at the office and couldn't go home. Movie stars were frequent visitors at the houses because Francis maintained a strict code of secrecy, which allowed them to come and go as they pleased without being besieged by photographers or fans.

After Lee Francis was jailed for thirty days on a morals charge, Ann Forrester (known as the "Black Widow") stepped in and became Hollywood's top madam in the late 1930s. It was said that Forrester's operations grossed more than $5,000 every week. By 1940, though, Ann had been jailed for pandering. This occurred despite Mayor Fletcher Bowron's request that she be given a light sentence because "her information was of great value in determining the identity of those police department members whose honesty was questionable."

The Black Widow's protégé, Brenda Allen, took over her operation in the 1940s. A former teenage streetwalker, the red-haired Allen became Hollywood's most famous madam. Using a series of luxurious houses located above the Sunset Strip, Brenda catered to the city's wealthiest clients, including many notable Hollywood personalities. Allen was reported to gross more than $9,000 a day, one-third of which was earmarked for bribes, physician and attorney fees, and bail bondsmen.

Brenda maintained secret client files in case she ever got into legal difficulties and had to call on one of her influential clients for help. As an added insurance policy, she had an ongoing affair with LAPD Sergeant Elmer Jackson of the vice squad, a trusted aide of Lt. Rudy Wellpott, commander of administrative vice and a confidante of Assistant Chief Joe Reed. But not all of the cops were in on the order to leave Allen alone. She began to be investigated by Sgt. Charles Stoker, who had no idea that Allen was sleeping with one his superiors.

Only a few people knew Brenda's address or her private telephone number, but her Hollywood exchange number had been advertised in the Players Directory, and Stoker was able to obtain her private number and address from an employee at the telephone exchange. He discovered that Allen worked out of an apartment in the upscale neighborhood behind the Ambassador Hotel. Allen also maintained a nearby bungalow court at 836 Catalina Street, where a number of her girls who worked the Ambassador Hotel stayed - the hotel was just a half-block from the bungalow. While staking out Allen's communication center, the enterprising Stoker posed as a deliveryman. He pretended to ring the doorbell while he leaned against the door, trying to listen to what was going on inside. He could hear the telephone ringing and could hear Brenda answering the calls.

A few days later, Stoker returned with an independent electronic surveillance expert named James Vaus, Jr., and they managed to enter the basement of Allen's apartment building and place a tap on her phone. That was how Stoker learned that Allen was having an affair with Sgt. Jackson. Stoker had heard the rumors, but he had discounted them; now he knew the stories to be true. He was also shocked to learn that some Hollywood starlets also worked for Allen and that many of her customers were movie stars, studio executives and major business and financial figures in the city. An honest cop, Stoker tried to have Brenda Allen arrested for her vice activities but he was warned by members of LAPD's notorious Gangster Squad to cease his unauthorized investigation. He was transferred out of Central Division a short time later.

The Gangster Squad had a dark history within the LAPD. Formerly called the Intelligence Unit, it purportedly worked closely with the chief and administrative vice in gathering intelligence information about criminal elements operating within the city. But in time, under the command of Chief James E. "Two Gun" Davis, the Intelligence Unit became the enforcers of Chief Davis' corrupt regime and the protectors of vice in the underworld. In 1938, it was learned that members of the Intelligence Unit attempted to assassinate grand jury investigator Clifford Clinton, who was investigating LAPD corruption and payoffs to City Hall. The unit was disbanded and replaced by the Gangster Squad. But under the new regime of Chief Clemence Horrall and Chandler's aide, Assistant Chief Joe Reed, only the name had changed. Horrall continued to use the Gangster Squad as enforcers and protectors of police corruption.

Starting in the 1930s, corruption among Los Angeles officials was epidemic and Chief Davis was right in the thick of it, along with scores of other police officials. Genuine attempts at reform were feeble and infrequent. Even most of the city's newspapers sided with the mob, supporting the crooks at City Hall against their detractors.

In 1933, Councilman Frank Shaw ran for mayor on a platform of honest government, "free from graft and private exploitation." He announced plans to appoint a police chief "who will run the gangsters and racketeers out of town and put a stop to commercialized vice." Despite loud opposition from mobsters, Shaw was elected. He immediately appointed his brother, Joe, a former naval officer, as his private secretary. He appointed James E. Davis, who had headed the police force during most of the 1920s, as his new chief of police.

The mobsters of LA immediately understood - a new era of corruption was just beginning. It was not quite business as usual since the price of bribes and payoffs was higher, but organized crime began doing business on an executive level. Payoffs weren't going to the street cops anymore; they had to go straight to the bosses. Joe Shaw became the mayor's bagman. Crooks began buying off cops, judges and politicians with suitcases filled with cash. By 1937, the mob bosses' biggest headache was where to stash the millions of dollars that were overflowing from their coffers.

Into this cesspool came Clifford Clinton, the son of Salvation Army missionaries and a strait-laced and kindly man. Clinton opened the Cafeteria of the Golden Rule, the first cafeteria in Los Angeles, which offered generous portions of food at rock-bottom prices. During the depths of the Depression, he became the city's most-admired citizen after he announced that patrons in "financial distress" would be served even if they couldn't pay. He also saved thousands of the poor from malnutrition, and even starvation, with "five-course dinners" (bread, soup, salad, Jell-O and coffee) for a nickel.

Clinton and Shaw were destined to collide. For appearance's sake, Mayor Shaw was obligated to make a cosmetic effort at ending corruption. When he was re-elected in 1937, he empaneled a new grand jury, filled with his cronies and stooges. To back his claim of honesty, however, Shaw also appointed Clinton and three other genuine reformers. It was a huge mistake.

Clinton and a few of his courageous followers tried to investigate corruption when they targeted mobsters under Shaw's protection, but the district attorney denied them funds to pay for the investigation. Clinton dug into his own pocket and formed a strike force, the Citizens Independent Vice Investigating Committee. He recruited about five hundred church, community and business leaders and to get hard evidence on corrupt police and politicians, he hired Harry Raymond.

Raymond was an unusual man. He was a fearless investigator and incorruptible - no amount of money would buy him - but he was also a hot-headed brawler who, while he was a cop, once knocked out another officer and sometimes arrested suspects that he knew were guilty, even though he had no evidence to prove it. In the years after World War II, he was the police chief of Venice by the Sea (which was then separate from Los Angeles), but was fired amid unsubstantiated charges of extortion and false arrest after taking important mobsters into custody. In 1920, Raymond was hired - and then fired - by Los Angeles Police Chief George Home, who was himself dismissed a few months later. Raymond became San Diego's police chief, serving several years before resigning to become a private investigator.

In 1937, Clinton directed Raymond to document a maze of police corruption that led all the way to Mayor Shaw's office. His investigation painted a lurid picture of graft and corruption. Through Mayor Shaw's brother, the racketeers of gambling and prostitution paid huge sums of money to Shaw. In return, Shaw appointed their hand-picked straw men to the police commission. Commissioners appointed James Davis as the chief of police, a man that the mob controlled. Davis then put his loyal followers into key positions on the vice and police intelligence squads. The money flowed, the rackets flourished and any cop that tried to do an honest job was bribed, transferred or fired.

Clinton issued a "grand jury minority report" that was signed by three other jurors, detailing the situation in the LAPD and similar corruption in the district attorney's and Los Angeles county sheriff's offices.

Mob leaders were furious. Mayor Shaw pulled a few strings and the county assessor clapped Clinton's cafeteria with an additional $6,700 in property taxes. A license to open another cafeteria was refused without explanation. Several people inexplicably "fell down" the steps of the restaurant and sued Clinton for damages. Other "customers" complained of food poisoning and they too filed lawsuits. A stink bomb canister was set off in the cafeteria, causing a stampede of sickened patrons. A few days later, another stink bomb was set off in the kitchen. Clinton's family got threatening letters and telephone calls. When he brought witnesses before the grand jury, the police arrested them on trumped-up charges and some were beaten while in custody. One was held in seclusion for five days before being arrested on a phony vagrancy charge. Clinton himself was cited for contempt before the grand jury, but even after all that, he refused to stop his campaign.

Then on October 27, 1937, a bomb went off at Clinton's home, destroying the first floor and the basement. Clinton and his family were sleeping upstairs and were unhurt by the blast. He still refused to be intimidated and told newspapers, "I refuse to stop now."

Meanwhile, Harry Raymond was investigating connections between the LAPD Intelligence Squad and the mayor's office. But he had all of the corrupt powers at City Hall against him. Ordered to discredit or destroy Raymond was Capt. Earl Kynette, head of the Intelligence Squad. Kynette promptly put a tap on Clinton's phone and sent men to Raymond's Boyle Heights neighborhood. They rented the house across the street from him and began tailing him around the clock. They did nothing to keep their activities secret. Practically everyone in the neighborhood knew the police were leaning on the grand jury investigator - and Raymond knew it too.

Raymond was scheduled to give testimony about the sources of Shaw's campaign funds in late January 1938. He had by then unraveled the entire sordid story. Shaw and Davis could not let him testify and gave orders for Kynette to make sure he was stopped.

Early in the morning on January 14, Raymond stepped out of his house and walked to the small garage at the rear of the property. He opened the garage door, climbed into the front seat of the car, turned the key in the ignition - and was blown into the air by a tremendous explosion. The car and the garage were blown apart. Raymond was bloodied, deafened, bruised and severely injured, but somehow, he survived. His near-death upset the public. They might tolerate booze, broads and bookmaking, but they drew the line at bombs. Raymond was wheeled into court and testified about payoffs and bagmen. A special prosecutor, Joseph Fainer, was appointed. The mob immediately threatened his family, so he put them on a cruise ship bound for Hawaii and promised to find the men who had tried to kill Raymond.

Chief Davis ordered his cops to be silent. Undaunted, Fainer got a court order to confiscate Kynette's files. In them was direct evidence that linked

Kynette and one of his subordinates to the bombing. After a sensational trial, the pair were sentenced to ten years in prison.

Every newspaper in the city, except the *Los Angeles Times*, attacked the Shaw administration. The Chandlers were tied too closely to the corrupt administration, which they had largely put into place, and they had a vested interest in Shaw. They stuck by him until his rapid exit from politics.

Clifford Clinton put together a broad coalition of community leaders and launched a petition to push Frank Shaw from office. Less than a year after his re-election, Shaw became the first big-city mayor in the country to be thrown out of office. His brother Joe was convicted of sixty-six counts of corruption in connection with the sale of patronage and bribes. He got ten years in prison. Also implicated was LAPD Lt. Pete DelGado, who fled to Mexico and was never prosecuted.

The man who took over for Shaw was another handpicked Chandler crony, Fletcher Bowron, who made a show of wanting to get rid of corruption - but little changed. However, he did appoint Arthur Hohmann as his police chief. In a whirlwind two-day period in 1939, Hohmann replaced the Vice Squad with an eighteen-man task force dedicated to arresting gamblers; reorganized the LAPD's fourteen patrol divisions into six; abolished 398 temporary department positions; and promoted, fired, demoted or transferred five hundred men. The lantern-jawed former Marine was denied permission to fingerprint and photograph every citizen in Los Angeles, which he wanted to do because he said it would cut down on the time that it took to arrest criminals. Later, Hohmann replaced the city's fourteen precinct captains with handpicked officers and set up a ninety-day rotation for all cops, a scheme designed to eliminate graft.

Needless to say, Hohmann only lasted two years in a department that thrived on corruption.

The departure of Frank Shaw as mayor did not end vice in Los Angeles. It simply meant that mobsters, politicians and dirty cops had to figure out a new way of doing things, which, of course, they did.

After being transferred to the Hollywood Division, Sgt. Stoker soon observed that Brenda Allen's girls mingled with the guests at Hollywood parties and were available for special house calls to those on the "A" list. One of Allen's biggest clients was Columbia Studio boss Harry Cohn, who took Brenda's girls on cruises aboard his luxury yacht, along with assorted Hollywood pals and visiting debauchers.

One of the Hollywood hopefuls who stumbled on her way to fame was curvaceous blonde starlet Barbara Payton, who became a prostitute and literally died in the gutter from drug addiction. Beth Short met Barbara Payton through Lucille Varela at Al Green's Nightlife Bar and Grill. "Al Green" was Albert Louis Greenberg, a former bootlegger for Ben Siegel and

Meyer Lansky. He had a long rap sheet and carried out robberies and murders for Siegel.

When Beth met her, Barbara had already become a starlet on the casting-couch circuit. She introduced Beth to some movie and radio fringe people and taught her where she should go to be seen by the "right people." One of those places was the Formosa Café, across the street from Samuel Goldwyn Studios at the corner of Santa Monica Boulevard and Formosa Avenue. Stars and executives from the Goldwyn lot often drank and dined there and the Formosa bar was a rendezvous spot for Hollywood lowlifes looking to get high. In the 1940s, the backroom was a bookie joint and Ben Siegel kept a well-guarded office upstairs, where he kept his books, ran the Extras Guild and conducted the vice business for the New York Syndicate in Los Angeles.

It was at the Formosa that actor Franchot Tone encountered an alluring young woman with jet-black hair. Tone was starring in *Phantom Lady* with Ella Raines, which was shooting on the Goldwyn lot, when he entered the bar and spotted Beth Short. Tone struck up a conversation with her as she was sitting at the bar and told her that one of his Hollywood associates was looking for young women with "your kind of looks." He suggested that they go to the associate's apartment and Elizabeth eagerly agreed. Tone was, after all, a prominent movie star and he was going to introduce her to someone who could get her career started! Tone later recalled, "I thought it was a pickup from the start - she came with me so easily, but to her, it wasn't anything of the kind."

When they arrived at the apartment, the "associate" wasn't there. The apartment was a place that Tone used for trysts. He admitted that he tried to kiss Beth a couple of times and to lure her to the couch, but she resisted and scolded Tone for only having "that" in mind. He gave her some cash, put her in a cab and she was gone. Years later, he said that he considered the encounter to be a strange and rather unsettling experience. He added, "There was something sad and pathetic about her."

In hindsight, some of the men who knew Beth called her a "tease," but being a tease was a role she played in her game of survival. She had her own set of rules. Her cache of love letters revealed a romantic who dreamed of finding the right man - someone she could trust and give her heart to in a lasting relationship. While she could be a tease as a B-Girl and in her attempts to advance her movie career, she apparently valued herself and chose not to have relations with men that she didn't find attractive. At the same time, she enjoyed the attention that her looks inevitably aroused. Later on, even with trysts that were arranged for her, Beth refused to give up on the idea that the "right man" was somewhere out there.

During her stay in Hollywood in 1944, Beth frequented the Hollywood Canteen, where she danced with servicemen and met some of the movie star

The Hollywood Canteen, where Beth volunteered during her second stay in Los Angeles

volunteers. Located in an old barn at the corner of Sunset and Cahuenga Boulevard, the Canteen had a Western motif, with wagon wheels hanging from the ceiling and light fixtures made from lanterns. More than three million men and women in uniform visited the Canteen from the time it opened in October 1943 until it closed the day after Thanksgiving in 1945. Many celebrities were on staff, including Bette Davis, John Garfield and Irene Dunne. It was at the Canteen where Beth met actor Arthur Lake in September 1944. Lake played Dagwood Bumstead, the bumbling husband in Columbia Studios' successful string of *Blondie* films, based on the Chic Young comic strip characters. Beth was able to get free meals at the Canteen by becoming a junior hostess like a young woman named Georgette Bauerdorf, who was also acquainted with Arthur Lake. Beth and Georgette were both attractive twenty-year-olds when they became Canteen volunteers in 1944. Both girls were popular with servicemen on leave, who competed for the chance to cut in with them on the dance floor.

One night in September, Beth danced with Lt. Joseph Fickling, a pilot stationed at the Army Air Base in Long Beach. Although it was against Canteen rules, they began dating and predictably, Beth fell in love. But like so many other wartime romances, their relationship was put on hold when Fickling received orders to ship out and was sent to England. They corresponded and their love affair was documented in Beth's memory book and in the packet of letters that was lost with her luggage.

It was shortly after Fickling's departure that Georgette Bauerdorf was murdered on October 12, 1944. Her body was found floating in the bathtub at her West Hollywood apartment. She had been raped, beaten and

Georgette Bauerdorf

asphyxiated by a cloth shoved down her throat. The cloth turned out to be bandage material of the type used at military hospitals, and detectives suspected that her killer was a serviceman who had followed her home from the Hollywood Canteen. Several soldiers that Georgette had met at the Canteen were questioned, but no arrests were made and the murder remained unsolved.

Soon after Georgette's murder - perhaps spooked by her brush with horror - Beth abruptly left LA and arrived home in Medford in time for Thanksgiving with her mother and sisters. She then returned to Miami during the winter season of 1944-1945, and she once again stayed at the El Mar Hotel. Investigators found no record that she held a job while in Miami, but she was often seen at a beachfront bar called the Grotto, which was operated by mobster Meyer Lansky. She returned to Medford in March 1945 and worked as a waitress at St. Clair's restaurant in Cambridge. It was at St. Clair's that Beth met another waitress named Marjorie Graham, whom she

85

Beth returned to Medford in the spring of 1946 (shown here with her mother) before meeting Lt. Joseph Fickling and returning to Los Angeles for the last time.

would later encounter in Hollywood and room with at the Hawthorn Hotel, a notorious enclave for Syndicate prostitutes.

In September 1945, Beth returned to Florida and spent the winter at the Colonial Inn, an upscale hotel that was owned by Ben Siegel and Meyer Lansky. It was known to the FBI as a mob-owned gambling establishment. There was no record that Beth was employed during her stay there.

Beth returned to Medford the following spring for a short time. She shipped her luggage to Indianapolis on June 1, 1946. According to her mother, Lt. Joseph Fickling was returning to the United States and Beth was going to meet him in Indianapolis during the first week of June. There is no record that this ever happened. The next record of Beth Short was in Chicago, where she stayed at the Park Row Hotel from June 24 to July 9. She returned to Los Angeles for the third time on July 12, 1946.

During the five months that Beth was in LA, between July 12 and December 6, police investigators discovered that she resided in at least eleven different locations and had at least fifty different male acquaintances. Was her killer really a "person unknown," as stated at the coroner's inquest, or did Beth know her killer all too well? Harry Hansen was convinced that the location where her body was found, the secret of the autopsy and the manner in which the body was displayed meant that her killer was someone she knew.

A number of detectives from administrative vice were assigned to the Hollywood area to trace Beth's whereabouts and her contacts prior to her sudden trip to San Diego on December 6. The detectives had far more questions than answers. Where did she live? Who did she know? Was she a B-Girl or a prostitute? Was she involved in drug trafficking? Was she in some kind of trouble when she suddenly left for San Diego? It was almost impossible to get a solid fix on the Black Dahlia. According to Detective Vince Carter, "Elizabeth Short was always on the move, and she hadn't established any close relationships that we could pin down. Nobody seemed to know her very well, but they all remembered what she looked like. She made a vivid impression, but was very secretive about her private life. She was a loner."

Beth arrived back in Los Angeles on July 12, 1946. She checked into #21 at the Washington Hotel at 53 Linden Avenue in Long Beach. Much like the hotel where she stayed in Miami, the Washington was near the ocean and a promenade lined with hotels, cafés and cocktail lounges that were frequented by servicemen. A local druggist, Arnold Landos, remembered Beth Short and told the *Examiner*, "She lived down the street at the Washington. She'd come into our drugstore frequently. She'd usually wear one of those two-piece beach costumes, which left her midriff bare. Or she's wear black, lacy things. Her hair was jet-black and she liked to wear it high. She was popular with the men who came in here and they called her the 'Black Dahlia.'" The manager at the Washington Hotel, Fred Smelser, recalled that a number of servicemen visited her at the hotel and there was "one army officer who saw her frequently."

That officer was Lt. Joseph Fickling.

Phoebe Short had told Hansen and Brown that Beth had gone to Long Beach to meet Fickling, who was scheduled to be discharged from the Long

Beth at the beach in the later summer of 1946. Shown here with friend, Marge Dyer

Beach Army Air Base at the end of August. She believed that Beth and Fickling had plans to get married. When Capt. Donahoe was informed about Fickling, the army officer was quickly moved into the position of prime suspect, which had recently been vacated by Red Manley. But Fickling was no longer in the city. Hansen and Brown managed to track him to Charlotte, North Carolina. Local detectives were asked to question him about his whereabouts at the time of Beth's murder.

The Charlotte police found Fickling living with his parents. He denied that he had been in Los Angeles in January 1947 and told the investigators, "I met Betty in 1944 before I went overseas. We met again when I got back last year. We carried on a long correspondence, but there was never any talk of marriage." It seemed that, once again, Beth had dreamed a wartime romance into a lasting commitment. In her mind, their love was true, but for Fickling, she was a fun, pretty girl who was willing to "shack up" with no strings attached.

Under questioning, he admitted that he had met up with Beth in Indianapolis when he returned to the States in June 1946. He told the police that Beth had taken a bus from Chicago to Long Beach where he was scheduled to be discharged. He said that he picked her up at the Long Beach bus station and took her to the Washington Hotel, where he visited her often

Lt. Joseph Fickling.. when he left Beth behind in Los Angeles and returned home to North Carolina, Beth began the final descent that eventually led to her death.

when he was off-duty. When Fickling had a week-long leave in August prior to his discharge, he stayed with Beth at the Brevoort Hotel in Hollywood, near Vine Street. Hansen and Brown found a registration card at the Brevoort that was signed by Fickling. It noted that he had registered there with his "wife" from August 20 to August 27, 1946. Fickling insisted that this was the last time that he had seen Beth. When he was discharged from the service at the end of August, he returned to his parents' home in Charlotte and started working for 20th Century Charter Airlines, which ran flights between Charlotte and Chicago. Witnesses confirmed that Fickling was on flight assignments to Chicago when Beth disappeared and was subsequently murdered.

Fickling insisted that he had told Beth that marriage was out of the question and had written her a letter to that effect in December 1946. The letter stated, "Time and again I've suggested that you forget me, as I've believed it's the only thing for you to do to be happy." He said that he had received a response from Beth while she was in San Diego, dated December

13. In it, she had written, "I do hope you find a nice young lady to kiss at midnight on New Year's Eve. It would have been wonderful if we belonged to each other now. I'll never regret coming west to see you. You didn't take me in your arms and keep me there. However, it was nice as long as it lasted."

In the same letter, she told him that she desperately needed money and Fickling told the police that he had wired her $100 while she was staying in San Diego with the Frenchs.

The last letter that Fickling received from Beth was mailed from San Diego and was postmarked January 8 - the day before she vanished. She told him that he should not write to her at the San Diego address again. She added, "I am planning to go to Chicago to work for Jack." Fickling told the investigators that she had once told him that she knew someone called Jack who lived in Chicago and operated a modeling agency.

Beth's December letter to Fickling seemed to say that she had finally let go of the dream of them being together permanently. But did she mean it? It was a sweet, almost maudlin note and there was no way that Fickling could know that his devastating rejection of her in late August - playing house with her in a hotel for a week and then leaving the city without her - was the beginning of her final slide into the depths of Los Angeles' darkest side.

It was on August 28, the day after "Mr. and Mrs. Fickling" checked out of the Brevoort, that Beth Short checked into the infamous Hawthorne Hotel, owned by Nate Bass and operated by the mob. And it was at the Hawthorne that a mysterious man who drove a 1936 or 1937 black Ford sedan began paying Beth's rent.

The Hawthorne Hotel was located just south of Hollywood Boulevard, behind the Roosevelt Hotel. It was known as a rendezvous for prostitutes who worked the Roosevelt and its popular nightclub, the Cinegrill. Hawthorne desk clerk Jim McGrath told reporters that Beth Short had shared a room with two young women, Marjorie Graham and Lynn Martin. Graham had known Beth when they had worked together as waitresses at St. Clair's in Cambridge. Graham later explained that they had run into one another in a store on Hollywood Boulevard in August 1946. After Fickling left her, Beth had moved into the Hawthorne, where Marjorie was sharing a room with Lynn Martin. Beth had no money but the two girls took her in. Two men who also lived at the Hawthorne, Harold Costa and Donald Leyes, told police detectives and reporters that they were the boyfriends of Beth's roommates. Costa told reporters, "Whenever we took the girls out to dinner, they always asked us if they could bring Beth along. They said the kid was broke and hungry."

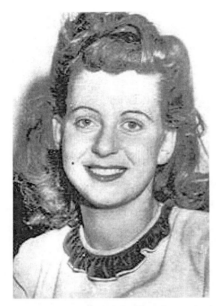

Beth's roommates at the Hawthorn Hotel, Marjorie Graham (Left) and Lynn Martin

Beth stayed at the Hawthorne for a month. She checked out on September 28 and when the cops tried to find Marjorie and Lynn, they found out that the girls had left soon after Beth. McGrath, the hotel clerk, recalled, "Miss Short was always getting behind in her rent. Whenever she did, a short, dark-complexioned man - about thirty-five or forty - came in and paid her bill. He used to drive an old, black Ford sedan and park it in front. When Beth left the hotel last September, she piled her baggage in the short, dark-complexioned man's car and drove off."

Whoever this "mystery man" was, he drove Beth to a house at 6024 Carlos Avenue, behind the Florentine Gardens supper club on Hollywood Boulevard. The 600-seat venue for dining and dancing featured elaborate floorshows with scantily clad showgirls. Its proprietor, Mark Hansen (no relation to Detective Harry Hansen), owned the house on Carlos Avenue, as well as the Marcal Theater on Hollywood Boulevard, the Roseland Ballroom in downtown Los Angeles, and a number of apartment buildings and rooming houses in the Hollywood area. Hansen was in his early fifties at the time and had an eye for pretty girls. Some of the showgirls - as well as the B-Girls - from the Florentine Gardens lived in Hansen's apartments and some of them stayed as guests at his house on Carlos Avenue. Nils Thor Granlund, credited by the *New York Times* as being the creator of the modern nightclub, managed the Florentine Gardens and produced its extravagant shows. He was known for finding the most beautiful girls in Hollywood to appear in

The Florentine Gardens

them. Garlund had an apartment above the garage at Hansen's Carlos Street residence, where he frequently entertained girls.

For Hollywood hopefuls in the 1940s, it was considered a step on the way to becoming a star to get in with the Granlund/Hansen crowd. Betty Hutton, Yvonne DeCarlo, (the actress who went on to play Lily in the CBS television series *The Munsters*), stripper Lilli St. Cyr, Mailia "Vampira" Nurmi, Gwen Verdon, and Marie "The Body" McDonald were among those who got their start in the floorshows at the Florentine Gardens. In that era, it rivaled Earl Carroll's dinner theatre as one of Hollywood's most popular nightspots. But despite the fact that it often booked Hollywood headliners, the Florentine Gardens never seemed able to escape its tawdry reputation as a hangout for Hollywood lowlifes. The floorshows were only one pasty spangle above burlesque and the B-Girls and the hookers were always there to make sure that the booze kept flowing and the customers were happy - no matter what it took. There was also a secret card room upstairs where customers were regularly fleeced. It was run by Jimmy Utley, a pal of Ben Siegel.

While the Florentine Gardens was operated on the surface by Mark Hansen and Frank Bruni, it was commonly known in the underworld that they were fronting for the mob. Ben Siegel and Mickey Cohen had their own special tables at the club where they were seen in the company of a bevy of pretty girls, including Marie McDonald, who was Virginia Hill's rival for Siegel's attention. Because Siegel controlled the Extra Guild, a Hollywood labor union, he could get the girls from the Florentine Gardens a little work in the movies at the drop of a G-string, so to speak. Nils Granlund, who staged shows for Syndicate nightclubs across the country, could get the girls good jobs in a number of venues.

Judy Walters, a prostitute who once worked for Mark Hansen, revealed how things worked around the club. She explained, "I was supposed to have been another discovery like Betty Hutton or somebody. I was promised spots in NTG's (Nils Thor Granlund) shows at the Gardens instead of wet-nursing the customers. The drinks were watered, and the food wasn't fit for a dog, and we were supposed to see that the suckers left in good spirits and with empty pockets. Bugsy Siegel was around there once or twice - I don't know, maybe more than that, and I was looking for a way to get to Vegas, to work for Siegel and Moe Sedway, who was living at the Roosevelt Hotel then. I know they wanted NTG to head the Flamingo, so I stayed on, but whatever promises were made to anyone at the Gardens it didn't ever happen. Instead of getting in the chorus and being a showgirl, I ended up dancing with winos and sex fiends at Hansen's Roseland Ballroom downtown."

According to Walters, an assistant manager at the Florentine Gardens was an "enforcer cop" friend of Mark Hansen's. Judy said, "The cops were on the take and this undercover cop would keep his eye on what was going on just to make sure that the juice wasn't getting watered down. The real gangsters were the cops."

Beth Short stepped into this sordid mess on September 28 when she was moved to Hansen's house on Carlos Avenue by the short, dark-complexioned man that drove a black Ford sedan. Beth found herself sharing a room with a pretty Hollywood starlet named Ann Toth, who was one of Mark Hansen's many girlfriends. Not long after Beth arrived, she arranged for her friend, Marjorie Graham, to also move into the house as another of Hansen's non-paying "guests."

Robert Slatzer, a young Ohio man who came to Hollywood to be a screenwriter, was a frequent customer at the Florentine Gardens. He dated Ann Toth for a while before dating another Hollywood hopeful, Norma Jeane Doughtery. At that time, Norma Jeane had only recently signed on as a starlet with 20th Century Fox. Soon after, the studio changed her name to Marilyn Monroe. Slatzer later recalled, "Marilyn liked going to the Florentine Gardens and enjoyed the shows and liked dancing in the conga line. Though she was relatively unknown then, Mark Hansen knew who Marilyn was and occasionally he'd ask us over to his table, where there'd always be three or four attractive women, and some questionable, flashy-looking characters."

Ann Toth, one of Mark Hansen's girlfriends, befriended Beth at the house on Carlos Avenue.

Years earlier, when the former Norma Jeane Mortenson married her first husband at sixteen, the Florentine Gardens was where the wedding party went to celebrate after the ceremony.

Slatzer remembered Beth being at Hansen's table on several occasions. He said she was attractive but she never seemed to have much to say. However, he did remember some interactions between Beth and Monroe. He said, "Elizabeth Short and Marilyn spoke several times and she would ask Marilyn what she should do to get a studio contract, but Elizabeth didn't have Marilyn's driving ambition. She dreamed of being a film star, but wasn't willing to make the effort. She seemed to have a defeated attitude, as I recall, and she hung around a bad crowd."

Ann Toth probably knew Beth the best during the time that she was living at Hansen's house. She later told reporters, "We used to think the world of that kid. She was always well-behaved and sweet when I knew her. But Beth could not stand up to trouble, and she was always in hot water... she was skeptical of people, but despite that often stumbled into trash." Ann said that Beth had been promised extra work in the movies and a role in the next Florentine Gardens revue. It had been implied in the press that Beth was one of Mark Hansen's girlfriends, but Hansen denied this. He told the papers, "She dated many different men while she was living here, mostly hoodlums whom I wouldn't even let in my house." Of course, this was ironic, coming from a man who was pals with Ben Siegel and other mobsters. Hansen's definition of "hoodlums" could well have been lowlife thugs who weren't as well connected as his gangster friends.

Ann Toth was asked about Beth's visitors and she spoke of the man who had paid her rent at the Hawthorne Hotel and who took her to Hansen's place. She described him as a "short, dark-complexioned man in his late thirties, five feet six inches tall, of medium build... a little fellow. He drove an older model black sedan. Beth called him 'Maurice' and he promised to 'set up' Beth in an apartment in Beverly Hills." Ann was the first person to put a name to this mysterious man. Did he drive the same 1936 or 1937 black Ford sedan that was seen by paperboy Bobby Jones as it remained parked for a few minutes at the spot where Beth's severed body was found in the pre-dawn hours of January 15? Detective Harry Hansen came to believe that "Maurice" was the connection between Beth's Hollywood acquaintances and her murder.

Witnesses at the Florentine Gardens were uncomfortable talking about "Maurice" or even mentioning his name. He was connected, some said, and a dangerous man. That's because "Maurice" turned out to be Maurice Clement, a minion of Ben Siegel and Mickey Cohen and a procurer for the call-girl ring run by Brenda Allen. Although Maurice was never publicly named by Capt. Donahoe or the press as a suspect in the murder, the Black Dahlia files released by the LA County District Attorney's Office in 2003 placed him high on the suspect list. Other suspects listed by investigator Jemison included police officers, servicemen and six physicians.

Former Columbia Studios employee Al Nolan stated that Maurice Clement worked for the studio's talent department. But the kind of "talent" that he managed was not the kind that would be seen on the silver screen. He arranged liaisons for Brenda Allen's girls with the studio brass and their friends. Nolan definitely remembered that Beth knew Clement and that she was one of the girls that he chauffeured around. At that time, it was common knowledge on the Columbia lot that a number of Allen's girls maintained an apartment on North Gower Street, near the studio's main gates.

Information in the District Attorney's files shed more light on Clement and on Beth's stay at Mark Hansen's house. When questioned in 1949 by Frank Jemison for the grand jury, Ann Toth said that she knew Beth was dating a number of different men, but Toth knew little about them because Mark Hansen was very jealous and Beth had to be careful about bringing her boyfriends around his house. This was in spite of the fact that Hansen claimed Beth was never one of his girlfriends. Ann testified, "Beth had to be cautious.

Everybody picked her up a block away, and everybody dumped her off a block away... because she wouldn't dare bring anybody to the house."

When asked to explain this, Ann stated, "Well, Mark wouldn't like it. I mean he more or less possessed her from the time she came there, so naturally, she didn't have anyone call for her there at the house ever... If it hadn't been for Mark, I would have found out lots of things because they would have called there, you know what I mean? I would have got acquainted with them, but he warned her not to bring anybody down there, not to go out with anybody else."

Ann added that when Hansen was not home, Beth made secretive telephone calls. She often called someone in Beverly Hills, Ann said, and she often called Maurice Clement, a man she described as small, dark-complexioned and driving a black Ford sedan. Ann was asked if she remembered Beth going to the doctor and was questioned about several of the doctors that were later found to be on the suspect list. Ann didn't recognize any of the names. She did admit, however, that she had taken Beth downtown for a doctor's appointment near the Biltmore Hotel about two weeks before she left for San Diego. She didn't give Ann a reason why she needed to go there, and Ann assumed that it was to meet Maurice.

Although California law requires that grand jury testimony remains sealed unless there is an indictment, it was leaked to the press at the time that a "wealthy Hollywood man" had become the prime suspect in the Black Dahlia case. The district attorney's files revealed that the "wealthy Hollywood man" was Mark Hansen. On December 16, 1949, Frank Jemison took Hansen's testimony in the presence of Sgt. Ed Barret of the LAPD Homicide Division.

During the interview, Hansen said Beth had initially come to his house after a fellow brought her and another girl (Marjorie Graham) over because they had no place to stay. They had stayed, he said, for a week or ten days in October 1946. Hansen said that Beth was "fair-looking, average. If it wasn't for her teeth. She had bad teeth. Other than that, she would have been beautiful."

Hansen asked the girls to move out because Marjorie had a drinking problem and also because Beth always seemed to have some undesirable character waiting for her outside and bringing her home. One particular character, he recalled, really seemed to be up to no good. He drove a 1938 or 1939 Chevrolet or Ford couple. Hansen only saw him at a distance, though. He couldn't describe him at all. He added that he had no hard feelings toward Beth. He asked her to move out mostly because her friend Marjorie was always "liquored up." He said he tried to speak to her about the caliber of men she had been seeing but she told him that she had been around and knew what life was about.

Jemison asked Hansen if she was having intercourse with these men, or was working as a prostitute. Hansen replied, "No, uh-uh. She was - she appeared to be a more domestic-type girl." He said she told him that she was engaged to a flyer named Gordon Fickling and gave Hansen the impression that she was saving herself for him. When Beth and Marjorie moved out of Hansen's house, he said they moved, "to that apartment-hotel."

The "apartment-hotel" was the Guardian Arms at 5217 Hollywood Boulevard and they moved into room 726. They shared the room with two men they had met on the street - Bill Robinson and Marvin Margolis. Robinson told the police the girls were broke, and he had Margolis had tried unsuccessfully to find them a place to stay. Eventually they allowed them to share their small apartment at the Guardian Arms, which had only a sitting room and a small bedroom. Robinson said that Beth slept on the couch and he "slept in the bedroom with Marge." They moved in on October 10 and moved out again on October 22. It was his understanding that the girls had gotten their fill of Hollywood and planned to return home to Massachusetts, but only Marjorie had the money to make the trip. On October 22, she boarded a Greyhound bus back to Boston - leaving Beth behind.

Until Beth could afford a ticket home, she needed a place to stay and the tiny apartment was just too cramped. Margolis said that he drove Beth back to Mark Hansen's house. Claiming to be Beth's cousin, he asked Hansen if Beth could leave her luggage there overnight.

Hansen remembered things a little differently, or so he told the investigators. According to Hansen, Margolis told him that Beth wanted to leave her suitcases at his place because she was leaving town the next day. However, when he came home that night, Beth was in the house and told him that she had no place to stay. Hansen let her move back in for a while and then kicked her out a second time. He claimed that he told Beth he didn't like the men she was going around with and that she was attracting a bad element to the house. Beth left, and moved back to the Chancellor apartments, where she had stayed before. One evening, Beth was back at his house when he walked in. He found her with Ann Toth, crying and insisting that she had to get out town. She told Hansen that she was very scared and was going to Oakland to visit her sister. Feeling sorry for her, Hansen paid for her to have dinner with Ann and then drove her back to her apartment at the Chancellor. She told Hansen that she was going to see her sister, and asked if she could stay with him again when she came back to town. Hansen told her that she couldn't; he didn't like the men she brought around. Hansen dropped her off on the street outside the apartment building and according to his story, he never saw her again.

Before the interview was over, Jemison asked him if he had any knowledge of the medical profession or knew anyone who performed abortions. Hansen stated that he did not. He said that he didn't know anyone

At some point during her last summer in Los Angeles, Beth had a collection of photos taken of herself for a portfolio. More than anything else, she wanted to be an actress and the photos show a pretty young girl with the whole world ahead of her. Tragically, they were found among her belongings when her bags were collected from the Greyhound station. These are the last known photos of Beth that were even taken.

Beth in the summer of 1946 in front of Graumann's Chinese Theater

connected to the medical field and he never had any connection with women who sought out the service of abortionists. Considering the circles he moved in, it's likely he was lying through his teeth. Hansen was released after that. In time, he dropped very low on the list of possible suspects for Beth's murder.

Beth left for San Diego on the day after her last visit to Hansen's house. She told Ann Toth and Mark Hansen that she was scared, which was the reason she was leaving. The next day, December 6, she checked out of the Chancellor after telling one of her roommates, Linda Rohr, that she was frightened. What was it that had scared her so badly? She never told anyone, but it might have had something to do with Maurice Clement.

Another of Beth's Chancellor roommates, Sherryl Maylond, said that one of Beth's frequent callers while she was living there was Maurice, and on the night of January 15, shortly after the headlines about the murder hit the streets, a man calling himself "Clement" entered the Hollywood bar where she worked and told the bartender that he wanted to "speak to Sherryl." It was Sherryl's night off, but the man returned the next night and told her that he had to speak to her about Beth Short. Frightened, she refused to talk to him and avoided him until he left the bar. Sherryl described him as a "slight, dapper, olive-skinned man."

Harry Hansen's notes in the 1949 grand jury files say that he questioned Maurice Clement about his relationship with Beth, and Clement admitted that he had seen her in the days just before she suddenly left the city.

Witnesses said that Beth frequented Brittingham's, which was just around the corner from Columbia Studios on Sunset and Gower. The restaurant was with Columbia studio executives and employees. George Bacos, an usher at CBS across the street, told the police that he had often seen Beth there. A Brittingham's waitress, Nina Blanchard, agreed that she had spotted her there many times. On several occasions, Beth had been in the company of Max Arnow, who was in charge of the Talent Department.

Max Arnow was notorious for supplying Harry Cohn and Columbia's studio heads with girls. Maurice Clement, also on the Talent Department payroll, was Brenda Allen's procurer and he drove girls to wherever Arnow told him to go. A witness saw Clement and Beth Short talking together at Brittingham's on at least four occasions early in December 1946, just before she fled to San Diego.

Because of the witnesses, Clement admitted to Harry Hansen that the meetings took place, but he lied to the police when he said that he first met Beth on December 1 at Brittingham's. She was broke, he said, and he paid her dinner check. Of course, this was a lie. Ann Toth and the desk clerk at the Hawthorne stated that he had been seen with Beth in September, when he occasionally paid her rent and reportedly offered to set her up in an apartment in Beverly Hills. Ann also believed that it was Clement who was meeting Beth at a doctor's office near the Biltmore Hotel shortly before Beth went to San Diego.

Maurice Clement was high on the "person or persons unknown" list for the detectives. And there was reason to believe that when Beth was dropped off at the Biltmore Hotel on January 9, 1947, she was waiting for him to pick her up. Did he?

If it was Clement, he might have been one of the last people to see her alive.

10. HERE IS DAHLIA'S BELONGINGS... LETTER TO FOLLOW

By the tenth day of banner headlines, the Black Dahlia case had made a small fortune for the Hearst newspapers, but after the inquest and the dismissal of Red Manley as the lead suspect, interest in the story was starting to wane. The public was still transfixed by the gruesome murder, but there were no new clues or theories that the police could offer. When cornered by the press, Harry Hansen was asked if he had any new suspects. He uttered his favorite response to reporters - "No."

But Capt. Donahoe, never one to let a chance to see his name in the papers pass him by, told Aggie Underwood, "We believe that the killer may have been a woman. The murdered girl was known to have been in the city from January 9 to January 14 without her baggage and makeup kit. It seems logical that the Short girl may have been staying with a woman where she could get a change of clothes." In support of this half-baked theory, Donahoe suggested that the girl's body was severed after death by a small female who was not strong enough to lift the entire one hundred and twenty-three-pound corpse. This theory forgets, though, that this "weak" woman would have had to subdue Beth, tie her up, and place her in a bathtub, where Dr. Newbarr was convinced she was then bisected. Donahoe based this on the actions of three of the most infamous mutilation killers in Los Angeles history, all whom were women - Winnie Ruth Judd, Clara Phillips and Louise Peete.

Winnie Ruth Judd was a medical secretary from Phoenix, Arizona, who murdered two of her former roommates in 1931 after an argument over a man. She dismembered one of them, stuffed both bodies in trunks and took them to Los Angeles on the Golden State Limited train. Alerted by a foul odor, station agents forced her to open the cases, revealing the body parts. Judd eventually became known as "The Trunk Murderess."

Clara Phillips, dubbed the "Tiger Woman" by the newspapers, became something of a celebrity after she carried out the vicious murder of her husband's mistress, a pretty bank clerk named Alberta Meadows. Twenty-three-year old Clara tricked her rival into taking a ride with her into a quiet area north of downtown LA. When they arrived, Clara got Meadows out of the car and attacked her with a claw hammer. She hit her in the face and the head and then used the claw hammer's head to disembowel the young woman. She hit her again and again with such force that the hammer broke off in her skull. Unbelievably, Alberta was still not dead, so Clara choked the last bit of life out of her. Hardened detectives and newspaper reporters were so sickened by the sight of the corpse that they noted that it looked as though Meadows had been attacked by a tiger, hence the nickname that was given to her killer.

Louise Peete came from a wealthy Louisiana family. The first hint of trouble came when she was expelled from school for sexual misbehavior. In 1903, she married a traveling salesman who committed suicide after discovering his wife with another man. She then spent time in Boston, working as a high-class prostitute and stealing from her clients. She later moved to Waco, Texas, where she became involved with a wealthy oil baron, who was later found murdered, with his jewelry missing. She was accused of his murder, but convinced a grand jury that she had been defending herself from rape. In 1913, she married a hotel clerk, who also committed suicide after finding her with another man.

In 1915, in Denver, she married salesman Richard Peete. They had a daughter, but Louise abandoned them and moved to Los Angeles. There, she lived with another oil magnate, who disappeared in 1920. By the time his lawyer had police search his house, Peete had returned to her husband in Denver. The missing oil magnate's body was found, and Peete was charged with his murder. She was sentenced to life imprisonment, but was released after serving eighteen years. During her time in prison, her husband killed himself.

After her release, Louise went to work as a housekeeper for a man who died a short time later. An elderly co-worker also died under suspicious circumstances. Peete then worked for Emily Dwight Latham, who had helped to secure her parole. Latham also died. Peete then became a housekeeper in Pacific Palisades, California, for Arthur C. Logan and his wife, Margaret, and married a man named Lee Borden Judson. Margaret Logan disappeared. Suspicion was aroused by poor forgeries of her signature that Peete presented on checks and letters to her parole officer. Louise's husband was acquitted of any involvement in the crime, but he committed suicide the day after he spoke to police. Louise was arrested and found guilty of the Logan murders. She was executed in the gas chamber at San Quentin State Prison at age 66 - one of only four women executed in the California gas chamber.

Donahoe's theory that Beth was killed by a woman was not exactly substantial, but it got attention and it forced detectives to start a search for Beth's old roommate at the Hawthorne, Lynn Martin, who had mysteriously vanished on the day after the murder story broke in the papers. She was last seen by her former Hawthorne boyfriend, Harold Costa, at about 5:00 p.m.

on January 15, as she was getting into a taxi near the corner of La Cienga and Sunset Boulevards. Donahoe claimed that Lynn Martin had a "bitter dislike for Miss Short" and he considered her a prime suspect. He told the press that "an intense search was underway for Miss Martin, who is still missing despite an ever expanding check on her whereabouts."

After getting an anonymous tip, the police picked up Lynn Martin at a North Hollywood motel, where she had gone into hiding after the murder. She was grilled by Hansen and Brown and it was learned that her real name was Norma Lee Myer and that she was a sixteen-year-old runaway from Long Beach. She was an aspiring nightclub dancer and singer who passed herself off as being in her early twenties. Like Beth, Lynn had been a B-Girl, but had slipped a rung down the Hollywood ladder and started turning tricks. She had once lived at the Chancellor Apartments and then had moved to the Hawthorne, where she shared a room with Beth and Marjorie.

She told the detectives that she had only shared the room with Beth for a week or two and didn't know her very well. She admitted that there were times that the two of them didn't get along, but she had no hard feelings toward her. The police located Marjorie Graham, who had left Hollywood on October 22 and returned to Massachusetts. She said that she was unaware of any bad feelings that Lynn might have had toward Beth. She denied Capt. Donahoe's allegations that there was animosity between the two of them. She added, "I don't thinks so. At least it didn't appear so to me when I was still in Hollywood."

Lynn turned into a few days of good copy for the newspapers, but little else. She may have fit into Donahoe's theory about the killer being a woman, but Hansen and Brown knew the young girl had nothing to do with the crime.

After in-depth discussions with the medical examiner, Dr. Newbarr, Hansen came to the conclusion that the bisection of the body had been done with medical instruments by someone with advanced medical knowledge. During his 1949 grand jury testimony, Hansen stated, "I think a medical man was involved - a very fine surgeon. I base that conclusion on the way the body was bisected... It was unusual in this sense, that the point at which the body was bisected is, according to eminent medical men, the easiest point in the spinal column to sever (between the second and third lumbar vertebrae) and he hit the spot exactly."

Hansen said that Dr. Newbarr concurred that whoever had sawed Beth's body in half had medical instruments and was a trained surgeon. He stated that it had been a fine piece of surgery that could not have been done in less than an hour. The FBI agreed with this opinion. After examining the autopsy photos, along with Dr. Newbarr's report, FBI experts determined that the body had been bisected by someone with medical knowledge. The FBI report noted: "The murderer had some training in the dissection of bodies. It is felt that the murder was committed indoors, where water, drainage facilities, and perhaps medical equipment was available."

However, this knowledge about the body being bisected by a "fine piece of surgery," carried by a trained surgeon, was never made known to the public. These observations did not come to light until the district attorney's files were opened in 2003. It may not have been announced to the public, but it was known to the homicide detectives. Contrary to Donahoe's ridiculous statements, he knew that Lynn Martin, a runaway and high school dropout, did not have the medical knowledge or experience to have committed the crime. Detective Hansen believed that the girl knew too much about Beth's friends and her shady connection and dropped out of sight when she saw the newspaper reports about the murder. She may have feared that she would be next.

While in the custody of juvenile authorities, Lynn Martin gave an interview to the *Herald-Express* in which she made some insightful - perhaps even dangerous - observations about Beth and some of the things she herself had seen while working as a B-Girl and prostitute:

There are a lot of girls in Hollywood who could end up like Beth Short... Hollywood draws them from all over the country.

Hollywood is a lonely place when you come to it without home ties or friends and very little money. There are few places for a lonely girl to go except into a bar.

Girls pick each other up in a store or a bar and start rooming together like old friends. It doesn't matter if they don't know anything about each other. It's somebody to talk to and share rent with - like Beth, Marjorie and I. Sharing rent means more money for something to eat or a new pair of shoes.

Even more important than food sometimes is having makeup and being able to keep your hair looking good, because if you look good, you can always get a man to buy you a big thick steak, some French-friend potatoes and a cup of coffee. Nothing ever tastes so good - at first. But the guys you pick up all insist you order steak or chops, and you get so sick of meat - meat all the time, and after a while you can hardly get it down.

You don't drink at first, because you don't like liquor. You don't like the taste. But you drink when you're on a date in a bar because you have to order something, and when you're out on a date the first thing is always a couple of drinks - and then a couple of drinks.

You're always lonely in Hollywood, even when you're out with people. They don't belong to you - those people. None of them really care what happens to you. Lots of time you can hardly stand the man you're with, but you can forget about that after a few drinks.

Lots of times the girls talk to each other about getting out of Hollywood and starting all over again. They're going back home, or they're going to get married to someone. Down in the heart of all of them is sort of a hazy dream about a husband and a house and a baby.

They talk about it, they dream about it, but somehow they almost never do it. This life is like a drug. You can't give it up. It's not like having a nine to fiver. They can sleep late if they want - they're on their own time. And if they have family back home, they never want their family to know the kind of life they're leading - so if they write home, they make up stuff.

Most of the girls are pretty innocent and well-meaning at first. The road downhill is gradual. They know their life isn't right, but after a while you take the easiest way.

Sooner or later, they become pregnant, and many of them resort to an illegal operation - and sometimes some of them end up like Beth Short.

For a girl that was hiding out from trouble, Lynn liked to talk a lot - maybe too much.

After the juvenile authorities returned her to her family in Long Beach, she disappeared once again and this time, she vanished for good. Some believe that she revealed a little too much about the life that Beth Short - and the girls like her - had been leading on Hollywood's dark side.

Aggie Underwood loved to shake things up. It was her job, after all, to get to the truth of each story that she worked on and sometimes it was necessary to make things happen. Aggie knew that there had never been another murder in LA's bloody history quite like the Black Dahlia case, but there was another unsolved murder of a young woman that had a connection to Beth Short. That was the murder of Georgette Bauerdorf, a volunteer with Beth at the Hollywood Canteen in 1944. Georgette was the attractive daughter of wealthy Wall Street financier George Bauerdorf, who had made a fortune in the oil industry. He was a close friend of Aggie's boss, William Randolph Hearst. Georgette's body had been discovered in the bathtub at her West Hollywood apartment on October 12, 1944, just a little over two years before Beth Short was killed. Georgette had been beaten, raped and asphyxiated by a cloth that had been shoved down her throat. Her body had been left in the bathtub and the killer had turned on the water before he fled the scene.

Aggie featured the Georgette Bauerdorf case in a front-page article that she wrote for the Herald-Express on January 23, 1947. Under a headline that read "Werewolves Leave Trail of Women Murder Victims in LA," she included the Bauerdorf case and seven other female victims of unsolved murders in recent Los Angeles history. The article raised the question of the LAPD's

Aggie Underwood

competency and asked whether or not the streets of the city were safe for young women.

As far as the police were concerned, the article could not have come at a worse time. There was already a growing concern about the number of unsolved murders on the books of the LAPD. Capt. Donahoe and the sheriff's department were doing their best to assure the public that they were making every possible effort to solve the Black Dahlia murder. More than four hundred officers were out knocking on doors, searching for witnesses and asking questions. Literally hundreds of suspects were questioned. Because it was considered a sex crime, the usual herd of known flashers, gropers, window-peepers and assorted perverts were rounded up and interrogated. Beth's friends and acquaintances were questioned as the detectives tried to reconstruct her final days and hours. Every lead that seemed promising ended up leading nowhere and the cops were further hampered by the lunatics whose crazed confessions were still pouring in. After thousands of police man-hours, the authorities had nothing to go on.

Administrative Vice Officer Vince Carter recalled, "Miss Short's life in Hollywood seemed to follow a pattern. She didn't have any visible signs of employment, she'd be broke, and then suddenly have some money. Her roommates, the bartenders, and the hotel clerks all came up with the same story. She was secretive - never one to confide. She never said what she was really doing, or who she was really going out with, or where she was going. Several of Elizabeth's girlfriends at Carlos Avenue and the Chancellor said there were days when she would disappear. Each time she would be gone for a day or two after saying she was going to hitch a ride downtown to Sixth Street. Upon her return, she was always loaded with money and would pay all her bills. 'We never knew where she went, or where she got the money,' one of the girls said. 'She didn't have a job and didn't act as if she was looking for work. She would often borrow money from her friends, but always paid it back later.'"

Carter knew there was more to the case than simple murder. He said, "I believe there were some acquaintances who knew her tragic story - like Lynn Martin, Mark Hansen and some of her roommates at the Chancellor but they were afraid to talk about it because it involved some powerful and dangerous people. The Dahlia case was very complex. It went way beyond the Werewolf Killer story reported in the papers, and Sgt. Harry Hansen knew a lot more than he ever confided to anybody - including Big Jack Donahoe and Finis Brown."

A week had passed, which Jim Richardson of the *Examiner* knew was an eternity in the newspaper business. The Black Dahlia case had managed to snag headlines since the body had been discovered, but it was starting to fade. The Dahlia stories had already slipped down the front page until it was below the fold. As the days passed, he knew it would sink deeper and deeper into the paper unless a miracle happened and new clues came to light. But then, on Thursday, January 24, Richardson received a telephone call that changed everything.

He was putting the next day's edition of the *Examiner* to bed when he picked up a ringing phone and heard a mysterious voice on the other end. It might have been a coincidence that it was a full moon because the so-called "Werewolf Killer" was on the other end of the line.

"Is this the city editor?' the called asked.

Richardson said that he was and gave his name when the man asked for it.

The caller went on, "Well, Mr. Richardson, I must congratulate you on what the *Examiner* has done in the Black Dahlia case."

Richardson impatiently thanked him, wondering what the point of the call was and probably thinking about the work that still needed to be completed to finish up the next day's edition.

"You seem to have run out of material," the caller remarked.

"That's right," Richardson snapped.

"Maybe I can be of some assistance," said the caller and chuckled. Richardson later said that the menacing little laugh sent chills up his spine.

"We need it," Richardson managed to say.

The caller said, "I'll tell you what I'll do. I'll send you some of the things she had with her when she, shall we say, disappeared."

Richardson wildly scrambled for a loose piece of paper on his desk. He scrawled the words, "Trace this call!" and waved it in front of his secretary. She hurried away. Richardson now needed to try and keep the man on the telephone. "What kind of things?" he asked.

"Oh, say her address book and her birth certificate and a few other things she had in her handbag."

"When will I get them?"

"Oh, within the next day or so. See how far you can get with them. And now I must say good-bye."

Richardson frantically cried, "Wait a minute!"

"But aren't you trying to trace this call?" The caller said - and then the line went dead.

On that Thursday evening, Richardson wasn't sure what to make of the call. The police weren't the only ones who had been getting crazy calls from lunatics and crackpots. But he had every reason to believe that he had spoken to the killer when an envelope arrived at the *Examiner* office postmarked January 24. It contained some of the contents known to be in Beth Short's handbag when she vanished, including the claim stubs for her luggage that had been checked at the Greyhound station on January 9.

The envelope had been mailed from the main branch of the post office downtown and was addressed to the "*Los Angeles Examiner* and other Los Angeles papers." It had been partially opened - apparently by accident - and postal inspectors intercepted it and passed it on to the police. The envelope opened at police headquarters in the presence of Capt. Donahoe, reporters and detectives. There was a message inside, formed from words and letters cut out of various Hearst newspapers and pasted onto a sheet of paper. It read: "Here is Dahlia's belongings - letter to follow."

Included in the envelope with the Greyhound claim stubs were Beth's identification, her birth certificate, social security card, the Matt Gordon obituary that she always carried in her purse, her address book and business cards from several male acquaintances, including a man she had met at the Hacienda Club in Mission Beach shortly before coming back to LA. Although the sender had soaked the envelope in gasoline to remove any fingerprints,

(Top) The bizarre letter sent to the newspapers. (Below Left) The belongings that were mailed - all soaked with gasoline so that no fingerprints would remain. (Below Right) Beth's birth certificate and the address book stolen from Mark Hansen.

the detectives found a few smudged prints, which were sent to the crime lab but were never identified.

It was assumed that only the killer could have the contents of the purse that Beth was carrying when she was last seen alive, but when he thought about it, Richardson wasn't so sure. Were those items still in the handbag when someone tossed it in the alley behind the restaurant? Or when the police found the purse in the city dump? It just all seemed too convenient for the skeptical newsman - the anonymous phone call, the envelope and mysterious note - right when the case had started to cool. It seemed like a once-in-a-lifetime break, but was it? Captain Donahoe had seized on Beth's address book, in which she had written numerous names, addresses and telephone numbers. After flipping through the book, Donahoe announced, "This book is going to be dynamite!"

It was rumored that more than seventy-five names of prominent citizens and Hollywood personalities were listed in its pages. Donahoe refused to divulge the names for fear of "embarrassing persons not connected to the case," and the contents of Beth's address book were never made public and were never examined by reporters. Richardson did learn, however, that several names and addresses had been deliberately cut from the book at some point before it was placed in the envelope, leading some to suspect that among the excised names was the killer's.

When it was discovered that the name of Mark Hansen, owner of the Florentine Gardens, was embossed in gold on the cover of the address book, Donahoe immediately placed Hansen back at the top of the suspect list. When he was shown the address book by detectives, Hansen identified it and said that it had "once been sent to me from Denmark, my native country." He claimed that it had been stolen from his desk about the time that Beth moved out of his house in October. He insisted, "There were no entries in the book, no names of any individuals, when I last saw it." And police handwriting experts determined that all of the entries in the book were written by Beth Short.

The message from the killer - or whoever had the items - along with the contents of Beth's handbag, had been a stroke of good fortune for Richardson and the *Examiner*, but lightning struck again on Monday, January 27 when a second message was received. A postcard arrived at the *Examiner* that had also been mailed from the main post office in downtown Los Angeles. There was a handwritten message scrawled in black pen that read: "Here it is. Turning in Wed. Jan. 29 10 a.m. Had my fun at police. Black Dahlia Avenger."

Capt. Donahoe told the press that he believed the postcard was legitimate and constituted the "letter to follow" that had been promised in the envelope that contained Beth's belongings. Donahoe said, "The fact that the postcard was written by hand, rather than lettered with words cut out of newspapers also supports the theory that the killer intends to turn himself in, and no longer needs to take pains to conceal his identity." In his press statements, Donahoe was optimistic about the suggestion that the killer was about to surrender. He theorized, "In signing the postcard 'Black Dahlia Avenger,' he is indicating that me murdered Elizabeth Short for some avenged wrong, either real or imagined. So far, we haven't seen any evidence of that, but we hope that the killer who is writing these notes keeps his promise to turn himself in on Wednesday."

The implication was that the killer was going to surrender to the *Examiner,* and as the days passed and Richardson - as well as the rest of Los Angeles - tensely waited for 10 a.m. on Jan. 29, the Dahlia headlines and the public's fascination with the case peaked again.

Donahoe used the press to send a public message to the killer. He promised, "If you want to surrender as indicated by the postcard now in our hands, I will meet you at any public location at any time or at the homicide detail office at City Hall. Communicate immediately by telephone - MI 5217, extension 2521 or by mail."

Of course, if the killer had actually tried to call, he would have gotten a busy signal - the line was flooded with calls from crackpots, nutcases and hoaxers.

By 9:00 a.m. on Jan. 29, Donahoe had posted detectives at all of the *Examiner* doors, waiting to grab the killer as soon as he showed up. At the same time, reporters from other newspapers were attempting to sneak into the Hearst building, hoping to beat the *Examiner* onto the street with the story. Richardson chased them out and then called Donahoe and told him to get his men out of the building too. He told him, "Nobody's going to turn themselves in with them standing there all eagle-eyed. If he comes, I promise I'll call you!"

Donahoe reluctantly agreed. He warned the editor, "But understand I'm taking him out of there at once. No deal this time. You can't hide out a murderer without getting yourself into real trouble. You know that, don't you?"

Silence fell over the city room as the clock on the wall ticked closer to 10:00 a.m. Will Fowler remembered, "All that morning the city room was unusually quiet. I don't think any of us really believed the killer would show, but there was always the outside chance that he would."

The designated hour, and then noon, came and went but the "Black Dahlia Avenger" never appeared. Richardson waited patiently by his phone in case he called again. He never left his desk that day, waiting until midnight, when the next day's edition had to be put to bed. The killer never showed - and neither did anyone else. Richardson finally gave the order to roll the presses for the Thursday morning run. He knew that someone had made a fool of him, but whether it was a crackpot, the "Werewolf Killer" or Capt. Donahoe, he didn't know.

11. SIN, SHADOWS AND L.A. SMOKE & MIRRORS

It was a known fact that Jim Richardson had little admiration for Jack Donahoe and the upper echelons of the LAPD, but he often found himself forced to play their games and he sometimes ran stories in his paper that led to nothing but dead-ends. The false leads and planted stories all served a purpose, he was assured, but there were other leads that were never investigated at all. Will Fowler was very aware that some aspects of the Dahlia story were never assigned to anyone and he later told an intriguing story about Richardson, City Hall, William Randolph Hearst and the Black Dahlia case.

Richardson got his start in the newspaper business thanks to his uncle, Friend Richardson, a newspaper editor and protégé of William Randolph Hearst before becoming governor of California from 1923 to 1927. It was Governor Friend Richardson who appointed Fletcher Bowron to the judge's bench prior to Bowron's run for Los Angeles mayor in 1939. The governor's nephew, Jim Richardson, became a close friend of Bowron during the years when Richardson was rising through the Hearst ranks to become managing editor of the *Examiner*.

According to Will Fowler, Richardson had once been a fiercely independent Hearst reporter and editor before succumbing to the newspaperman's curse - alcoholism. In 1937, he was fired by Hearst because of his drinking. After drying out, he worked for the Warner Brothers publicity department for a time and then his friend, Mayor Bowron, intervened with Hearst and persuaded him to hire Richardson back - with the condition that he never touch alcohol again. Richardson stuck with the agreement and he never drank again - but he was never a fiercely independent newsman again either. He was in debt to Mayor Bowron, and according to Will Fowler, there were leads in the Black Dahlia case that pointed toward City Hall that Richardson knew would never be chased down.

Until the Black Dahlia case, Aggie Underwood at the *Herald-Express* has also managed to maintain her independence and her integrity. Her article about the unsolved murders of young women in the city may have angered some people at City Hall and at the LAPD, but she felt that it was her duty to report the story. It was during her research into the recent open murder files that Aggie re-discovered the links between the Georgette Bauerdorf and Elizabeth Short murders. And once she started to publicize those links, she found herself maneuvered into silence and forced to compromise her journalistic integrity.

Beth and Georgette were both born in 1924. Georgette came from a wealthy New York family and had lived on Park Avenue before moving to Los Angeles. Beth, of course, came from a family with a missing father and a mother who worked whatever jobs she could find and fed her children on welfare. While Beth had been waiting tables in Miami, Georgette was attending the exclusive Westlake School for Girls in Bel Air.

But in many ways, the two young women were alike. Both had dark hair and made friends easily. Both enjoyed the company of attractive men in uniform. But unlike Beth, Georgette had gone to finishing schools and all her bills were paid by her indulgent family. At the time of her death, she lived alone in her family's apartment in a fashionable Spanish Baroque-style building at 8493 Fountain Palace in West Hollywood. The apartment building, El Palacio, had been the transitory home of a number of film stars and celebrities, including Joan Crawford, John Garfield, Franchot Tone and Evelyn Keyes. Mobster Johnny Roselli became a resident of El Palacio after his release from prison in 1947. Because the building was in West Hollywood and just outside the jurisdiction of the LAPD, the Bauerdorf murder investigation was handled by the LA County Sheriff's Department.

Georgette's body was discovered by Mr. and Mrs. Frederick Atwood, the building managers who lived downstairs from her apartment. The Atwoods told detectives that they were awakened some time after midnight on Wednesday, October 11, 1944 by a "commotion" and what sounded like a crash of "something metallic." The next morning, they found Georgette's door was partially open and they could hear the sound of running water coming from inside. Mrs. Atwood knocked on the door, and when there was no answer, she and her husband cautiously entered the apartment. They found that the place was flooded with water that was pouring from the bathtub. And then, to their horror, they found Georgette's body submerged face-down in the overflowing tub.

When the detectives from the sheriff's department arrived, they determined that Georgette had been assaulted and raped in the bedroom and then asphyxiated by a piece of cloth that was shoved down her throat. Bloodstains were found on the floor near the bed, along with her cut and ripped pajama bottoms, which had been sliced by a knife. Apparently, the killer fled after placing the body in the bathtub and turning on the water. Since the water had been left running, the detectives surmised that the killer might have been frightened off by something. Georgette's neighbor, prominent Hollywood drama coach Stella Adler, recalled that she had returned to her apartment at a little after midnight and noticed that

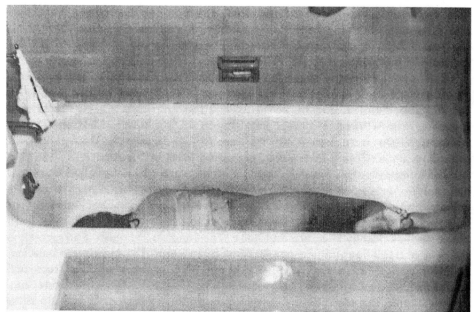

Georgette was found raped, strangled and her body dumped into a bathtub with the water left running. Her murder – like Beth Short's – has never been solved.

Georgette's door was partially open. This would have been a very short time after the Atwoods heard the loud sounds coming from her apartment.

During the inquest, it was determined by Medical Examiner Frank Webb that Georgette's murder had taken place around midnight and that the official cause of death was "obstruction of upper air passages by inserted cloth." Dr. Webb stated, "Abrasions of the knuckles of the girl's hands showed that she fought desperately against the attacker. Thumb and finger marks on her face, lips, abdomen and thighs indicated the attacker was powerful with almost ape-like hands... The victim had been asphyxiated prior to the time that the body had been placed in the bathtub."

Georgette's purse was found on the floor near the bedroom door and its contents were strewn about nearby. Her car keys were missing and her green Oldsmobile coupe, which she normally kept in the Palacio garage, was gone. Three days later, the car was found parked at the curb in front of 7281½ East Twenty-Fifth Street, south of downtown Los Angeles. The keys had been left in the ignition and sheriff's detectives concluded that it had been abandoned there by the killer.

Georgette had last been seen alive by her coworkers at the Hollywood Canteen. She had left at approximately 10:30 p.m. on Wednesday evening,

October 11. Like Beth Short, she served as a junior hostess and would socialize and dance with the servicemen on leave in Hollywood. Her friend, June Ziegler, who worked in the classified department of the *Los Angeles Times*, was also a volunteer hostess. She told detectives that she had seen Georgette dancing with a number of different servicemen that evening, just as she always did.

Detectives found dozens of fingerprint samples in Georgette's apartment and car. Although it was against Canteen rules, Georgette sometimes invited servicemen whom she met at the Canteen to come home with her if they needed a place to stay. Although her friends warned her not to, she sometimes gave lifts to hitchhiking men in uniform. It's not surprising that there were so many fingerprints in her apartment and car. What was unusual were the fingerprints that were found on an automatic nightlight on the porch leading to Georgette's apartment. The bulb had been partially unscrewed so that it would not come on, leaving the area around the entrance in shadows. Investigators believed that the killer may have been someone that Georgette would recognize, so he unscrewed the bulb and stood in the dark to avoid recognition before forcing his way in when the door was opened. The prints of the killer, though, were never identified.

It was the fact that Georgette's body had been found in the bathtub that compelled Aggie Underwood to try and renew interest in the story in the wake of the Black Dahlia murder. She began to suspect that the Bauerdorf murder might have a connection to Short's. The method the killer used was quite different, of course, but there was a bathtub in that case, too. And Aggie had heard through her contacts in the sheriff's department that detectives had found and confiscated Georgette's diary, which documented that she had known Beth Short when they were both working as volunteers at the Hollywood Canteen in the fall of 1944.

According to Aggie's source, both girls had been familiar with a Hollywood celebrity whom they had met at the Canteen. The celebrity, a well-known actor at the time, because a suspect in both the Bauerdorf and Black Dahlia cases and was brought in for questioning. Although it was never mentioned by the sheriff's department, the LAPD, or the press, the celebrity was Arthur Lake, who was under contract to Columbia Pictures and played Dagwood in the *Blondie* movies.

Arthur Lake had been born Arthur Silverlake, Jr. in 1905 while his father and uncle were touring with a circus in an aerial act known as the "Flying Silverlakes." His mother, Edith Goodwin, was an actress. His parents later appeared in vaudeville, traveling with Arthur and his sister, Florence, throughout the South and Southwest. Arthur first appeared on stage as a baby in *Uncle Tom's Cabin* and he and his sister became part of the act in 1910. Their mother brought the children to Hollywood to get into films when

Arthur and Patricia Lake. His close connections with William Randolph Hearst – through his wife – likely kept him out of the investigations into the deaths of Georgette and Beth, even though he knew both girls.

Arthur was twelve. He made his screen debut in the silent film, *Jack and the Beanstalk* in 1917.

Lake's first Hollywood contract was with Universal Pictures, where he acted in westerns and as an adolescent character actor. His last name was changed to Lake because studio head Carl Laemmerle, Sr., thought Silverlake sounded too Jewish. Shortly after the founding of RKO Pictures in 1928, he signed with that studio and made *Dance Hall* and *Cheer Up and Smile* in 1929 and 1930. During this early sound film era, he typically played light romantic roles in films such as *Indiscreet* with Gloria Swanson. He also had a substantial part as the bellhop in the 1937 film, *Topper*.

Lake became best known for his portrayal of Dagwood Bumstead in twenty-eight *Blondie* films that were made by Columbia between 1938 and 1950. He was also the voice of Dagwood on the radio series and later played the character in a short-lived television series.

After Beth Short's murder, Hollywood Canteen records were checked by sheriff's investigators. A former hostess recalled that Arthur Lake socialized with both of the murdered girls. When Lake met with investigators, he reluctantly told Detective Frank Esquival that he "may have talked to Elizabeth Short and Georgette Bauerdorf at the Canteen." Beyond that, he said, there was nothing that he knew that could help the investigation.

Esquival later said, "Dagwood looked us straight in the face from one to the other and said he wanted us to understand that his wife, Patricia, was the niece of Marion Davies, a close friend of William Randolph Hearst and George Bauerdorf, the murdered girl's father." Lake said that any further questions that the detectives had for him needed to be handled through his attorney. He didn't add that he was also a close friend of Hearst, was a frequent houseguest of the newspaper magnate or that he and his wife had been married at Hearst's Castle in San Simeon in 1937.

Investigators believed that there was a link between the Bauerdorf murder and the Black Dahlia case and that Arthur Lake should be questioned further, but Detective Esquival told Aggie that the investigation into both cases had been blocked and that all logical avenues of investigation had been shut down.

After Aggie wrote the article about the unsolved murders of Georgette Bauerdorf, Beth Short and a number of other young women, she began working on a story about the similarities between the Bauerdorf murder, the Black Dahlia case and the Arthur Lake connection. But before she could complete the article, she was told by managing editor Lou Young to kill the story. He also told her that she was being pulled off the Black Dahlia case altogether.

When Aggie demanded to know why the story had been killed - and why she was being taken off the Dahlia murder - she was told that it was on orders from the boss. Of course, the "boss" was William Randolph Hearst. Aggie initially suspected that Hearst killed the story connecting the Bauerdorf and Short murders because of his friendship with Georgette's father, who hated notoriety. But why was Aggie pulled off the Dahlia case? Whatever the reason, she was angry - so angry that she considered quitting and taking her considerable talents to another newspaper.

Before she could, though, she was promoted from reporter to city editor.

Aggie later recalled, "They kicked me up the ladder... it made my head spin. But did I want to be city editor of the *Herald*, or did I want to be a reporter with my thumb on the doorbell?" No woman had ever been appointed city editor at a major metropolitan newspaper before, and Aggie found the promotion difficult to resist. She asked what would happen to the Bauerdorf case and Young told her that it would not be mentioned again. Young told her in no uncertain terms, "We will not recognize that name anymore at the *Herald*."

Aggie Underwood knew that her silence was the price of her promotion, but she accepted it anyway. She later said, "I decided that I wanted to be the city editor at the *Herald*. That's all that I'd ever say about the Bauerdorf or the Dahlia case. But I'd lay awake many a night wondering if I did the right thing."

Aggie strongly believed that there was a connection between Arthur Lake and the murder of Georgette Bauerdorf and Elizabeth Short, although it would be many years before she learned what the connection was and why Hearst had killed the Bauerdorf story and had taken her off the Dahlia case.

When Beth Short's killer failed to show up at the *Examiner* on January 29, the Black Dahlia case finally started to run out of steam. Paste-up notes that supposedly came from the killer continued to arrive at the Hearst paper offices, but Detective Harry Hansen considered them all to be hoaxes.

After examining the first four notes, Ray Pinker's crime lab stated that they had come from the same person, which led Capt. Donahoe to dramatically state, "We are dealing with a homicidal maniac who craves attention for his crime and may come forward in a bold and spectacular manner for his curtain call after he has wrung out the last drop of drama from his deed."

Jim Richardson wasn't satisfied with the official line from Donahoe. He hired Clark Sellers, an esteemed questioned document examiner, to look at the one handwritten note that was among the first four messages. In Sellers' report to the *Examiner*, he stated, "It was evident that the writer took great pains to disguise his or her personality by printing instead of writing the message and by endeavoring to appear illiterate. But the style and the formation of the printed letters betrayed the writer as an educated person."

According to Will Fowler, Richardson privately believed that the phone call that purportedly came from the killer, the first four paste-up notes and the mailing of the contents of Beth's purse had been contrived by Donahoe. Fowler stated, "Richardson suspected that Donahoe was covering up the murder, which was connected to the mob and some big-shot at City Hall -- but it was an avenue that Richardson didn't pursue."

It wasn't long before the press began receiving copycat paste-ups from various nuts and cranks. More than a dozen notes were sent to the *Examiner* and the *Herald-Express*, and each was more ludicrous than the last. After a while, it became difficult to discern between the first four notes and the spurious paste-ups that followed.

For the record, the first four notes included the paste-up that came with Beth's belongings, which promised a "letter to follow," the handwritten note that told of the surrender of the "Black Dahlia Avenger" and two others. The third and fourth notes were also paste-ups and read:

"Dahlia's killer cracking, wants terms"

"To Los Angeles Herald-Express, I will give up in Dahlia killing if I get 10 years. Don't try to find me."

These were believed to be from the same person. The police claimed they were from the killer. Jim Richardson believed they were sent by Capt. Donahoe.

While this was going on, the confessors, nutcases and cranks continued to line up to take credit for the murder and Donahoe continued to release his absurd, headline-grabbing announcements. On February 1, 1947, he stated:

It appears impossible that the Short girl was murdered in the city. We are forced to this conclusion by the failure of anyone to report a possible place where she was killed within the city limits. If she was slain in a house or a room or a motel in the city, it seems impossible that some trace has not been reported or found. This leads us to the conclusion that she was killed outside the city. The killer could not have emerged from the place in clothing worn when the murder was committed and the body drained of blood. He could have been too easily detected and stains would have attracted attention.

By placing the murder outside of the city, Donahoe got the LAPD partially off the hook for not solving the crime and apprehending the "homicidal maniac." Donahoe began to disclose various sites outside of the city as suspected murder locations - and then abruptly eliminate them. He kept floating new theories about the murder, rambling for the press, which was happy to listen to him since they had nothing else to go on in the case. At one time or another, he said that the murder, "may not have taken place in Los Angeles," "may have been committed by a woman with lesbian tendencies," and "may have been committed by someone she knew."

Finis Brown later noted that Harry Hansen didn't mind Donahoe babbling to the press. He was just happy that he didn't have to talk to them. Donahoe could say anything he wanted, as long as it didn't interfere with Hansen's investigation. On the other hand, Hansen didn't trust Donahoe and felt that he was deliberately manipulating the facts. Hansen believed that the murder scene was somewhere near the site where Beth's handbag and shoes had been discovered, in the alley near Pico and Crenshaw. Predictably, Donahoe seemed to go out of his way to dispel that notion.

Robert Manley had positively identified the purse and the shoes found near the incinerator as those worn by Beth Short on January 9, when he had last seen her. However, several days after Manley's positive identification, Donahoe brought Elvera and Dorothy French from San Diego to also identify the handbag and shoes. The Frenchs were not certain whether or not the items belonged to Beth, so on January 28, Donahoe sent out a press release stating that the handbag and shoes had not belonged to Beth after all and Manley must have been mistaken. But it should be noted that the Frenchs last saw Beth on January 8 and they had not seen her, or what she was wearing, when Manley dropped her off at the Biltmore Hotel the next day.

While Harry Hansen had little regard for Donahoe, there was an element in the LAPD that held him in high esteem. According to Vince Carter, it was well known to a number of officers in administrative vice that the upper echelons of the LAPD were receiving payoffs from the mob and that those payoffs were arranged by their operative at Central Division - Capt. Jack Donahoe. Carter stated, "The old-line vice payoff from the Mafia to corrupt police officials had tapered off after a new territorial vice map had been drawn up by Charles "Lucky" Luciano and Meyer Lansky in the '30s. But when Captain Jack Donahoe came into power at Central in 1945, he seized the opportunity to reorganize and juice up the vice take by key police officials, which included Chief Clemence B. Horrall, Assistant Chief Joseph Reed, and Captain William Burns of the Gangster Squad." As the vice take enforcer, Donahoe did the dirty work and squeezed the juice that kept everybody happy, except the honest cops, who knew they'd never rise above the rank of sergeant, and had to deal with gangsters on the street, as well as those within the LAPD - like "Big Jack" Donahoe, as he was often called within the department.

Carter went on to say that many of the officers that he worked with in administrative vice knew that Donahoe was misleading the press and the public in regard to the Black Dahlia case, but they were afraid to come forward. No one dared to expose Donahoe because of his connections in the underworld. Carter explained, "Donahoe had a reputation as a killer, and he was a close friend of another killer - Jack Dragna, who was Luciano's West Coast representative. Somewhere along the way, Jack Dragna and Captain Jack Donahoe became friends. Dragna had control over the narcotics business, and Donahoe was an important contact... It was Dragna who introduced Donahoe to Chickie Stein, Dragna's narcotics distributor in LA, and she and Donahoe became quite close. Chickie was a beautiful Sicilian woman with dark brown eyes who was brought up in a New York whorehouse. Her mother had been one of Luciano's whorehouse madams... Chickie was introduced to Dragna by Luciano when she was in her early twenties. Luciano trusted her completely, and when Luciano was arrested by Thomas Dewey, and Chickie's mother's prostitution business folded, Chickie came to Los Angeles as Luciano's West Coast heroin connection under Dragna's guidance. Donahoe and Chickie became close friends, and he presented her with a gold medallion with the Christ crucifixion on one side and the Star of David on the other. Chickie wore this around her neck on a fine gold chain. On one occasion she showed it to me, and Captain Jack Donahoe's name was engraved on one side of the medallion. Chickie was as proud of it as if it had been given to her by one of the mob bosses - which in my opinion was not too far off the mark."

Part of Donahoe's strategy in misleading the press and the public in the Black Dahlia case involved his repeated references to Beth Short as a suspected lesbian. Will Fowler and *Herald-Express* reporter Bevo Means were told by a Donahoe underling and a deputy coroner that Beth couldn't have sex with men. The contact stated, "Something in the autopsy indicated a lesbian pathology."

Will Fowler recalled, "It was a leak and Bevo jumped on it figuring that if she couldn't have sex with guys, she was having sex with women." Following Donahoe's calculated plant of this sensational and misleading information, a number of stories appeared in the newspaper indicating that the autopsy report revealed that Beth had undeveloped sexual organs and therefore, could not have normal relationships with men. This misinformation - started by Donahoe - was spread by journalists and writers for more than fifty years. In 1988, Will Fowler finally acknowledged that Beth's purported inability to have normal sexual relations with men was pure fiction. He wrote to author Mary Humphrey, "Regarding my telling you that Elizabeth Short had "infantile sex organs"... That is untrue, and a ploy I use to shock all of faint stomachs, and phony would-be biographers and article writers."

But beyond shocking people and throwing the competition off-track, this ploy also managed to allay suspicions that Beth may have been pregnant when she was murdered. All of the lesbian stories in the press did the same thing. Hearst reporter Sid Hughes was told to canvas all of the known lesbian bars in the city in an effort to establish that Beth was a frequent customer. In addition, author and screenwriter Ben Hecht wrote a Dahlia article for the *Herald-Express* in which he labeled Beth a lesbian and maintained that she was murdered by a lesbian acquaintance. It was a direct connection to Donahoe's claims that a woman had killed Beth, but everyone seemed to ignore this connection at the time.

The Hecht article, which ran in the paper on February 1, 1947, was fairly ridiculous for such a talented and established writer and was filled with double-talk and pseudo-science that may have sounded impressive to everyday people at the time, but could never be taken seriously today. Remember that in the late 1940s, homosexuality was still considered a mental illness by the scientific establishment, which meant, of course, that such people might be capable of anything - or so Hecht implied. He wrote: "The manner in which the 'Black Dahlia' was done to death, befouled and butchered after expiring under diverse torture, bespeaks the looks, sex, height, weight, coloring and even type of hair of the killer. It was a crime done by a lesbian - and not intended to be a crime. The killing itself may well have been part of the didoes to which the 'Black Dahlia' had submitted herself. She, too, was an odd one, and because of her physical and glandular and psychic make-up given to humoring the fancies of women..."

Using "science," Hecht went on to even greater heights of absurdity by theorizing that the killer was a woman who was "a hyperthyroidic type of human, with an over developed thymus gland at work - driven into a thyroidal storm by some great shock."

Hecht proceeded to find faulty grammar as an indication that the killer was female. Citing the handwritten note to the *Examiner* in which the killer stated, "Had my fun at the Police," Hecht maintained that the killer's grammatical error in using "at" instead of "with" could only have been a "female malapropism, and an infantile one (an over developed thyroid bespeaks infantilism). Little girls often say, "Give it *at* me!'"

Hecht then went on to provide a detailed description of the killer: "She is a woman of forty. She is 5 feet 6 inches tall. She weighs 115 pounds. She is thin, almost gaunt. She has a rudimentary bosom. Her face is long and narrow. She has a receding chin. Her teeth are slightly oversized. She has brown and very wavy hair. Her fingers are long. And she has large eyes - unusually large and arresting eyes. And she has a 'European' accent, as well."

Even though the Hecht article was obviously the writer's attempt at a blatant con job, there was an odd note at its convoluted conclusion. After having his fun with the reader, Hecht switched gears and negated everything that he had previously said about the murder and tersely stated that the killer wasn't a woman - it was a man. He added that he knew the killer's name and the reason behind the gruesome murder, but that he was unable to disclose "a second version of the crime and its perpetrator, which I am unable to offer this, or any other paper."

It was a weird ending to a weird article. At the time, Hecht was one of the highest paid writers in Hollywood, having written the screenplays for movies like *Scarface, Nothing Sacred, Wuthering Heights,* and *Notorious.* He had not written a crime story for a newspaper since his time as a Hearst crime reporter in Chicago in the 1920s, and he may have done the article with the lesbian allegation as a favor to someone. He was friends with William Randolph Hearst, as well as Gene Fowler and his son, *Examiner* reporter Will Fowler. He also hit the Hollywood nightspots with Ben Siegel, Mickey Cohen and mobsters who ran the Brenda Allen prostitution ring. Gangsters were glamorous in Hollywood in those days. Hecht may very well have been telling the truth when he said he knew who killed Beth Short and the reason why she was killed.

Detective Harry Hansen

By the end of the investigation's third week, Capt. Donahoe had to confess to the press that the police were stymied. They had no suspects, no leads, no witnesses, no clues and not even a murder scene. The case files were overflowing with false confessions, played-out suspects, and leads that went nowhere, but they didn't have a single piece of real evidence. Finis Brown said, "No lead had any conclusions. Once we found something, it seemed to disappear in front of our eyes. Following any of those leads was like going down one-way streets with dead ends."

Harry Hansen believed from the beginning that the only way to identify the killer in the Black Dahlia case was to learn everything about the victim - but it was difficult to know Beth Short. She was a very private person, who lived in her own dream world. She was constantly on the move to the next dream, the next scheme, the next guy and the next hotel. Nevertheless, Hansen followed his own leads and believed that he was making progress. Finis Brown spoke about his partner, "He was a brilliant detective, a smart, smart man; but a loner and an odd bird. He wasn't liked - not that he was disliked - he just wasn't liked. He was too removed and too above others in his thinking and in his way of holding himself and his opinions about others and police work in general."

One of Hansen's biggest problems in the LAPD of the era was that he was an honest cop, devoted to his work, which he saw as his true calling. He always defended police work, yet he had to deal with the corruption that surrounded him. He had an intense dislike for his boss, Capt. Donahoe, but kept his silence. The secret of the sealed autopsy established a motive for the murder and provided avenues of investigation that Hansen believed Donahoe and his cronies were blocking. When Hansen discovered that Finis Brown was reporting everything he was investigating to Gangster Squad commander William Burns, he began to suspect that Brown was an operative for the squad. Soon after, they had a falling out. Hansen stopped confiding in Brown and locked up his private Dahlia files.

Brown later recalled, "I was personally concerned that Harry kept saying he was going to yank the papers from the morgue. I said, 'Harry, you can't monkey with the coroner'... He said I was a fine one to talk about ethics, and I was lucky I wasn't in jail, or off the force... Then he laughed, but he was serious."

Former reporter Chuck Cheatham, who wrote about the Black Dahlia case for the *Long Beach Independent* recalled, "Harry Hansen was well liked by some, and hated by others. I liked Harry. He wasn't on the take - not Hansen. Some people say they were all on the take, the police. They all had their circles of people they protected. But not Harry - as straight as they come. His partner, Finis Brown, that's another story."

The district attorney's files on the Black Dahlia case, not opened for more than fifty years after the murder, confirmed Hansen's suspicion that Finis Brown was a secret operative for the Gangster Squad. In 1949, Sgt. Conwell Keller was called to testify before the grand jury and he admitted that the squad had their own records about the murder and that Brown was assigned to their detail and fed them information about Hansen's investigation.

Suspicion about Brown and Donahoe was enough to keep them out of many aspects of Harry's own investigation. He continued to pursue his own leads and things began making sense to him. He knew that someone with advanced medical knowledge had methodically bisected the body. He knew the approximate site where the murder had occurred. And he knew what secret had been hidden in the sealed autopsy files. He also knew that more than one person had been at the scene on Norton Avenue where Beth's body had been dumped. He suspected that one of them was a short, dark-complexioned man who drove the old black Ford sedan - Brenda Allen's procurer, Maurice Clement.

By the early part of February, the Black Dahlia case had sunk to well below on the fold on the front pages of the LA papers. New and diverting stories about the murder had been hitting the headlines until the public grew tired and confused. In the ensuing weeks, Dahlia stories became sporadic and only showed up in the back pages, as other murders and scandals made the headlines.

On February 10, 1947, the murder of Jeanne French became the lead story. A construction worker found her nude body in an isolated area of Culver City. She had been kicked and stomped to death. The killer had written "Fuck you PD," and "Tex" on her torso in red lipstick. Jeanne French was originally from Texas, but whether "Tex" referred to her or to someone else was unknown. Capt. Donahoe publicly stated that the Black Dahlia murder and the so-called "Red Lipstick Murder" of Jeanne French were related but it was obvious to Harry Hansen and the other investigators that there was no relationship between the two cases. The killer's method was totally different. Jeanne French's murder was one of pure rage. There were no knife wounds or surgical incisions. The victim had been kicked to death at the site hours before her body was discovered - the opposite of how Beth Short had been tortured for an extended period of time before being killed and her body dumped at another spot.

Donahoe worked hard to spread the theory about the two cases, but that turned out to be his last connection with the Black Dahlia case. On February 19, he was removed from his position as commander of the homicide division and transferred by Chief of Detectives William Bradley to the robbery detail. According to Vince Carter, Donahoe's problems began when Hansen learned that Donahoe had arranged for two officers from the Gangster Squad to conduct advance interviews with some of the people found in Beth's Short's address book. When Hansen went to question them, he found that in many cases, they had already been questioned by Gangster Squad officers Archie Case and James Ahern. It was believed that Donahoe was afraid that when Hansen questioned the people whose names had been left in the book, they might come up with something that would lead him to the names that had been removed. This was a blatant violation of procedure and Hansen was furious. He took his complaints to the Chief of Detectives, William Bradley. Hansen found out that Case and Ahern had been assigned by Assistant Chief Joseph Reed and Donahoe to find out how much certain people in the address book knew about connections between Beth and an important public figure on the police commission. One of those interviewed by Case and Ahern was actor Arthur Lake, a close friend of William Randolph Hearst and Chandler family heir Norman Chandler, the publisher of the Los Angeles Times and head of the police commission.

After that, things became antagonistic between Hansen and Donahoe and Hansen refused to have anything to do with him. Eventually, Donahoe was transferred to the robbery detail.

Following the murder of Jeanne French, there were a number of gangland shootings, earthquakes and Hollywood scandals that snagged the LA headlines. On February 22, 1947, a mysterious shooting made the news. It was reported that Brenda Allen's friend, Sgt. Evan Jackson of the vice squad, shot and killed a robber with his service revolver. According to the newspaper stories, Jackson was sitting in a car with a female acquaintance by the name of Marie Blanque when a thug approached the car with a gun. Sgt. Jackson managed to shoot the would-be robber, who died instantly, but an accomplice escaped in a second car.

Although the stories of what seemed like an attempted holdup quickly disappeared from the papers, the shooting did not escape the attention of Sgt. Charles Stoker, who noted that it took place near the Ambassador Hotel and in front of Brenda Allen's apartment at Ninth Street and Fedora Avenue. Stoker decided to attend the inquest and saw that Brenda Allen was in attendance. He soon learned that she was the "Marie Blanque" that was in the car at the time of the incident. The inquest established that the dead man was Roy "Peewee" Lewis, a mob gunman from Chicago, and that the weapon that he was carrying was a machine gun. His intention had not been robbery; it was to kill the driver of the car - Brenda Allen.

It was obvious that the LAPD wanted to keep Brenda Allen's name out of the newspapers. Stoker assumed that this was because of police payoffs or because her association with Sgt. Jackson would have proved embarrassing to the department. The fact that Brenda Allen was the intended victim of a shooting - less than five weeks after the murder of Elizabeth Short - was not acknowledged, either by the press or by the police, until a year later when the *Los Angeles Daily News* broke the story as part of a series of reports that revealed corruption in the highest levels of the police department.

Stoker had heard the rumors from officers in administrative vice that the attempted murder of Allen had been contracted by Jack Dragna and it had something to do with Allen's knowledge about the murder of Beth Short and the site where the murder took place. Allen's apartment and her girls' bungalow court were approximately thirty blocks from Thirty-Ninth Street and Norton and fifteen blocks from the alley where the purse and shoes had been found. Shortly after the shooting incident, Allen moved out of the apartment and went into hiding. Several months later, Stoker heard that she had rented a place near Sunset on Cory Avenue, well within Ben Siegel's territory.

According to Robert Slatzer, the young screenwriter who once dated Beth Short's friend Ann Toth and Marilyn Monroe, there were rumors all over Hollywood that the Black Dahlia murder was connected to Brenda Allen and the mob. He recalled that Monroe became very disturbed after Beth's murder. She was convinced that Beth had "gotten herself into trouble" and was murdered by some of the underworld characters that hung around the Florentine Gardens. Slatzer said, "Marilyn became frightened by what had occurred and never went back there."

Then, five months after Beth Short's murder and four months after the attempted murder of Brenda Allen, Ben "Bugsy" Siegel was shot to death on June 20, 1947. It would be this murder that, for some theorists about the Black Dahlia case, put some of the final pieces of the puzzle into place.

In the meantime, although interest peaked every once in a while, by the end of 1947, one of the most infamous murders in Los Angeles history left homicide detectives without a suspect or a clue. The LAPD file on the Black Dahlia case was stamped "Open and Unsolved."

Officially, it remains unsolved today.

12. WHO KILLED THE BLACK DAHLIA?

Today, nearly seven decades after Elizabeth Short was brutally murdered in Los Angeles, it would be easy for us to ignore what clues exist in the case and write off her death to the act of a random predator, some depraved killer who saw her as a victim of opportunity and insanely tortured, killed and mutilated her. But such thinking is not only short-sighted, it ignores the wealth of evidence - both hard evidence and anecdotal evidence - that exists in regard to what Beth Short knew, what she did, and whether or not it got her killed.

So, in the pages ahead, we'll take a look at the various theories that have emerged over the years in regard to the Black Dahlia killer, leaving out the ridiculous "psychopathic lesbian" angle. While such ideas were already mentioned, it's hard to take them seriously, even though one of the suspects on the district attorney's "top 25 suspects" list was simply noted as "Queer Woman Surgeon." Newspaper stories of the time implied that Beth was a lesbian, or perhaps bisexual, but in the investigator's files, it bluntly stated that after questioning her friends, Beth "had no use for queers."

Who killed the Black Dahlia? You'll have to be the judge, but you'll see what direction that I lean toward in the chapters that follow. But here are some of the more popular and substantial (and some that are not so substantial) theories that have appeared over the years.

THE SERIAL PREDATOR

The theories of who killed Elizabeth Short fall into two basic categories: acquaintances and strangers. Early in the case, the lead suspect was, of course, Robert "Red" Manley, the traveling salesman who had been sleeping with Beth and who drove her back to Los Angeles from San Diego. He was the last one to see her when he dropped her off at the Biltmore Hotel. Since he had been with Beth for days before she was murdered, he had the opportunity. After two polygraph tests and a sworn alibi, Manley was set free - but he never dropped off the radar of some theorists. There is no denying that he had some serious psychiatric problems, which had gotten him discharged from the Army. After the scrutiny he faced in the Black Dahlia case, he suffered a series of nervous breakdowns and claimed to be hearing voices. In 1954, his wife committed him to Patton State Hospital and agreed to have him questioned under sodium pentothal, a drug that the CIA experimented with as a truth serum. While under the influence of the drug, Manley maintained that he was innocent of Beth's murder and was released. He died on January 16, 1986. The coroner attributed his death to an accidental fall.

There were other theories (explored in the pages ahead) that focused on various other men whom Beth knew in Hollywood, but there were also many stranger theories that suggested that she was picked up by a sadistic drifter or a Jack-the-Ripper-style serial killer. Capt. Jack Donahoe suggested a couple of startling theories - linking Beth's murder to both Chicago's "Lipstick" killer and the "Cleveland Torso Killer."

The "Lipstick Killer" had terrified the city of Chicago in the middle 1940s and in the minds of many crime buffs, he was never caught. Despite the fact that the police nabbed University of Chicago student William Heirens for the murders of the two women found slashed to death in their apartments on the city's North Side, many believe that the real killer got away.

Those two North Side murders were not ordinary crimes, especially in the days before the term "serial killer" was in common use. Each of the victims had been savagely slain and the killer had bathed their corpses. A message was found written in red lipstick on the wall at the second murder scene:

"For heaven's sake catch me before I kill more. I cannot control myself."

The police couldn't be sure if the killer was taunting them, or genuinely crying for help. But before they could find out came the day that has since become known as "the day Chicago locked its doors." It was on January 6, 1946, just twenty blocks north in the Edgewater neighborhood, that a six-year-old girl was taken from her bed in the middle of the night and cut into pieces that were found in storm drains and sewers all over the neighborhood.

The police were desperate to find the killer and came to believe that all three of these crimes were linked. When they arrested William Heirens, who had a long rap sheet for burglary, it seemed that the terror was finally over. But, was it? That remains a matter of conjecture to this day.

On June 6, 1945, the *Chicago Tribune* printed a small article about a forty-three-year-old woman named Josephine Ross, who had been murdered in her apartment at 4108 North Kenmore Avenue on Chicago's North Side. According to the article, someone had entered her apartment while she was sleeping in the afternoon and stabbed her to death. Her throat had been cut and the killer washed the blood from her body in the bathtub. When he was finished, he taped her flesh back together with adhesive tape. As the investigation progressed, several of Ross' boyfriends and her three ex-husbands were questioned but all of the leads quickly fizzled out. The victim had been found with several dark hairs clutched in her hand and two witnesses stated that they had seen a dark-haired man leaving the scene, but aside from those details, there was little else to go on. Soon, the case went cold.

Five months later, on December 10, 1945, another woman was killed in her apartment, which was only five blocks from where Ross had been killed. Frances Brown, a former Navy WAVE and an office worker at a copy machine company was found dead in her apartment at 3941 North Pine Grove Avenue. The killer had gotten into her apartment late at night, climbing from a fire escape into her bedroom window, six stories above the street. Frances had been shot in the head and stabbed. The blade of the knife had been driven into her throat with such force that it came out the other side of her neck. The petite young woman was found completely nude, but she had not been sexually violated. Chief of Detectives Walter Storm quickly noted the similarities between the murder of Frances Brown and that of Josephine Ross. The victims had both been stabbed to death, each body was carefully washed in the bathtub and then the wounds were taped back together again.

On the wall next to Frances Brown's bed, the police found the chilling words that had been written in the victim's lipstick. The crimson message would be seared into the memory of the cops - and into the memory of every Chicagoan who picked up a newspaper the next day.

The Brown murder, now linked to the slaying of Josephine Ross, galvanized the city. Newspaper headlines warned of a new "Jack the Ripper" stalking the city and began calling him the "Lipstick Killer." Detectives began rounding up sex offenders and mental cases, but little progress was made. The only bit of physical evidence that had been left behind at the scene was a single fingerprint, smudged onto a door jamb. Unfortunately, it didn't match any of the prints the police had on file and the fingerprint led to another dead end.

A month later, the "Lipstick Killer" was replaced in the headlines by one of the most horrific atrocities ever committed in Chicago. On January 6, 1946, six-year-old Suzanne Degnan was kidnapped in the middle of the night. At some point after 9:00 p.m., her abductor had slipped into the window of the Degnan home at 5943 North Kenmore Avenue and had taken the little girl away. Her parents found her gone, and the window of the bedroom standing open, the next morning. A scrawled ransom note was found on the floor of Suzanne's bedroom:

"Get $20,000 reddy & waite for word.
Do not notify FBI or police. Bills in $5's and $10's.
Burn this for her safty."

Little Suzanne Degnan, murdered and dismembered in Chicago a few years before the Black Dahlia murder.

James Degnan went on the radio to plead for the safe return of his daughter. Later that morning, a man telephoned the Degnan house several times, asking about the ransom money, but he hung up before any real conversation could take place.

Meanwhile, scores of policemen and volunteers scoured the North Side neighborhood and just after dark that evening, an officer made a gruesome discovery. Behind a building on the west side of Kenmore, south of Thorndale, the policeman saw a catch basin that appeared to have been tampered with. When he lifted the lid and peered inside with his flashlight, he found the severed heard of a little blond-haired girl floating in the water. The head belonged to Suzanne Degnan and officers were alarmed as more body parts began to turn up. Suzanne's right leg was found in another catch basin in the same alley and her left leg in an alley east of Kenmore. Her torso was discovered in a storm drain at the northwest corner of Kenmore and

Chicago police detectives discovered some of Suzanne's remains in a sewer catch basis

Ardmore. Her arms would remain undiscovered until the following month, when they were found near Hollywood and Broadway.

The public was outraged by this new development. The newspapers screamed for vengeance and the police commissioner and the state's attorney both went to the Degnan home and vowed to capture whoever had carried out such a horrific crime and bring them to justice.

As the investigation continued, it was found that the kidnapper had taken Suzanne to an apartment building at 5901 North Winthrop Avenue, just a block from her home, where he dismembered her with a hunting knife in a basement laundry room. Efforts had been made to clean up the scene, but investigators found traces of blood in a laundry tub. The police focused on anyone with access to the room. The crudely written, badly misspelled ransom note led them to focus their attention on the building's 65-year-old janitor, a Belgian named Hector Verburgh. Although tenants described him as a kindly old man, he was taken to the Summerdale District police station and cops spent forty-eight hours trying to beat a confession out of him. He refused to admit that he had anything to do with the crime.

On January 10, lawyers from the Janitor's Union managed to free Verburgh and it was later determined that he could not write English well enough to have penned the ransom note. He sued the police for brutality and was eventually awarded $20,000.

Detectives started all over again and new information soon came to light. On January 5, just one night before Suzanne was kidnapped, a burglary had occurred at an apartment near the Degnan home - an apartment that overlooked Suzanne's bedroom window. Not much had been taken during the break-in, other than a scrapbook of wartime photos, but detectives believed that if they could find the scrapbook, it might lead them to Suzanne's killer.

Months passed, and after several dead ends and false clues, the case was growing cold. In late January, the police answered the question of the mysterious telephone calls that came into the Degnan house on the morning after Suzanne's abduction. Still working on the idea that the killer might have committed other crimes in the area, detectives routinely picked up ex-cons and petty criminals. After several false leads, they found two neighborhood youths who admitted to making the ransom calls, but they had nothing to do with the kidnapping. They had made the calls as a prank. The mystery of the telephone calls had been solved, but investigators were no closer to finding the killer.

Hundreds more were questioned but it was not until June 27 that another viable suspect appeared. On that day, a University of Chicago student named William Heirens was arrested following a burglary in Rogers Park. Two days later, he was the leading suspect in the murder of Suzanne Degnan - and soon he was believed to be the "Lipstick Killer," as well.

William Heirens, born in 1928, had a troubled history of burglaries and break-ins, starting when he was just thirteen years old and was arrested for carrying a loaded gun. He was eventually sent away to a strict religious school, where he was a model student. While he was away, his family had moved to 1020 West Loyola Avenue, which was six blocks from where Suzanne Degnan would later be murdered. Unfortunately, the time at the private reform school had little positive effect on Heirens. He began a new series of burglaries and break-ins after he was released in 1943, all of which occurred during the time the two women were murdered in their apartments. He was arrested for burglary and his proximity to the earlier crime scenes led the police to link him to not only the two "Lipstick" murders, but also to the kidnapping and murder of Suzanne Degnan.

The initial connections were circumstantial, but more links were found between Heirens and the victims when detectives began investigating his background. They learned that Heirens had lived near the Degnan home and

A teenager named William Heirens was arrested, tried, convicted and died in prison for the "Lipstick Murders" and the murder of Suzanne Degnan, but the question remains whether or not he committed them all.

also near both the Ross and Brown apartments. Although Frances Brown and the Degnan family lived nearly three miles apart, Heirens had burglarized homes on both of these blocks. To the investigators, it seemed hard to believe this could be a coincidence. State's Attorney William Touhy believed that they had the killer of Suzanne Degnan, Frances Brown and most likely, Josephine Ross, as well. He began building a case that would convince a jury of that fact.

Almost from the time of his arrest, Heirens claimed to be innocent of the murders, but the authorities were sure they had the right man. Worried about the evidence against him, Heirens' attorneys arranged for him to plead guilty, write up a confession for the three murders, and answer all of the questions that the state's attorney had for him. In return, he would receive essentially one life sentence for the murders, plus concurrent sentences for his burglaries. With good behavior, he would likely spend about twenty-five years in prison and could be released by the 1970s. With his lawyer's assistance, Heirens wrote up the confession and both he and his parents signed it. However, when the time came for him to answer the questions posed by the state's attorney, Heirens suddenly claimed that he couldn't remember anything. He simply refused to talk. Left with no other choice, State's Attorney Touhy regarded the plea agreement to be nullified and announced that he would press ahead with a trial for the murders of Suzanne Degnan and Frances Brown.

There is no question that Heirens should have answered William Touhy's questions and taken the deal because his written confession contained a piece of information that had been previously unknown to the police. In the confession, he said that he had cut up Suzanne Degnan's body with a hunting knife and that he had gotten rid of the knife by tossing it up onto the El tracks from the alley behind Winthrop Avenue. No one had ever searched at that spot.

When reporters from the *Chicago Tribune* learned of this, they immediately headed for the El tracks, arriving there before the police. They found a track maintenance man who told them that he had found a knife on the tracks at that area. In fact, the knife was still in a storage room at the Granville El station. The reporters determined that a knife of the same description had been reported stolen during one of Heirens' burglaries.

With new evidence, Heirens was offered one last plea bargain: three life sentences that would run consecutively. Heirens could escape execution, but he would never get out of prison. On the advice of his lawyers, Heirens took the new agreement.

On September 4, with his parents and the victim's families in attendance, Heirens admitted his guilt on the burglary and murder charges. That night, he unsuccessfully tried to hang himself in his cell. The following day, he was formally sentenced to three life terms in prison.

As soon as he went to prison, Heirens began to claim that he did not commit the murders. He claimed that he was beaten and coerced into confessing to crimes that he didn't commit. Others joined his efforts, stating that Heirens was a convenient scapegoat who was easily framed by the police, who were under siege by the public and the press for their inability to find the real killer. Despite his efforts, Heirens died in prison at age 83 in 2012.

We will never know if any of Heirens' claims were true, but it seems very unlikely that the "Lipstick Killer" and the murderer of Suzanne Degnan were the same person. The "Lipstick Murders" were obviously the work of one man, an experienced burglar who committed murder when he found that the apartment that he was robbing was occupied. Heirens likely killed twice and may have been overwhelmed with guilt after the murder of Frances Brown, which caused him to leave the lipstick message on the wall. But did he kill Suzanne Degnan?

The abduction, murder and dismemberment of the little girl seemed to be completely different from the crimes of the "Lipstick Killer." While Heirens was certainly in the neighborhood of the Degnan home around the time of the kidnapping, as evidenced by the burglary of the nearby apartment, this may have been merely a coincidence.

Heirens was not even the main suspect in the Degnan murder. Before he became a suspect, the police interrogated a forty-two-year-old drifter named Richard Russell Thomas, who was passing through the city at the time of the murder. Police handwriting experts noted the similarities between his Thomas' handwriting and the ransom note. When questioned, he confessed to the murder, but he was released from custody after Heirens became the prime suspect.

In hindsight, it's very possible that Thomas might have been the killer. In addition to his handwriting possibly linking him to the murder, he had previously been convicted of attempted extortion, using a ransom note that threatened the kidnapping of a young girl. When he confessed to the crime, he was in jail awaiting sentencing for molesting his daughter. He had a history of violence, including spousal abuse. He was a nurse who sometimes posed as a surgeon and was known to steal surgical supplies, which matched the initial profile of the Degnan killer as having surgical skills or being a butcher. Thomas also frequented a car agency near the Degnan residence and parts of Suzanne's body were found in a sewer across the street from the agency.

Unfortunately, Chicago detectives dismissed Thomas' confession after Heirens was blamed for dismembering the little girl, in addition to the "Lipstick Murders." Thomas died in an Arizona prison in 1974. His prison record, and most of the evidence of his interrogation regarding the Degnan murder, has been either lost or destroyed.

Even if William Heirens did not kill Suzanne Degnan, he still deserved to go to prison for the assaults and burglaries that he confessed to. There was also no doubt that the "Lipstick Murders" came to an end after Heirens went to jail, which makes him the most likely suspect in those cases. His was a tragic case of a boy who went wrong at an early age.

But how did the "Lipstick Killer" get mixed up in the Black Dahlia case? We can thank the inventive Capt. Donahoe for that. At the time, he was busy throwing out every possible suspect he could come up with to the press. Some theorists believe this was an effort to draw attention away from the real culprit. Regardless, he stated that Beth's murder was "likely connected" to the sadistic murders in Chicago. Despite the fact that William Heirens was arrested in 1946, Donahoe based the connection on his own analysis of the "Black Dahlia Avenger's" handwriting and - bizarrely - on the fact that one of the victims in Chicago was named Suzanne Degnan and Beth's body was found three blocks away from Degnan Boulevard.

In Donahoe's defense, there were other similarities too, including the fact that the two adult victims were cut up and then washed in a bathtub. Suzanne was also dismembered, and the killer had written notes to the police. But all of this added up to a weak connection and turned out to be nothing more than Donahoe deflecting attention away from the LAPD's inability to bring in a killer.

Kingsbury Run in the 1930s

But this was not the only infamous crime wave that Donahoe attempted to link with the Black Dahlia murder. The other was one that received a lot more attention - namely because the "Cleveland Torso Killer" was never caught and his identity remains unknown today.

The murders in Cleveland took place in a part of the city known as Kingsbury Run. When they began in 1935, Kingsbury Run was a wasteland-like ravine on the city's east side. It cut through the rugged area, sometimes plunging to depths of sixty feet, and was scattered with overgrown weeds, patches of wild grass, tumbling pieces of old paper, piles of garbage and the occasional skeletal remains of an abandoned car. Along the edges of the ravine were ramshackle frame houses, built close together and of such shabby construction that they seemed to be teetering on the brink of collapse. As the ravine angled toward downtown, it emptied out into the muddy waters of the Cuyahoga River, where concrete and steel bridges, tanks and old factory buildings dotted the banks.

Kingsbury Run was a forbidding and shunned place in those days, and yet among the refuse and decay was a shantytown built by homeless men, victims of the Great Depression. They squatted there in cardboard boxes and in shacks made from scavenged wood, huddling near small campfires and trying to ignore the lonesome cries of the freight trains that passed nearby.

It was through this desolate region that two young boys walked home from school on a warm afternoon in September 1935. As they ambled along a weed-covered slope known as Jackass Hill, one challenged the other to a race and they plunged down the steep incline to the bottom. The older of the two, James Wagner, reached the bottom first and as he stopped running, he noticed something white in the bushes a short distance away. He peered a little closer and was stunned to see that the white shape was a naked and headless corpse.

The police arrived soon after and started their investigation. The body was that of a young, white male, clad only in a pair of black socks. The man's head and genitals had been removed. The body had been positioned on its back with the legs stretched out and the arms placed neatly at its sides. As the police began searching the area, they discovered another shocking surprise -- just thirty feet away from the first body was another corpse, this time that of an older man. This body was placed in the same position as that of the young man, and the head and genitals had also been removed.

Nearby, the police discovered the heads of the two dead men. They had been wrapped in clothing and placed in a paper bag. They also found the men's severed genitals, which looked as though the killer had tossed them away like garbage.

One thing the search did not reveal was the murder site. It appeared as though the men had been killed somewhere else, because no blood was found on the ground or on the bodies. The corpses had obviously been washed and left in the ravine.

The forensic examination that followed revealed even more puzzling evidence. The body of the older man was badly decomposed and the skin was discolored from some sort of solution that the pathologists believed had been used to try and preserve it. His age was placed at about forty-five. He had been dead for about two weeks, and yet someone had kept the body, only dumping it when it had reached a point of advanced decay. The younger man had been dead for about three days. The police were able to identify him through his fingerprints as Edward W. Andrassy, age twenty-eight. Andrassy had once been arrested for carrying a concealed weapon. He lived near Kingsbury Run and had a reputation for being a drunk and for frequently getting into fights.

The most chilling discovery came when the pathologists realized that Andrassy was still alive when his head was cut off. He had been bound hand and foot by ropes, and abrasions on his wrists and legs showed that he had

The decapitated body of Edward Andrassy, found at the bottom of Jackass Hill

struggled violently. The decapitation was done very skillfully and the investigators suspected that the killer might be a butcher, a surgeon, or at least someone familiar with killing animals.

The older man turned out to be impossible to identify, but the police hoped that it would be easy to find Andrassy's killer by following the dead man's trail through the sleazy bars and gambling parlors that he frequented. He was known to be a pimp and he had admitted to having male lovers. Detectives followed lead after lead, pressing for answers from people who bore Andrassy a grudge, including a husband who had vowed to kill him for sleeping with his wife. The investigation led nowhere, though, and the leads all came to dead ends. The murders both went cold - just as all of the murders that followed would do.

The press, with its usual delight in a good, bloody murder, began calling the killer the "Mad Butcher of Kingsbury Run."

Four months after the first two bodies were found, on a cold Sunday afternoon in January, the howling of a dog led a woman who lived on East Twentieth Street (not far from Kingsbury Run) to make a gruesome discovery. She found the dog trying to tear open a basket that was on the ground near the wall of a factory. After a brief glance inside, she told a passing neighbor that the basket contained hams. The neighbor recognized the "hams" for what they really were - human body parts. A burlap bag in the basket

Human remains found in a basket, which a passerby first thought was "hams."

contained a female torso, from which the head, the left arm and lower legs were missing. The police were able to trace the fingerprints on the remaining right arm to a forty-one-year-old prostitute named Florence "Flo" Polillo, who was well known in the local dives and gin joints. Once again, there were plenty of leads to follow in the investigation but once again, they all led nowhere. Two weeks later, Polillo's left arm and the remainder of her legs were found discarded in an empty lot. Her head was never recovered.

The discovery of the woman's body had dire repercussions for the detectives assigned to the earlier murders. Since the original victims had been men - with their genitals removed -- they had been convinced that they were dealing with a homosexual killer. Now, with the latest victim being a woman, it appeared that the killer's motives were going to be harder to pin down. To make matters worse, a cold case from September 1934 was recalled in which the torso of an unknown woman was found near Euclid Beach on the shore of Lake Erie. The newspapers began by calling her "Victim Zero," but they later settled on the more poetic-sounding "Lady of the Lake." She had apparently been the first of the Mad Butcher's victims.

The biggest advantage in the case, as seen by the citizens of Cleveland, was that since the double murder in September, a new director of public safety had been appointed to oversee the police department. His name was Eliot Ness. He had achieved fame a few years before for cleaning up Chicago with the assistance of his "Untouchables." He had come to Cleveland to fight that city's gangsters, gambling and corruption but soon found himself

Famous "Untouchable" Eliot Ness

embroiled in the hunt for a sadistic killer. The newspapers and the people on the street were confident that Ness would make Cleveland safe again.

Ness was not so confident. It soon became clear to him that hunting down a lone killer was not like battling organized crime. The Butcher struck at random, leaving no clues behind, and despite well-organized searches and investigations, the killer managed to stay several steps ahead of the police.

The killing began again that summer. One June 5, two boys discovered the head of a young man wrapped in a pair of trousers beneath a bridge in Kingsbury Run. The body was found a quarter mile away. He had been dead for about two days. This time, it was obvious from the pool of blood at the scene that the victim had been killed at the site. Like Edward Andrassy, he had died as a result of being beheaded. But unlike Andrassy, he could not be identified. It was estimated that he was about twenty-five and was heavily tattooed.

Three weeks later, a hiker discovered another decapitated male body in the ravine. The head was found nearby and again, the victim could not be identified. The body was so decomposed that examiners realized that he had

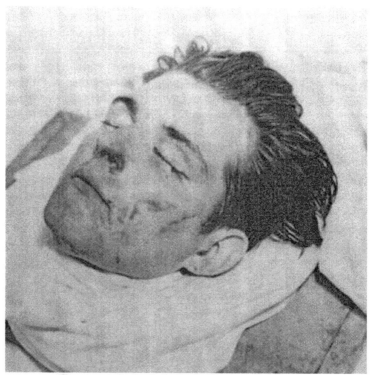

The severed head of the Mad Butcher's fourth victim

been killed before the previously discovered victim, whom the papers were calling "The Tattooed Man."

The Butcher struck again in 1936. The body of a man who was thought to be about thirty was found in Kingsbury Run. His genitals had been severed and his body was sliced completely in two. A hat that was lying nearby gave detectives a lead. It was identified by a woman who lived nearby as being one that she had given to a homeless man. Not far from the site where the body was found was a "hobo camp," where those who rode the rails and drifted from town to town would sometimes sleep. Apparently, this was where the Butcher had found this latest victim.

Months passed, and while the Butcher was silent, the press was anything but. The string of gruesome killings had attracted the attention of newspapers all over the country. Just recently, Cleveland had been the scene of a Republican convention and the Great Lakes Exposition of 1936-37. The eyes of the nation were on the city and the police were being harshly criticized in print for their failure to catch the Butcher. Ness, who was used to being lionized as a crime-fighting hero, was feeling the sting of the public's disapproval for the first time. As no leads in the case panned out, the investigators could do little more than wait for the Butcher to strike again, and hope that he made a mistake.

They only had to wait until February 1937. Unfortunately, the Butcher was just as efficient as ever, leaving the body of a young woman along the frozen shore of Lake Erie. She was never identified. The eighth victim was identified by her teeth as Rose Wallace. Her body was found in a burlap bag in a pile of rocks under the Lorain-Carnegie Bridge in an area where the homeless camped that the papers called "Hoboville." She was a known prostitute and the killer's only black victim. Like the tattooed male body discovered by the hiker, it appeared that Wallace had been dead for about a year.

Victim number nine was a male and was likely another of the legion of homeless people who had been set adrift by the Great Depression. His body was discovered in the river and his head was never found. The corpse had been badly mutilated. The detectives were sent into action by what seemed to be a promising lead when a witness spoke of seeing two men in a boat on the river the night before, near where the body was found. The sighting never panned out, though, and the investigation continued to go nowhere.

The Butcher was not heard from again until later that year. Several months passed, and then a leg was pulled out of the river. Three weeks after that, two burlap bags were found that contained more body parts. The coroner was able to determine that the body had belonged to a woman, about twenty-five years of age. This would mark another period of inactivity for the killer, lasting more than a year.

But he would return to strike two more times in Cleveland. In August 1938, the dismembered torso of a woman was found in a dump along the lakefront. A search of the area revealed the body of a man. The remains of the twelfth victim were found wrapped in a quilt, but neither body was ever identified.

Finally certain that the Butcher was selecting his victims from the homeless and transients of Kingsbury Run, Ness took a drastic step. Two days after the police found the last two bodies, officers raided the shantytown in the ravine. They arrested hundreds of vagrants and burned down their makeshift shelters. Whether it was a coincidence or a brilliant move on the part of Eliot Ness, the murders stopped.

The Cleveland Torso Murders were officially never solved, but that has not stopped scores of crime historians and investigators from speculating as to the identity of the "Mad Butcher." Detectives in the case believed that they were close to catching the killer several times. They spent many hours searching for the killer's "laboratory," believing that the Butcher was slaughtering his victims in a convenient location and then dumping the bodies somewhere else. At one point, they believed they had found it. They found a photographic negative that had been left behind by one of the early

The "Hoboville" shanty town that was located in Kingsbury Run. Desperate for a solution to the murders, Ness ordered it burned.

victims, Edward Andrassy. When it was developed, it showed Andrassy reclining on a bed in an unknown room. The photo was published in newspapers and was identified as being the bedroom of a middle-aged homosexual who lived with his two sisters. Detectives searched the house and found bloodstains on the floor of the room and a large butcher knife hidden in a trunk. Unfortunately, the blood turned out to be the suspect's (he was prone to nosebleeds) and the knife showed no traces of blood. To further prove the man's innocence, another Butcher victim turned up while the man was in jail for sodomy and it became obvious he was not the killer.

Investigators found another suspect while backtracking through the last days of Flo Polillo and Rose Wallace. They discovered that the women frequented the same saloon and that Andrassy had also been a regular there. Another connection was a man named Frank Dolezal, who was known to carry knives and often threatened people with them when he was drunk. He was not only a regular at the saloon, but he also had lived with Flo Polillo for a time. He was quickly arrested and a search of his home found a brown substance that resembled dried blood in the cracks of the bathroom floor. The search also turned up several knives with old bloodstains on them. Finally, after hours of intense questioning, Dolezal confessed to killing Flo Polillo. The newspapers hurriedly announced the capture of the Butcher.

144

Then the case against Dolezal began to fall apart.

Forensic tests showed that the "dried blood" on the bathroom floor was not blood at all and Dolezal's so-called "confession" was riddled with holes and full of errors as to where and how the body was found. In August 1939, Dolezal hanged himself in jail. An autopsy revealed that he had four cracked ribs, which suggested that perhaps his "voluntary" confession had been obtained the old-fashioned way --- by force.

Who was the depraved killer? His identity was never discovered and sadly, the Kingsbury Run murders started the downturn of Eliot Ness' earlier illustrious career. He never really got over the stain that the unsolved murders left on his reputation. The last decade of his life was marked by poverty and frequent disappointment. Ironically, considering his destruction of the Prohibition era bootlegging gangs, Ness became a heavy drinker and suffered from poor health. He resigned from the position of Cleveland's public safety director in 1941, after a scandal having to do with his involvement in a hit-and-run accident. He tried running for the office of the city's mayor in 1947 was badly defeated. A year later, he was even turned down for a $60-a-week sales job. At one point, he was reduced to selling frozen hamburger patties to restaurants. In 1953, after five years of poverty and obscurity, he became involved with a papermaking company, and through a friend who worked there, he had a chance meeting with a journalist named Oscar Fraley. The two would later collaborate on a highly dramatized autobiography entitled *The Untouchables*. It came out in 1957 and was an immense success, becoming a bestseller and inspiring two television series and a popular film. Tragically, Ness would never learn of this success. He died of a heart attack at age fifty-four on May 16, 1957, six months before *The Untouchables* was published.

The identity of the Mad Butcher remains a mystery, but many believe that the killings did not end in Cleveland with the destruction of the shantytown in Kingsbury Run. On June 30, 1939, the bones of a dismembered woman were found in a dump in Youngstown, Ohio, along the rail line that ran straight from Cleveland. On October 13, 1939, the nude body of a headless man was found in the weeds near the train tracks in New Castle, Pennsylvania. On May 3, 1940, three decapitated bodies were found in an abandoned train in the town of McKees Rocks, in Allegheny County, Pennsylvania. From evidence collected at the scene, it was determined that the victims had been murdered while the train was in the yard at Youngstown, Ohio, in December 1939. The remains of a headless woman, dead for about a year, were found in a New Castle swamp in 1941. The body of a headless man was found next to the train tracks in Pittsburgh in 1941.

Did the Mad Butcher's murders continue? And if so, did they stop in Cleveland because the killer left the area and began traveling the country? And could he have been in Hollywood in 1947? Some believe so, citing the similarities of the Butcher's crimes to the murder of the Black Dahlia - the dismembering of the body, the public display of the corpse, and the murder and bisection of the body taking place in one location and then the body being left in a vacant lot.

It truth, though, any connections between the murders seem tenuous. The Mad Butcher case had been in the headlines - like the Lipstick Killer - in the years leading up to the sensational murder of the Black Dahlia. It was not surprising to see a connection made between the notorious crimes, especially because in both cases, the killer was never captured.

In the end, the LAPD did not find a way to connect Beth's murder to these infamous cases, but this does not completely rule out the fact that she could have fallen victim to an unknown predator. It just might explain how the killer managed to elude capture - he simply packed up, left town and never returned to Los Angeles again.

THE "MAD DOCTOR"

As mentioned earlier, among the list of suspects put together by the LAPD and the district attorney's office were a number of doctors and suspected abortionists that may have had a connection to the murder, or been the actual killers. Three of the doctors were linked to Beth through Mark Hansen and a couple of them were taken seriously by the police, at least for a time.

Naturally, Hansen himself was one of the leading suspects in the murder. Hansen was a Hollywood nightclub and theater owner who knew Beth while she was in Los Angeles. She lived in his home on several occasions in 1946, sharing a room with Hansen's girlfriend, Ann Toth. During Hansen's interviews with the police, he made a number of contradictory statements about his relationship with Beth and her connections with his nightclub and with some of the characters that hung around there. An address book embossed with Hansen's name was among Beth's belongings that were mailed to a newspaper after the murder. The address book had been a gift to Hansen, but he had never used it. Short had apparently filched it from his desk. According to the district attorney's files, Hansen tried to seduce Beth, but she rejected him. These things combined to make him a prime suspect - one of the first in the case - and for many investigators, he remained on the suspect list until 1951. No charges were ever filed against him, though, and he had no criminal history or record of violence. He died of natural causes in 1964.

As mentioned, there were several medical doctors who appeared on the list of Dahlia suspects and they were linked to Beth Short through Mark Hansen. Most of them were ruled out right away, but one of them, Dr. Patrick O'Reilly, knew Beth through Mark Hansen and became part of the investigation. According to the district attorney's files, O'Reilly was a good friend of Hansen's at the time of the murder and he frequented the Florentine Gardens. Allegedly, O'Reilly "attended sex parties at Malibu" with Hansen, but there's no record of Beth being present at these parties. O'Reilly did have a conviction for assault with a deadly weapon in conjunction with "taking his secretary to a motel and sadistically beating her almost to death for apparently no other reason than to satisfy his sexual desires without intercourse," the files stated. In addition, it was said that O'Reilly's right pectoral had been surgically removed, which some investigators found similar to the mutilation of Beth's body. O'Reilly did not stay on the suspect list for long. He was quickly ruled out, which fanned the flames of conspiracy for some theorists because he had once been married to the daughter of an LAPD captain. Some have claimed that his connections to the case were covered up.

Another physician became part of the list of suspects after his death. In 1996, Larry Harnisch, a copy editor and writer for the *Los Angeles Times*, began studying the case and came to believe that Dr. Walter Alonzo Bayley could have been Beth Short's killer. Bayley was a Los Angeles surgeon who owned a home just one block south of the vacant lot where Beth's body was found. He had moved out in October 1946, but his estranged wife still lived there at the time of the murders. And there were other connections as well. Bayley's daughter was a friend of Virginia Short, Beth's sister, and was the matron of honor at her wedding to Adrian West. When Bayley died in January 1948, his autopsy showed that he was suffering from a degenerative brain disease. After his death, his widow alleged that his mistress knew a "terrible secret" about Bayley and claimed that this was the reason why the mistress was the main beneficiary in his will.

Bayley was never an official suspect in the case, although many medical doctors and others with medical training were. During his testimony at the 1949 grand jury hearings, Harry Hansen gave the opinion that the killer was a "top medical man" and a "fine surgeon." Bayley was sixty-seven years old at the time of the murder, had no known history of violence or a criminal record of any kind. In addition, he was not known to have ever met Beth Short, even though his daughter and Beth's sister were friends.

Larry Harnisch became convinced of Bayley's guilt after many hours of research. However, critics of his theory question whether Bayley's mental and physical condition at the time of the murder would have been consistent with this type of crime. But it should also be considered that one of the early theories in the official investigation surmised that the body was cut in half because the killer wasn't strong enough to move it intact. Could this give strength to Harnisch's theory? Harnisch theorized that Bayley's neurological deterioration contributed to his violence against Beth Short. Could Bayley have known Beth? It's possible --- some have suggested that the secret that Bayley's mistress knew about him was that he was performing abortions, which were illegal at the time. She may have been blackmailing him and this may have been how Beth came into contact with him. A number of her acquaintances suggested that Beth may have gotten herself "into trouble," which was a term commonly used at the time for an unplanned pregnancy. Did she go looking for a doctor who could help her? Of course, the police files all claimed that Beth was not pregnant and there is no evidence that Bayley ever performed abortions, so that avenue of the investigation has come to a dead end.

FAMOUS SUSPECTS

With so much of the drama of the Black Dahlia case taking place in Hollywood, featuring characters who were involved with celebrities and the Hollywood studios, it should come as no surprise that some of the accused suspects have been famous ones.

According to the LA County district attorney's files, folk singer Woody Guthrie was one of the many suspects in the murder of Beth Short. Guthrie drew the attention of the police because of some sexually explicit letters and tabloid clippings that he sent to a woman in Northern California that he was allegedly stalking. The letters disturbed the woman so much that she showed them to her sister in Los Angeles, who contacted the police. Guthrie was pulled in and questioned by the police about the Black Dahlia, but was quickly cleared in the matter. However, various authorities did attempt to prosecute him, with minor success, on charges related to sending prohibited materials through the mail.

In 1999, author Mary Pacios, a former neighbor of the Short family in Medford, Massachusetts, suggested filmmaker Orson Welles as a suspect. Her theory was based on Welles' violent temperament and his creation of mannequins three months before Beth's murder that supposedly featured lacerations that were almost identical to those in the Black Dahlia murder. The mannequins were used in his "house of mirrors" set for *The Lady From Shanghai*, a film that Welles was making with his ex-wife Rita Hayworth around the time of the murder. The scenes containing this set were later cut from the film by studio head Harry Cohn. According to Short family members, in one of Beth's last letters home, she claimed that a movie director was going to give her a screen test. But, of course, it's pretty hard to take such claims seriously, based on the number of lies that Beth spun about her burgeoning acting career.

Pacios used other information about Welles to link him to the murder. She stated that he was familiar with the site where the body was found and that he used "sawing a woman in half" as part of the magic act that he performed to entertain soldiers during World War II. She theorized that the bisection of Beth's body was part of the killer's signature and that he was acting out an obsession. Welles applied for a passport on January 24, 1947 - the same day that the killer mailed a packet to the Los Angeles newspaper - and then left the country for an extended stay in Europe that lasted ten months. He left without completing the editing of *Macbeth*, a film that he was both directing and starring in, and ignored repeated efforts by Republic Pictures to get him to return to Hollywood and finish it.

According to witnesses that Pacios interviewed, both Welles and Beth Short frequented Brittingham's Restaurant in Los Angeles. Waitresses there believed that Beth was going out with someone at Columbia Pictures during this time. Was the famous director really the Black Dahlia killer? Probably not, but it makes for some compelling reading as the author puts the puzzle pieces together.

LESLIE DILLON

One of the most unusual and compelling suspects in the Black Dahlia case was Leslie Dillon, a twenty-seven-year-old bellhop, aspiring mystery writer and former mortician's assistant. He became a suspect in October 1948 when he began writing letters to LAPD police psychiatrist Dr. J. Paul de River. When the correspondence began, Dillon was living in Florida with his wife and baby, but he had previously lived in Los Angeles. Dillon read an article about the case in the October 1948 issue of *True Detective* magazine in which de River was quoted and he wrote to the psychiatrist about his theories in the case, signing the letter "Jack Sands." He mentioned his intense interest in sadism and sexual psychopathy and wrote that he hoped to write a book on the subject. Dillon was no headline chaser or "confessing Sam." He never confessed to the crime. Instead, he offered up another man as a likely suspect - an acquaintance named Jeff Connors.

De River was a friend of LAPD Chief Horrall, who put him in charge of the so-called "Sex Offense Bureau," making him responsible for the psychiatric examination of all persons arrested on suspicion of "morals offenses." In addition to the *True Detective* article, de River had written a series of articles for the *Herald-Express* in which he theorized that Beth Short's killer was a sexual sadist with a taste for necrophilia. As the letters between the two went back and forth, de River began to believe that "Connors" was a figment of Dillon's imagination and that Dillon had committed the murder himself. In December 1948, Dillon agreed to meet de River to discuss his theories and he was given the choice of three cities - Phoenix, Los Angeles or Las Vegas - as a place to meet. Dillon expressed reservations about coming to Los Angeles and chose Las Vegas instead. De River sent him an airline ticket and then went to Las Vegas to meet him, along with Sgt. John J. O'Mara of the LAPD, who posed as de River's chauffeur. The two men met in Las Vegas and Dillon agreed to accompany the psychiatrist on a drive back to California, but only if they could go to San Francisco first so Dillon could point out Jeff Connors to de River.

After reaching San Francisco, they searched for Connors, but could not locate him. Needless to say, Dr. de River was not surprised. After several

The suspect who really wasn't a suspect – Leslie Dillon

fruitless days, during which de River asked him a series of questions that ran the gamut from the inane (What kind of hairstyles did he like on women?) to the macabre (How did he think the killer had disposed of the piece of skin with the tattoo on it that he cut from Beth Short's leg?), Dillon was handcuffed by an undercover officer and officially taken into custody for a trip to Los Angeles. The police held Dillon in a hotel room for days, where he was brutally questioned in an effort to wring a confession out of him. Desperate, Dillon sailed a postcard out the window with a plea for help on it; it was discovered by a passerby and turned over to a lawyer who helped get Dillon released.

Soon after Dillon's arrest, police investigators discovered that the "imaginary" Jeff Connors was a real person - and his real name was Artie Lane. Lane had lived in Los Angeles at the time of the murder and worked at Columbia Studios, a favorite hangout of Beth Short's, as a maintenance man. Leslie Dillon, it later turned out, was likely in San Francisco at the time of the murder.

Dillon later filed a $100,000 claim against the City of Los Angeles, but he quickly dropped the lawsuit when it came to light that he was wanted by the Santa Monica police for robbing the vault of a local hotel while he was employed there as a bellhop a few years earlier. This was the real reason why he didn't want to meet de River in Los Angeles.

The scandal caused by de River's missteps with Dillon partially triggered the 1949 grand jury investigation of police handling of the Black Dahlia case and several other unsolved murders of the time. De River lost his job with the LAPD in 1950, after being found guilty of illegally writing morphine prescriptions for his wife. Dillon eventually faded into obscurity and became a bizarre footnote in the strange and convoluted case.

GEORGE KNOWLTON

There is little reliable information available about George Knowlton, other than that he lived in the Los Angeles area at the time of the Black Dahlia murder and he died in an automobile accident in 1962. He was never listed as a suspect by the LAPD and never investigated by any of the initial detectives who worked on the case. However, in the early 1990s, George Knowlton's daughter, Janice, began claiming that she had seen her father murder Beth Short, a claim that was based on "recovered memories" that surfaced during therapy. A story in the *Los Angeles Times* in 1991 stated, "Los Angeles Police Detective John P. St. John, one of the investigators who had been assigned to the case, said he has talked to Knowlton and does not believe there is a connection between the Black Dahlia murder and her father. 'We have a lot of people offering up their fathers and various relatives as the Black Dahlia killer,' said St. John, better known as Jigsaw John. 'The things that she is saying are not consistent with the facts of the case.'"

The LAPD dismissed Knowlton's claims, but the Westminster Police Department took her seriously enough to dig up the grounds of her childhood home, looking for evidence. They found nothing that could tie George Knowlton to the crime, but this did not stop Knowlton from publishing a book called *Daddy was the Black Dahlia Killer* in 1995. In the book, Knowlton, a former professional singer and owner of a public relations company, alleged that her father had been having an affair with Beth Short and that Beth was staying in a makeshift bedroom in their garage, where she suffered a miscarriage. Knowlton said she was later forced to accompany her father when he disposed of her body. She also went on to claim that a former member of the Los Angeles Sheriff's Department told her that her father was considered a suspect by investigators, but this claim was never supported by any of the files of the case. She further claimed that this same source told her that future LAPD chief and California politician Ed Davis and LA County District Attorney Buron Fitts were also suspects.

In the years that followed the book's short-lived release, Knowlton also made claims in public forums that, on Halloween 1946, she was sold as a nine-year-old child prostitute to a Satanic cult in Pasadena. She frequently alleged that she was used as a child prostitute by a long list of dead celebrities and notables including movie musical producer and lyricist Arthur Freed, cowboy star Gene Autry (whose name she misspelled as Autrey) and Walt Disney.

In 2004, Janice Knowlton died of an overdose of prescription drugs in what was deemed a suicide by the Orange County, California, coroner's office.

GEORGE HODEL

Janice Knowlton has not been the only person to claim that her father was the Black Dahlia killer. In 2003, author Steve Hodel claimed that it was his father that killed Beth Short - not Knowlton's. And not only did he kill Beth Short, Dr. George Hodel also killed at least thirty-one other women. Unfortunately, little authentic evidence exists to back up those claims.

Unlike George Knowlton, Dr. George Hodel actually was investigated by the police in regards to Beth's murder. He came under police scrutiny when he was arrested on a morals charge in October 1949. At the time of his arrest, Tamar Hodel, the doctor's fifteen-year-old daughter, told the police that she had been involved in an incestuous relationship with her father - and he had murdered the Black Dahlia. This occurred just as the Black Dahlia case was about to go to the 1949 grand jury and the LAPD hoped that Hodel might rescue them from the scandal caused by the arrest of Leslie Dillon. The molestation case led the LAPD to include Hodel, a physician specializing in public health and sexually transmitted diseases, among its many suspects in the Dahlia case. At the time of Beth Short's murder, Hodel was medical director and chief of staff for the First Street Medical Clinic, a venereal disease clinic in Los Angeles. Hodel was placed under surveillance by the police and recording devices were planted in his house. But after many hours of investigation and the questioning of dozens of witnesses who knew Hodel, it became evident that he was not connected to the crime.

At Hodel's trial for incest and immoral behavior, three witnesses testified at his trial that they were present in the room and saw him having sex with Tamar. Another witness, who had previously admitted that she had participated in sex acts with Tamar, recanted and refused to testify. However, family members testified that Tamar was a pathological liar and Hodel was acquitted in December 1949. It was recommended that Tamar receive psychiatric care.

But Hodel was far from perfect. He had earlier been accused of playing a part in the death of his secretary, Ruth Spaulding. Spaulding died from a drug overdose and Hodel was investigated by the LAPD in 1945 for her

Dr. George Hodel

suspected murder. He was present when Spaulding died and had burned some of her papers before police were called. The case was dropped for lack of evidence, but documents were later found that indicated Spaulding may have been about to make public the accusation that Hodel was intentionally misdiagnosing patients and billing them for laboratory tests, medical treatment, and prescriptions they didn't need. Years later, Steve Hodel would suggest that Beth Short had been one of his father's patients.

But he was ruled out in the Black Dahlia case. In the final report to the grand jury, dated February 20, 1951, Lt. Frank Jemison wrote:

Doctor George Hodel, M.D. 5121 Fountain Avenue, at the time of this murder had a clinic at East First Street near Alameda. Lillian DeNorak who lived with this doctor said he spent some time around the Biltmore Hotel and identified the photo of victim Short as a photo of one of the doctor's girlfriends. Tamar Hodel, fifteen year old daughter, stated that her mother, Dorothy Hodel, has told her that her father had been out all night on a party the night of the murder and said, "They'll never be able to prove I did that murder." Two microphones were placed in this suspect's home (see the log and recordings made over approximately three weeks' time which tend to prove his innocence. Informant Lillian DeNorak has been committed to the State Mental Institution at Camarillo. Joe Barrett, a roomer at the Hodel residence cooperated as an informant. A photograph of the suspect in the nude with a nude identified colored model was secured from his personal effects. Undersigned identified this model as Mattie Comfort, 3423½ South Arlington, Republic 4953. She said that she was with Doctor Hodel sometime prior to the murder and that she knew nothing about his being associated with the victim. Rudolph Walthers, known to have been acquainted with victim and also with suspect Hodel, claimed he had not seen victim in the presence of Hodel and did not believe that the doctor had ever met the victim... See supplemental reports, long sheets and hear recordings, all of which tend to eliminate this suspect.

In 2003, George Hodel's son, former LAPD homicide detective Steve Hodel, published a book claiming his father, who died in 1991, had in fact committed the Black Dahlia murder as well as a host of unsolved murders over the better part of two decades.

Steve Hodel came up with the idea when he saw two pictures in his dead father's photo album that he said resembled Beth Short. However, the pictures in George Hodel's album look nothing like Elizabeth Short. Members of Short's family came forward to state with certainty that the photos "are not Betty - not even close."

In November 2004, CBS aired a segment in *48 Hours* about Hodel's claim that his father was the Black Dahlia killer. CBS hired a professional photo identification expert for the New York Police Department to examine the photos. Using a computer system for facial recognition, she examined the photos and then compared them to known photos of Beth Short. She then stated she was "85-percent certain that these two photographs are not of the same woman."

But the photos were only what started Hodel's interest in his father and whether or not he was a killer. He also had a lot of other pieces of questionable evidence. One of them involved the unsigned telegram sent from Washington, D.C. that was found in Beth's memory book after it was recovered by the police. Although there is no substantiating evidence, Hodel maintained that it was sent by his father in October or November 1945, when he was studying Chinese in Washington, D.C. On close examination, though, the telegram was evidently sent in July 1944, when Hodel's father was living in Los Angeles.

One of Hodel's strangest claims was that the Black Dahlia's murder was an homage to a photograph taken by the Surrealist artist Man Ray, who lived in Hollywood during World War II. George Hodel and Man Ray were friends and Hodel admired his artistry so much that he supposedly posed Beth Short's body as a tribute to Man Ray's *The Minotaur*, a surreal photo of a nude woman with her arms bent above her head like the horns of the mythological bull. Hodel claimed that this proves his father was the killer, writing, "Much as I wanted to deny it to myself or to look for other possible explanations, I now realized the facts were undeniable: George Hodel, through the homage he consciously paid to Man Ray, was provocatively revealing himself to be the murderer of Elizabeth Short. Her body and the way she was posed was George Hodel's signature - on his surreal masterpiece... in a 'still death' tribute to his master."

In reality, it's more likely that Beth's arms were bent back above her head because her wrists have been tied to bathtub shower pipes when she was bisected.

Naturally, Hodel also claimed that his father was the one who had sent the Dahlia notes to the *Examiner* and other Los Angeles newspapers. He employed handwriting expert Hannah McFarland to examiner nine of the notes that were sent to various newspapers and according to Hodel, McFarland verified that the handwriting on the paste-up notes originated with George Hodel. Therefore, Hodel stated, his father was the Black Dahlia killer. But when looking at McFarland's report, it becomes clear that what she actually said was that the results were inconclusive. Handwriting samples from George Hodel were taken from several different time periods and experts agree that handwriting changes throughout a person's life. In addition, McFarland never saw the original samples of the newspaper letters, only second and third-generation copies. Producers from CBS had the samples analyzed by two forensic experts and they concluded that there was no evidence that the notes were written by the same person. John Osborn, one of the most respected document examiners in the field, stated, "There is simply not enough evidence to prove one way or another whether his father was the writer or not the writer."

In September 1949, the *Herald-Express* ran a story that was based on information leaked from the 1949 grand jury investigations. In the article, it was released that investigators believed Beth's murder took place in a room that was less than fifteen minutes away from the vacant lot on where the body was found. Harry Hansen had always believed this. Steve Hodel claimed that the murder site was at his father's house in the Los Feliz district of Hollywood. This landmark home, built in 1926 by Lloyd Wright in the Mayan Revival style, is sometimes referred to as "the Jaws house," because its façade resembles the gaping jaws of a great white shark. The problem with Steve Hodel's claim that the house was where the murder took place was that it would have taken nearly thirty minutes in 1947 to drive from there to Norton Avenue. Based on this, Hodel was again eliminated as a suspect by the grand jury investigators.

Hodel also claimed that his father was the man who had accompanied Beth when she checked into the Hirsh Hotel on Washington Boulevard on January 12, 1947. Mr. and Mrs. Johnson, who ran the hotel, stated to the police that they had seen Beth at their hotel during her missing week. Beth and the man who was with her had checked in as "Mr. and Mrs. Barnes" just two days before the murder. Hodel claimed that detectives showed photographs of Beth Short and George Hodel to the Johnsons and they identified them as the couple that had checked in that day. However, a photograph of the Johnsons examining the photo that detectives used to identify Beth and her companion appeared in the *Examiner* on January 22 and the man in the photo is clearly not George Hodel. In addition, the Johnsons' testimony was later discredited by detectives when they described the woman they believed to be Beth as having "jet-black hair." The detectives knew that her hair had been hennaed and the Johnsons admitted their mistake. The district attorney's files clearly stated that in the follow-up investigations, all of the supposed sightings of Beth Short during the missing week had been disproved. The report read, "No one reported seen from January 9, at approximately 10:00 p.m., until the body found by Mrs. Bersinger at 10:30 a.m., January 15, has been definitely identified as Elizabeth Short."

Hodel also identified the old black Ford sedan that was seen idling at the curb on Norton Avenue where Beth's body was found as his father's. The problem was that Hodel was known to drive a post-war, black Packard sedan at the time of the murder. Obviously, it was not the same car that was identified by anyone at the scene.

Was George Hodel the "wealthy Hollywood man" who was considered a prime suspect and questioned by the grand jury? According to his son he was, but the district attorney's files reveal that Dr. Hodel was never questioned by the grand jury and he wasn't wealthy, either. In 1949, he suffered a series of financial reverses. The newspaper publicity about his incestuous relationship with his daughter had destroyed his business and the legal fees to defend him against the charge were costly. While under surveillance, he was seen selling a number of his belongings at auction. George Hodel was not the "wealthy Hollywood man" questioned by the grand jury - Mark Hansen was.

And perhaps most damning element to this theory is the fact that Dr. Hodel suddenly returned from China in September 1946 because he had suffered a serious heart attack. He was hospitalized in Los Angeles in

September and October 1946. It's not plausible that he had the physical strength to stalk and kill Elizabeth Short.

In spite of all of this, Hodel got some reputable people to go along with his theory. After reviewing the information presented in his book, Deputy District Attorney Stephen Kay proclaimed the case solved, but others have noted that Kay, who has since retired, formed this conclusion by treating Steve Hodel's many disputed assertions as established fact. Detective Brian Carr, the LAPD officer in charge of the Black Dahlia case at the time of Steve Hodel's briefing, said in a televised interview that he was baffled by Kay's response, adding that if he ever took a case as weak as Steve Hodel's to a prosecutor he would be "laughed out of the office." In a September 2006 television interview with investigative reporter Bill Kurtis, Carr added, "I don't have the time to either prove or disprove Hodel's investigation. I am too busy working on active cases."

While Hodel's case against his father seems too weak to even bother with, it has not stopped him from maintaining that it's accurate - raising the number of his father's alleged victims to more than thirty and also claiming that Dr. Hodel was responsible for a number of other high-profile murders, including the Zodiac slayings, which took place in Northern California during the late 1960s and early 1970s. Needless to say, his claim that his father was the Black Dahlia killer is more than a little hard to swallow.

Over time, all of the leads in the Black Dahlia case came to dead ends and the investigation fizzled, and then came to a halt. As most readers know, it remains unsolved today. But just because it's never been officially solved, it doesn't mean that some people don't know the identity of the killer.

13. HOLLYWOOD UNDERWORLD

The greatest era in Los Angeles' criminal history began in the 1930s, when the city was expanding at a tremendous rate. Newcomers arrived on a daily basis. There were "Okies" looking for work, scavengers looking for a quick buck and of course, dream-seekers who came to California looking for their big break. Hollywood continued to serve as a beacon for would-be starlets and dreamers, but death and scandal sometimes cast a shadow over even the brightest aspects of Tinseltown.

This was definitely the case with the death of actress Thelma Todd, who was brutally murdered in 1935. Though plenty of suspects and theories have been floated over the years, her murder remains unsolved. Combining the elements of gangsters, gambling, and a beautiful corpse, it was purely a Hollywood-style killing.

It was 1938 that became a turning point for LA crime. After private investigator Harry Raymond was nearly killed by a car bomb while looking into reports of police corruption, the ensuing investigation revealed proof of rampant bribery and vice throughout the police department and among city officials. Mayor Frank Shaw was implicated and he was eventually replaced by Fletcher Bowron. After that, raids increased on nightclubs and gambling spots, and as many mobsters lost their political connections, they headed out of town to Las Vegas.

While the heat was undeniably turned up for a time, it did not bring an end to crime and corruption in the city. As World War II loomed closer, reports of overseas fighting began to replace newspaper headlines about sensational crime. But the war began to expose other problems in LA, namely the situation with gangsters and the black market. Soon, readers were introduced to the king of the Los Angeles underworld, Mickey Cohen.

Cohen was the most recognizable of the city's gangsters and he always dressed and acted the part, wearing flashy suits, hanging out in all the right places and making enemies of all the right people. He became sort of a cult hero in LA during the 1940s and 1950s. Connected to almost every type of vice in the city, he was constantly in the newspapers and was trailed by both the LAPD and the sheriff's department, who busted him for small infractions that inevitably revealed larger crimes.

Cohen had the dubious distinction of escaping more attempts on his life than perhaps any other mobster in American crime history. He rose through the ranks as Ben Siegel's bodyguard and made himself scarce on the day

Los Angeles mobster Jack Dragna, an old school Mafioso, or what the younger gangsters of the 1930s and 1940s called a "Mustache Pete"

that Bugsy was wiped out in Virginia Hill's Beverly Hill mansion. Cohen began building his own empire within days of Siegel's removal, through gambling, prostitution and extortion rackets and never paid a dime to any of his LA superiors. Cohen inherited Siegel's numbers operation, but not much else. In spite of this, he set up his own operations, drawing the ire of Jack Dragna, who fancied himself the "Al Capone of Los Angeles."

Dragna was an old-school Mafioso. He had moved into LA at the start of Prohibition and had pushed out the loose outfits of organized crime that already existed there. He began a bloodbath that resulted in numerous deaths, including thirty men who were gunned down along Darwin Avenue in 1925 alone. This stretch of roadway became known as "Shotgun Alley."

Dragna was an immigrant from Sicily and the president of the Italian Protection League. He was the unofficial mayor of the Italian neighborhood in LA, dispensing wisdom, settling family disputes, and enforcing his own set of rules. He muscled in on the bootleg liquor market and gained the leadership of the first Italian crime family in Los Angeles. He and his gunmen managed to gain national prominence for the LA mob. Dragna's power was compromised with the arrival of Ben Siegel in the 1930s. Siegel dismissed Dragna's operation as the "Mickey Mouse Mafia" and soon took over control of the region. Siegel arrived with the blessings of Meyer Lansky and the

Syndicate based out of New York and Dragna understood that if he wanted to stay in business, he was going to have to turn over his bookmaking operations, casino interests, racetrack betting, and gambling ships to Siegel. In this way, Bugsy, who had made his presence known by assassinating Les Bruneman, a key member of the original LA operation, had solidified his control of the rackets by 1937. Dragna remained the head of the LA family, though, and continued to settle disputes, arrange hits, and oversee drug trafficking throughout the region.

Mickey Cohen never paid any respect to Dragna, even when he had to occasionally work with him under Siegel's orders. The animosity between the two men was mutual. Dragna refused to let Jews into his outfit, just as his Mafia predecessors had done in the past, and Cohen hated him for it. He also imitated the disdain that Siegel had for Dragna, further exacerbating the situation. Once Siegel was taken out, Dragna expected to inherit the operation that had been left behind, but Cohen had other plans. Soon, the two mob factions were at war.

Fortunately for Cohen, Dragna's attempts on his life were ineffectual. Cohen managed to cheat death at least five times. Twice, Dragna's hit men tried dynamiting Cohen's home, once with a homemade torpedo and once with dynamite. The torpedo never exploded but the dynamite went off. However, it had been placed directly under a concrete floor, causing the explosion to travel downward and sideways instead of up. The blast shattered windows throughout the neighborhood, but left Cohen, his wife, his dog, and the family maid unharmed. What upset Mickey the most was the loss of more than forty $300 suits that had been shredded to rags by the explosion. Neighbors jokingly dubbed him "Public Nuisance No. 1" after the bomb blast.

On another occasion, a Dragna gunman let loose with both barrels of a shotgun one night as Cohen was driving home. His Cadillac was peppered with holes but, incredibly, not a single slug touched him.

Cohen finally got the message and made overtures of reconciliation. However, he never offered to relinquish any of his territories or give any money to Dragna. This infuriated the Italian even more. Dragna sent Sam Bruno, a veteran hit man, to wait outside of Cohen's house with a high-powered rifle. Cohen arrived home just after 4:00 a.m. and Bruno opened fire on him. He blazed away at Cohen and left after three minutes, believing the mobster was finally dead. Somehow, once again, Cohen emerged without a scratch.

Dragna never did get Cohen. Even after Cohen was convicted on a tax rap and sentenced to serve five years in prison, a major corruption probe cost Dragna the police protection that he needed to take over his rival's operations.

Mickey Cohen became Los Angeles' most famous – and America's most shot at – gangster.

Cohen became a nationally known mob figure and was probably the most-quoted gangster of his day. In 1950, he appeared before the Kefauver Committee's hearings on organized crime. He was asked to explain why a Hollywood banker had given him a $35,000 loan without any sort of collateral. Cohen quipped, "I guess he just likes me."

Cohen was twice convicted on tax violations, serving four years of a five-year sentence on one occasion and ten years of a fifteen-year term on the other. When he was released from prison in 1972, he declared his intention to go straight. It wasn't really a matter of choice by that time. He was partially paralyzed as the result of a head injury that he received at the hands of another convict in 1963. Mickey Cohen died - of natural causes - in 1976.

Most crime writers tend to discount the effect that organized crime had on the movie industry, downplaying the amount of mob activity in the Los Angeles area during the first few decades of the twentieth century. Few chronicles of Hollywood life make much mention of the influence that gangsters had on the daily operations of the movie studios and how mobsters rubbed shoulders with celebrities by night and terrorized studio executives during the day. While actors and actresses were facing the "studio system" and the iron wills of their bosses, gangsters were intimidating the movie moguls into lucrative compliance. It was a situation that never really came to light until years after the mob's influence had diminished in the movie industry.

Organized crime's infiltration of the film business began when movies were still silent and existed through Hollywood's "Golden Age" (1920s-1950s), when most of the industry's power was held by a handful of major studios and their tight-fisted bosses. Thanks to this, the mob had well-defined targets to threaten and shake down and of course, they regularly did so.

By the 1920s, Hollywood was no longer just a second thought for the dominant East Coast movie business. The major studios were now all located in LA and were thriving during the years of Prohibition, when organized crime was growing in leaps and bounds all across America. The swanky movie colony was a prime marketplace for bootleg liquor and mob syndicates were making a fortune peddling narcotics to the film crowd.

With the repeal of Prohibition in the early 1930s, organized crime in New York and Chicago began looking for new ways to bleed cash from the movie industry. As they worked to control the movie business, they sought out contacts in the industry and one of the most famous was George Raft.

Born in 1895, the future movie star grew up in Manhattan's infamous Hell's Kitchen, where one of his childhood pals was Owney Madden, who went on to become one of New York's most vicious bootleggers and killers. Madden's rackets made him a feared and respected member of the New York underworld and his old friend George rubbed shoulders with gangsters for years. When Madden decided to distance himself from a brewing gang war in New York, he traveled to California in 1930 and brought George along. Raft had made an earlier trip to LA under mob orders to chaperone nightclub hostess Texas Guinan, who was about to make a Hollywood film. Guinan was famous for greeting patrons at her 300 Club at 151 W. 54th St. in Manhattan with a cheery, "Hello, suckers!" Raft had been "discovered" by Broadway and Hollywood talent scouts while he was working as a dancer at the club. This time, Madden ordered him to stay in Hollywood, where he would be out of the way of Madden's underworld rivals in Manhattan. He also believed that his good-looking pal had screen star potential.

In films like *Quick Millions* and *Scarface*, Raft quickly established his movie persona as a slick, well-dressed gangster. It was a part that he knew well. In addition, movie studio bosses appreciated a star with real-life mob affiliations playing a gangster. That way, organized crime would be tolerant of his celluloid representations and the studios would not be held responsible.

Although Raft had been married to Grace Mulrooney since 1923, the marriage fell apart. Being a staunch Catholic, Raft refused to divorce her. However, he had no qualms about carrying on torrid affairs with Hollywood starlets. With his almost-single status and his agility on the dance floor, the

Handsome actor George Raft didn't just play gangsters on the screen – he rubbed shoulders with them in real life and for years was the Mob's "man in Hollywood."

handsome and mannered actor was in constant demand on the Hollywood social scene. Film people were always intrigued by his connections to the underworld, and they loved the idea of brushing up against real danger. Raft's array of escorts over the years included Carole Lombard, Lucille Ball, Betty Grable, Norma Shearer and others. However, his greatest love was socialite and fledging actress Virginia Pine, with whom he unofficially shared a house in the late 1930s.

Raft circulated on the Hollywood scene with, among other underworld characters, Pasquale "Pat" DiCicco, who in 1941 married seventeen-year-old Gloria Vanderbilt. The fashion designer, artist and author later wrote that DiCiccio was physically abusive to her during their four-year marriage. DiCicco was affiliated with New York kingpin Charles "Lucky" Luciano. He was sent to LA posing as a manager and talent agent, but in reality, he was a front man for the rackets. From 1932 to 1934, he was married to movie actress Thelma Todd, who died mysteriously in 1935. Her death by carbon monoxide poisoning was ruled an accident, but there were rumors that she was murdered on orders by Luciano when she turned down his offer to turn her beachside restaurant into a gambling club. Later, DiCicco turned to film producing, which would some would stay is barely a step above gangster.

Another of George Raft's close pals was Benjamin "Bugsy" Siegel.

Born on February 28, 1905 in the Williamsburg section of Brooklyn, Siegel was the son of Russian-Jewish immigrants. He grew up in a teeming neighborhood of crowded tenements, pushcart peddlers and street thugs. Although he never finished school, he got a solid education in criminal activity on the streets. By the age of fourteen, he set up a protection racket for the local street vendors. Any of the vendors who felt they didn't need to pay his gang of kids for protection soon found their vending carts doused with kerosene and set on fire.

He formed an early alliance with two young men named George Raft and Meyer Lansky, and by 1920 they had formed a gang that specialized in bootleg liquor, gambling and auto theft. While Raft went on to play gangsters on the screen, Siegel and Lansky became the real thing. On occasion, Siegel and Lansky hijacked liquor shipments from other operations, before realizing that there was more money to be made by hiring out their gang as protection for the other outfits. Soon they were connected to rising Italian mobsters like Charles Luciano, Frank Costello, Joe Adonis, Albert Anastasia and others. After Luciano and Lansky created a national crime syndicate, they often assigned Spiegel to carry out murders that were used to gain control of various operations. In many ways, Siegel and Lansky were opposites. While Lansky was calculating and had a cool head for sinister business dealings, Siegel was a hothead who was capable of brutal violence. He relished the sight of blood and was so enthused by it that he was dubbed "Bugsy," although he was never called that to his face.

There was no question that Siegel enjoyed the more violent aspects of his work. When he agreed to murder his old friend Bo Weinberg in 1934 - as a favor for Dutch Schultz - he called Weinberg and invited him out for dinner. They took a shortcut on the way to the restaurant and Siegel stopped the car and started pistol-whipping Weinberg. He then pulled out a knife and slashed his face and throat. The bodies of his victims were seldom recovered. Borrowing from old-school Sicilian tactics, Siegel disemboweled his victims so that intestinal gases didn't cause the bodies to rise from the bottom of the East River. In a lengthy FBI file, Siegel was credited with at least thirty brutal murders before he left New York for Southern California.

In the spring of 1928, at the age of twenty-three, Siegel married his childhood sweetheart, Esta Krakower. Meyer Lansky was his best man. Initially, Esta had no idea what Siegel did for a living. She thought he operated a trucking business with Lansky on the Lower East Side. The truck rental business was very lucrative, or so it appeared, since Ben was able to keep a suite at the Waldorf and buy a fashionable home in Scarsdale. The

Benjamin Siegel started out in the rackets with Meyer Lansky and later became part of the national crime syndicate with Lansky and Charles "Lucky" Luciano. The handsome mobster became "Hollywood's favorite gangster" but behind his smooth exterior lurked a fiery temper and a brutal penchant for violence.

business, of course, was merely a front for bootlegging and hijacking for Siegel and Lansky. They soon expanded and joined forces with some of the most powerful mobsters in the city, including Luciano. Lansky and Luciano put together the Syndicate, which was essentially a mixture of the Sicilian mafia and the Jewish gangsters who worked for Siegel and Lansky.

While there were ethnic traditionalists within the Mafia - like Luciano's boss, Giuseppe "Joe the Boss" Masseria and others - who refused to join forces with the Jewish gangsters, they were quickly and efficiently eliminated. On April 15, 1931, Luciano invited Masseria to dine with him and discuss business at the Nuovo Villa Tammaro restaurant in Coney Island. Near the end of the meal, Luciano excused himself to use the restroom and Siegel and two gunmen then entered the restaurant. Siegel gunned down Masseria, leaving the new Syndicate in charge of the underworld.

For a period of time, the Syndicate proved to be a cooperative venture that became highly profitable, uniting major crime families from across the country. Millions of dollars rolled into their coffers each month. By the time Prohibition was repealed in 1933, the Syndicate was overwhelmed with cash. Even though bootlegging had come to an end, Lansky and Luciano agreed that millions more could be made in gambling, narcotics, prostitution and on the racing wires.

In the middle 1930s, Siegel was sent to California to run the syndicate's West Coast operations, including the lucrative racing wire service for bookmakers. Siegel was already in love with Los Angeles. His brother, Maurice, and his sister, Bessie, had moved to the area in 1933 and Siegel became a frequent visitor. After the end of Prohibition, it was Siegel who first envisioned the new underworld opportunities that waited on the West Coast. In 1934, he rented an apartment at the Piazza Del Sol, next to the Clover Club on the Sunset Strip. The handsome gangster loved the Hollywood nightlife and rubbing shoulders with movie stars who undoubtedly enjoyed "slumming it" with a real-life gangster. Siegel was suave and entertaining and he often hit the town with his old pal George Raft. He became friends with Hollywood celebrities like Jean Harlow, Clark Gable, Gary Cooper, Cary Grant and for a short time, Thelma Todd.

After the thwarted attempts (some say arranged by Siegel) to operate a casino at Thelma Todd's Sidewalk Café, and her untimely death in 1935, Siegel returned to the East Coast for several months. It was a difficult time to be a gangster in New York. District Attorney Thomas E. Dewey was turning up the heat on the mob and no amount of cash could buy him off. He was intent on wrecking the operations of organized crime and specifically, putting Luciano in prison. On December 10, 1935, Luciano was indicted for racketeering and on June 7, 1936, he was found guilty of compulsory prostitution in Manhattan Supreme Court.

Shortly after Luciano's conviction, Siegel made a permanent move to Los Angeles, where city government and the police department could still be bought off. He returned in the summer of 1936 with his wife, Esta, and their daughters, Millicent and Barbara. They rented a home on McCarty Drive in Beverly Hills from opera star Lawrence Tibbett. Siegel soon re-established himself as "Hollywood's favorite gangster."

While establishing a network of Syndicate bookie joints, brothels and casinos in Hollywood and the western side of the city, Siegel hobnobbed with film stars and studio bosses. He joined the exclusive Hillcrest Country Club, and was often seen at the Santa Anita Turf Club and in the fashionable Hollywood nightclubs on the Sunset Strip. As a partner at the Clover Club, he maintained a private gambling room upstairs. For many years, he was also a partner with Charlie Morrison at the Mocambo nightclub. The Mocambo underwent a dazzling $100,000 renovation in the early 1940s, and with its Brazilian-inspired décor and aviary of live parrots, macaws and cockatoos, it was *the* place to be seen on the Sunset Strip. He set up an old bootlegger pal named Billy Wilkerson at the Trocadero nightclub, Ciro's and La Rues on the Strip and they became fronts for the Syndicate. According to the California Crime Commission reports, the Syndicate owned more than thirty bars, at least seventy-five bookie joints, nineteen brothels, seventeen casinos and fourteen nightclubs in the Hollywood area - including the Florentine Gardens, which was operated by Mark Hansen.

When Siegel arrived in LA, Southern California was being run by Jack Dragna, whom local papers called "the Al Capone of Los Angeles." However, Dragna's operation (which Siegel later laughingly referred to as the "Mickey Mouse Mafia") was never well organized and was easily taken over by Siegel and his associates. Dragna had little choice but to cooperate. Luciano had demanded their obedience and according to Syndicate rules, refusal to follow orders could be punishable by death. On instructions from Luciano and Lansky, a vice map was drawn up that divided the city into territories, with some sections being controlled by Siegel and others being controlled by Dragna. Siegel got the western side of the city, which included Hollywood and Beverly Hills, while Dragna was given the central city, the valley suburbs and Long Beach.

Born in Corleone, Sicily, in 1891, Dragna was an old-school Mafioso. He was short, barrel-shaped and spoke broken English. He immigrated to the United States in 1914 and became associated with the Capone organization in Chicago before becoming the boss of Southern California during Prohibition. Ruthless in his rise to power in the local underworld, he fought his way in through murder, extortion and generous payoffs to City Hall. He lived with his wife, Frances, in an unpretentious home in Los Angeles at 3927 Hubert Street and also maintained a winery and a lavish ranch house in Cucamonga.

Although Dragna lacked the smooth polish of Ben Siegel, by the end of Prohibition he had built an extensive gangland empire in Southern California, controlling the gambling, prostitution and narcotics trades. He was best-known for the gambling ships that he operated three miles off the coast - in international waters - that were popular with city dwellers and the movie colony.

Dragna's second-in-command, Johnny Rosselli, had all the polish that his boss lacked and he was the mob's man in Hollywood before Siegel arrived. Rosselli, who was close to Harry Cohn at Columbia and Joe Schneck at Fox, had gained control of the International Alliance of Theatrical and Stage Employees union (IATSE), which supplied craftsmen and technicians to studio productions. With their domination of the labor force, Rosselli and union boss Willie Bioff began extorting money from the studios to ward off possible strikes. Even though Dragna warned Siegel not to muscle in on Rosselli's operation, he soon took over the Extras Guild and managed to weasel into the Screen Actors Guild with his pal, George Raft. The bad feelings between

Two of Siegel's girlfriends – actress Wendy Barrie (Left) and Marie "The Body" McDonald

Siegel and Dragna intensified when Siegel worked his way into his gambling ship enterprise and launched the *S.S. Rex*, which perched itself off the shoreline of Santa Monica. Only Luciano's insistence that Dragna cooperate prevented Dragna from resorting to violence and open war.

In 1938, Siegel moved with his wife and daughters to an elegant Mediterranean-style mansion in Holmby Hills. He also kept a suite of rooms at the Sunset Towers in Hollywood, which became a rendezvous spot with his various girlfriends that were mostly culled from the ranks of studio starlets and the chorus lines of places like the Florentine Gardens. It was easy for Siegel to find girls who were thrilled to be dating a real-life mobster.

One of Siegel's girlfriends was actress Wendy Barrie, who hoped to someday marry the volatile and elusive gangster. Another of his steady dates was Marie "The Body" McDonald, a voluptuous actress who got her start in the chorus line at the Florentine Gardens and who went on to make several forgettable films in the 1940s. However, Siegel was smitten with auburn-haired Virginia Hill, a crime syndicate bagwoman from Marietta, Georgia. This hard dame's career included a stint as a dancer at the 1933 Chicago World's Fair and being a bed partner to various underworld characters, including Frank Costello, Joe Adonis, and Frank Nitti. Siegel probably met Virginia for the first time in New York but their relationship heated up when she came to Hollywood in 1939, hoping to make it in pictures - or at least

Siegel couldn't stay away from mob bagwoman Virginia Hill, who, unknown to Siegel, had been sent to California to keep an eye on him for the Syndicate.

that's what she told Siegel. She had actually been dispatched to California by the Syndicate, with orders to keep an eye on the erratic Siegel. Virginia attended all of the best Hollywood parties, was a fixture on the nightclub scene and was usually seen in the company of Siegel and his buddy, George Raft.

Jean Harlow's former boyfriend Longy Zwillman introduced Siegel to Countess di Frasso (a.k.a Dottie Taylor of Watertown, NY). The Countess Dorothy Dendice Taylor di Frasso was a vivacious heiress, who had married the impoverished Italian Count Carlo di Frasso before heading to Hollywood and the high life. The highlight of Hollywood's social season was Marion Davies' annual birthday party for William Randolph Hearst, at which, in 1938, the Countess di Frasso was escorted by Ben Siegel. The countess and the gangster were also seen in the receiving line at the formal reception for the visiting Duke and Duchess of Windsor, held at Pickfair, the legendary Beverly Hills estate of Douglas Fairbanks and Mary Pickford.

The countess, no matter how questionable her title might be, provided Siegel with an air of respectability. Gossip columnists never referred to him as a mobster - instead he was a "sportsman" and a "bon vivant." Many in Hollywood knew that he had ominous mob connections, but didn't suspect that he was the one who called the shots in the underworld murders that occasionally plagued the city. Hollywood society flocked to the lavish parties that he threw at his mansion in Holmby Hills and it wasn't until he was arrested for the murder of Harry "Big Greenie" Greenberg in September 1940 that the film stars, celebrities and hangers-on realized that they had a notorious gangster in their midst.

Greenberg was the proverbial "man who knew too much." A former hired killer, Greenberg was broke and hiding from the law. He made the mistake of contacting his former boss, Louis "Lepke" Buchalter, and demanding some cash - or he was going to talk to the cops. At that point, Greenberg became a marked man and when it was discovered that he was hiding out in a Hollywood rooming house, the Syndicate got in touch with Siegel. He had the rooming house staked out by his brother-in-law, Whitey Krakower, who reported that Greenberg was in the habit of driving off each night around 8:00 p.m. to get a *Daily Racing Form*. On the night of November 22, 1939, Siegel and Abe "Kid Twist" Reles drove to Hollywood in a stolen Buick and met Allie "Tick" Tannenbaum and Frankie Carbo, who were waiting two blocks from the rooming house in a stolen Mercury. When they got to Greenberg's hideout, they parked on the west side of the street and didn't have long to wait before Greenberg pulled up and parked his Ford convertible coupe. Abe Reles recalled that Siegel quickly stepped out of the car, walked up to Greenberg and whipped him in the head four times with the butt of the gun. He then stepped back and fired a shot into his fractured skull. Greenberg was slumped over the wheel when Siegel got back into the Mercury and drove away. The only witness was a pedestrian who saw the car drive away with its lights off. Siegel's back-up men, Tannenbaum and Carbo, were never needed.

Greenberg's murder remained unsolved for months. Siegel would have continued to be a Hollywood "bon vivant" with a mysterious source of income if Abe Reles was not arrested on racketeering charges in New York and began offering information to the authorities to get a better deal. Reles wasn't much over five feet tall, but what he lacked in stature he made up for in ruthlessness. It was said he had gotten the nickname "Kid Twist" because of his penchant for strangling people who offended him, as well as his other favorite murder method of jamming an ice pick in his victim's ear and giving it a hearty twist. He had gotten into the business of murder for hire in his boyhood, when he accepted as little as $8 to "whack" someone. Reles had been involved in dozens of contract murders and he eventually filled twenty-five district attorney steno books with bloody tales of mob violence. One of the killers that Reles named was Ben Siegel, who committed dozens of murders, including that of recent Hollywood victim Harry Greenberg.

Siegel was booked on suspicion of murder on September 14, 1940. He was locked up at the old county jail building in downtown LA - a place where a little money went a long way. While under indictment for murder, Siegel was had his own apartment in the jail, had his meals catered by Lindy's in Beverly Hills and was frequently chauffeured to Hollywood nightclubs by uniformed deputies.

It turned out to be the *Examiner's* Jim Richardson who exposed Siegel's special treatment. Acting on a tip, he assigned reporters Sid Hughes and Howard Hertel to check things out. They waited outside the county jail until the reporters spotted Siegel exiting by a side door, accompanied by Deputy Sheriff Jimmy Pascoe. Siegel was nattily dressed in a tailored suit and a fancy silk tie. He drove off in the backseat of the deputy's unmarked car. The reporters followed them to Beverly Hills, where they spotted Siegel picking up actress Wendy Barrie at Lindy's restaurant. The couple then set off for a night on the town, chauffeured by Deputy Pascoe. When Siegel and Barrie walked out of Slapsie Maxie's nightclub around midnight, there were startled by the blinding flash of Hertel's camera. Siegel cursed and ran to Deputy Pascoe's car and sped off, but it was too late. The next day, the photo of Siegel and Barrie was on the *Examiner's* front page.

The people of Los Angeles may have been shocked - but they could hardly have been surprised.

Richardson discovered that the jail's physician, Dr. Benjamin Blank, had received more than $32,000 from Siegel in return for arranging for him to stay in the jail's private apartment, where a trustee was assigned to be his butler and to serve him gourmet meals that included roast pheasant and caviar. In addition to unlimited phone privileges and eighteen trips out of the jail during his first month of incarceration, under the pretext of seeing the dentist, Siegel was allowed female visitors, whom he entertained in his apartment while serving them lemonade spiked with whiskey.

The *Examiner* noted, "Siegel is not only permitted to keep an extensive wardrobe of costly 'mufti' for his trips outside the jail, but while in jail he wears a tailor-made uniform with notched lapels, razor-edged creases, and made of cloth far superior in quality to the usual jail denim. Siegel's shoes are shined each morning for him by his 'valet,' a trustee who keeps Bugsy's raiment in apple-pie order."

There were the usual investigations and reprimands, but the story quickly faded from the news. The murder charges against Siegel were eventually dropped - after Siegel donated $30,000 to the Los Angeles district attorney's election campaign. It also didn't hurt that Abe Reles somehow fell or was tossed out of a sixth floor window of a Coney Island hotel while under around-the-clock protective custody by teams of police officers. Reles had already testified against Louis Lepke Buchalter and was about to do the same against Albert Anastasia. The abrupt end to his short-lived career as an informant was gleefully noted by newspaper columnists, who called him "The Canary Who Could Sing but Couldn't Fly." With Reles dead, the prosecution was left without a witness, but Reles had disclosed that Siegel's brother-in-law, Whitey Krakower, was also involved in Greenberg's murder. Shortly after Krakower was brought in for questioning by the New York district attorney, he was gunned down in a Manhattan street. The murder of Esta Siegel's brother turned out to be the last straw in the destruction of the shaky Siegel marriage. Esta filed for divorce and moved back to New York with the children.

Although Siegel had threatened Jim Richardson in an attempt to keep his name out of the papers, the damage had been done and Siegel found himself being shunned by the Hollywood high society that had formerly lionized him. In 1941, he sold the five-bedroom mansion in Holmby Hills and moved to Florida. He and Virginia Hill purchased a house in Miami Beach from one of William Randolph Hearst's sons. Siegel and Meyer Lansky operated a number of lucrative Florida gambling ventures, including The Grotto and the Colonial Inn, a lavish casino hotel in Hallandale, where city officials were willing to look the other way in returned for payoffs and increased tourism revenue.

When Siegel moved to Miami, Jack Dragna may have thought he was free of his nemesis, but Siegel couldn't stay away from Hollywood. He soon returned and set up a headquarters above the Formosa Café. He began to expand his gambling, narcotics and prostitution operations, which included Brenda Allen's pricey call-girl ring. During World War II, Siegel and Hill were often seen at Sunset Strip nightclubs and Hill was known for dropping thousands of dollars for lavish parties at Ciro's, the Trocadero and the Mocambo. Often referred to in the gossip columns as a "Southern oil heiress" (in reality, her father was a horse and mule trader and her mother ran a boarding house) Virginia's elegant parties were popular with Hollywood society. Like Ben Siegel, though, Virginia had another side. Few knew that she was a cash courier for the Syndicate and was allowed to skim off a large percentage of the cash that she delivered and distributed.

Also like Siegel, Virginia Hill couldn't stay away from Hollywood. She played several walk-on bit parts in films at Universal before Bugsy "persuaded" Harry Cohn to give her a contract at Columbia, where she briefly attended acting classes with a very patient drama coach and did several more walk-ons before finally giving up the dream of a movie career.

Money poured in from Siegel's operations, but he wanted more. Using a former boxer named Mickey Cohen as his strong-arm man, Siegel became determined to infiltrate the race-wire system that sent racing results back and forth across the country. The race-wire was an intricate and tricky operation that involved spotters at the track who were able to quickly transmit odds and results from a communication post near the track. They sent them out on the Continental Wire Service, which was controlled by James Ragen and the Chicago mob. After Prohibition ended, the race-wire and the Syndicate network of bookie joints became one of the mob's most important operations. The combined take from the nation's bookies ran into the billions. It provided the only source of instantaneous information about all of the betting opportunities at all of the tracks in the country. The money made at the tracks paled in comparison to that which was being taken in by the bookies. Whoever controlled the race-wire controlled all of the bookies in America and Siegel had plans to put himself on top.

According to Mickey Cohen, "Benny Siegel began pushing another wire, the Trans-America Service, because he didn't have any cut with the Continental. Jack Dragna and Johnny Rosselli - the guys Benny was pushing out of action - did. Russell Brophy was Ragen's son-in-law and in charge out here. So Benny tried politely to talk to Ragen and Brophy and bring the matter about without any hassle. When he couldn't get no cooperation with Brophy, Benny just said, 'Well, we're going to break the whole thing up." So he gave orders to knock the service out."

With a carload of gunmen, Mickey Cohen charged into the Continental Wire Service office in downtown Los Angeles, where it was secretly located on the ninth floor of the Newmark Building.

Cohen recalled, "We tore that fucking office apart. In fact, we busted Brophy's head open pretty good because he got out of line a little bit. But actually, the instructions were to knock him in pretty good anyway. With the Continental joint out of commission, Benny figured that he would be able to get with Ragen in Chicago, but Ragen didn't see the light, so a truck went by and shot him down. When he didn't die fast enough from the hit and went to the hospital - he was poisoned. Ben Siegel's knocking over Ragen and the Continental was kind of s slap in the face to Dragna, who thought he was running the West Coast. Dragna was really from the old moustache-Pete days. The worst thing you can do to an old-time Italian *mahoff* is to harm his prestige in any way, and that's what took place when Benny came out here."

Perhaps the one thing that fanned the flames in the conflict between Siegel and Dragna was Siegel's takeover of Brenda Allen's prostitution ring. Allen had been operating in Dragna's territory behind the Ambassador Hotel, but Siegel and Cohen had enlarged her business by giving her connections within the moneyed Hollywood community. They saw this as good reason to

The Ambassador Hotel – Brenda Allen's call-girl ring operated in Jack Dragna's territory behind the hotel, but the Syndicate put Ben Siegel in charge of the operation. This was just one of the problems that had caused issues between Dragna and Siegel.

muscle into her lucrative operation. Although Allen was running over one hundred pricey call girls from her Hollywood telephone exchange, her communication center was in the middle of Dragna's territory - and yet the Syndicate cut was going to Siegel.

The animosity between Siegel and Dragna simmered for years, but it didn't turn into open warfare until Siegel abandoned his Los Angeles interests for the Nevada desert, where he planned to turn a sleepy watering hole called Las Vegas into a legal gambling paradise. It was not hard for him to convince Syndicate pal Meyer Lansky of the enormous potential in Las Vegas. Gambling had always been a huge moneymaker for the mob and in Nevada legalized gambling had a much lower overhead than anywhere else. There were no politicians or police officers that had to be paid off and legal gambling would be the perfect arrangement for laundering money. Instead of dingy back rooms with a few poker tables and a roulette wheel, the Las Vegas casinos would be glittering palaces - high-class "carpet joints" in mob parlance, with crystal chandeliers and chorus lines of high-kicking showgirls.

While Siegel was in Las Vegas, he appointed Mickey Cohen to handle the day-to-day operations in Los Angeles. Cohen, however, was no Ben Siegel. He lacked his mentor's style and discretion and he began aggressively moving in on Dragna's bookmaking operations.

Dragna decided to fight back. The first shots in the war were fired in May 1946 with the killing of Paulie Gibbons, a Syndicate bookmaker from the East Coast who worked with Cohen. He was gunned down in front of his Beverly Hills home on May 2. Then, on October 3, two other Siegel and Cohen associates, Benny "The Meatball" Gamson and George Levinson were wiped out when a gunman entered their West Hollywood apartment and shot them to death.

The murders - and attempted assassinations that followed - made headlines for days but none of them were ever solved. Allegedly, homicide detectives and reporters had no clue as to who was responsible, or at least that's what they said in the papers. Privately, most everyone agreed that it was the work of Jack Dragna.

Elizabeth Short returned to Los Angeles in July 1946, just at the underworld war was getting started. She had dreams of becoming a movie star, but she had no idea how things worked under the surface in the industry, where the studios, nightclubs, unions and many of the major talent agencies had been infiltrated by the mob.

Ann Toth later told detectives that Beth had questionable associations and "often stumbled into trash." Mark Hansen agreed, adding, "She dated many different men ... mostly hoodlums." With her heart set on becoming a star, she may have perceived Maurice Clement, who drove Brenda Allen's call girls around for Max Arnow at Columbia Studios, as her connection with the Hollywood studio elite. But if Clement truly had "offered to set her up in an apartment in Beverly Hills," as Beth told Ann Toth, he almost certainly had something else in mind. Naïve and out of her element, Beth had no concept of how dangerous the associations were that she was making - or that she could wind up as yet another casualty in the underworld war that was taking place in LA.

When Beth's mutilated and bisected body was discovered in Leimert Park, it was never mentioned by Capt. Donahoe, the detectives or the press that her remains were found approximately two hundred and fifty yards from Jack Dragna's home, which was near the corner of Thirty-Ninth and Norton. Nor was it ever revealed that the letter "D" had been carved into Beth's pubic area. The D is visible in police photographs that were released with the district attorney's files in 2003, but not at the time of the murder.

Did the D stand for "Dahlia" - or could it have stood for "Dragna?"

Whatever the killer's message, it was likely received loud and clear at the nearby home of Jack Dragna.

Just five months after the murder of Beth Short, Ben "Bugsy" Siegel was also dead - shot to death in Virginia Hill's Moorish-style mansion at 810 Linden Drive in Beverly Hills.

At the time of his death, Siegel was deeply immersed in his dream of a grand casino in the Nevada desert. Although he was spending most of his time in Las Vegas, he frequently visited LA to raise cash for his hotel project, which ran several million dollars over budget.

The land that would later be the site of Siegel's iconic Flamingo casino was originally owned by Billy Wilkerson, owner of the *Hollywood Reporter* and several nightclubs on the Sunset Strip. Wilkerson had hired George Vernon Russell to design a hotel that was more in the refined European style than the so-called "sawdust joints" that were located on Fremont Street. Russell planned a hotel with luxurious rooms, a spa, showroom, golf course, nightclub and upscale restaurant. Due to high wartime materials costs, though, Wilkerson began to run into financial problems almost at once, running almost $400,000 short. He began looking for new financing.

In late 1945, Siegel convinced Meyer Lansky to invest in Las Vegas. He first purchased the El Cortez on Fremont Street for $600,000 and later sold it at a hefty profit. At the same time, Siegel learned that Wilkerson had run out of money for his grand hotel and casino. Using the profits from the sale of the El Cortez, Siegel influenced Wilkerson into accepting new partners. With Lansky's blessing, Siegel talked the Syndicate into investing $2 million in the new property. Wilkerson was allowed to keep a nominal interest in the casino and, on the surface, would retain operational control. Everyone knew, however, that it was actually Siegel who was running the show.

Siegel took over the final phases of construction and convinced more of his mob associates to invest in the project. The problem was that Siegel had no experience in construction or design and the cost quickly spiraled out of control. There were still shortages on construction materials after the war. Siegel paid a premium for what he needed and things were made worse by price gouging from construction firms and suppliers, as well as companies who delivered by day, stole the materials back at night, and then re-sold them to Siegel again the next day. Rumors of such things ran rampant, as well as claims that Siegel was actually in on the scam, which allowed him to skim part of the construction money into his own accounts.

The project ran into delay after delay, falling far behind schedule. In September, rains pounded the area for days, flooding the building site over and over again. Construction problems taxed Siegel's patience. After deciding that the aisles in the hotel's kitchen pantry were too narrow, he had them re-constructed at a cost of $30,000 - the equivalent of $200,000 today. Walls that were found to block views were torn down and rebuilt with windows. When a heavy beam in Siegel's private penthouse was found to be less than six feet above the floor, Siegel pistol-whipped the foreman, had it torn out and replaced at a cost of $22,500. The construction budget had originally been $1.5 million, but by September 1946, the project had cost more than $3.5 million - and costs were still skyrocketing. After asking for more cash from Luciano and Lansky, the Syndicate bosses became increasingly skeptical about the project.

As construction costs soared, Siegel's bank account ran dry and checks began to bounce, including one to contractor Del E. Webb for $150,000. Desperate for cash, Siegel sold his interest in the Florentine Gardens for $100,000 to Barney Vandersteen, a friend of Mark Hansen. He also instigated a series of jewelry robberies, orchestrated by henchmen Albert Louis Greenberg and the McCadden Gang. Greenberg sold narcotics out of his Hollywood bar, Al Green's Nightspot, and had once been a bootlegger for Siegel before relocating to Hollywood when Bugsy moved west. Al had met Beth Short in 1944 when she was learning the B-Girl trade with Lucille Varela. And in 1946, Beth had frequented Al Green's Nightspot, which became the center for the jewelry thefts that Siegel carried out to help finance his casino. The McCadden Gang included Louis and Marty Abrams, who had long worked for Siegel and Lansky, and Greenberg's friend, a tall, lanky thug named Jack Anderson Wilson.

The theft of more than $150,000 in jewelry from an LA residence was pulled off by Greenberg on November 11, 1946. The jewelry was fenced through a Siegel pal named Maurice Reingold, who owned a high-end jewelry store next to Drucker's barbershop on Beverly Drive. Siegel sold off real estate holdings and borrowed money from George Raft so that he could promise Lansky and Luciano that the casino would be open for Christmas. He missed the deadline by one day.

Siegel finally opened the Flamingo Hotel & Casino on December 26, 1946 at a total cost of $6 million - more than triple the budget that he had promised the Syndicate. He named the resort after Virginia Hill, who loved to gamble and whose nickname was "Flamingo," which Siegel had dubbed her due to her long, skinny legs. Virginia allegedly helped Siegel skim money from the construction project and made frequent trips to deposit money for the mobster in Swiss banks. Hill may have been Siegel's favorite mistress, but she was not his only one. At one brief time after the casino opened, Siegel had four of his favorite girlfriends lodged in separate hotel suites. They were Virginia Hill, Countess Dorothy di Frasso and actresses Marie McDonald and Wendy Barrie, who frequently announced her engagement to Bugsy and never gave up hoping. Whenever she saw Wendy in the hotel, Virginia Hill would go wild and once she punched the actress so hard in the face that she nearly dislocated her jaw.

Unfortunately for Siegel, female trouble soon became the least of his concerns. The Syndicate began getting restless when, a year after the official groundbreaking, the resort had produced no revenue and had become a

Siegel's Flamingo Hotel in Las Vegas

drain on the resources of the investors. Then, charges were made at a mob meeting in Cuba that either Siegel or Hill was skimming the resort's building budget, an accusation that seemed to be substantiated when Hill turned out to have a $2.5 million bank account in Switzerland, where the skimmed money was believed to be going.

Charles Luciano and the other mob leaders in Havana asked Meyer Lansky what to do. Distressed because of his longtime ties to Siegel, whom he loved like a brother, Lansky reluctantly agreed that if someone was stealing, he had to go. However, he was willing to give Siegel a chance to come clean and make good on the investments. He persuaded the others to wait for the Flamingo's casino opening and if it was a success, then Siegel would have a second chance. Luciano agreed to the plan and the others followed along with him.

The splashy opening -- with a roster of stars scheduled to appear that included George Raft, George Jessel, Clark Gable, Lana Turner, Cesar Romero, Joan Crawford, Sonny Tufts and others - was a disaster. Two Lockheed Constellations had been chartered to fly in the celebrity guests, but heavy rains in Los Angeles grounded the flights. Only Sonny Tufts showed up because he drove across the desert in his car. Jimmy Durante, Rose Marie and Xavier Cugat's orchestra headlined the showroom - which was largely empty. Recalling the opening night, Rose Marie later said, "The show was spectacular, everything was great, but nobody came. We worked to nine or ten people a night for the rest of the two-week engagement."

During those two weeks, the casino at the Flamingo had more dealers than customers and Siegel became increasingly paranoid and violent. One incident involved a dealer that Siegel accused of cheating. His bodyguards had to restrain him so that he didn't kill the man. Furious at his press agent for the bad publicity - and for referring to him as "Bugsy" - he chased the man around the Flamingo pool several times before striking him in the head with the butt of his automatic. Westbrook Pegler made some derogatory comments about Siegel in his syndicated column and when Siegel spotted him in the Flamingo casino, he threatened to kill him and again had to be restrained by his bodyguards.

No matter what kind of big-name entertainment appeared at the Flamingo, it never seemed to be able to lure gamblers to the Nevada desert. To make matters worse, some of the construction had still not been completed and those costs - in addition to the loss from being open with few customers - caused the Flamingo to lose $300,000 in the first ten days of operation. Lansky managed to persuade the other mob chiefs to give Siegel one more reprieve and allow the Flamingo a little more time. During the first week of January 1947, the resort was closed until the hotel could be finished. Bugsy knew that he was in big trouble.

On January 6, 1947, Siegel returned to Los Angeles and according to Bernard Ruditsky, a private detective who worked for Siegel as a debt collector and managed Sherry's Nightclub on the Sunset Strip, he was acting irrationally. This was nothing new to those who knew and worked with him, but Ruditsky admitted that it was worse than usual. In addition to his financial problems with the Flamingo, on January 5, California's Governor Earl Warren announced that there would be no more offshore gambling. The *S.S. Rex* was impounded and all of its gambling equipment was dumped in the sea. At a meeting held at Siegel's home, attended by Ruditsky and Siegel's friend, Allen Smiley, there was a discussion on collecting a number of debts that were owed to Siegel. He desperately needed the cash. The meeting started off on a civil note, but escalated into madness with Siegel screaming obscenities, breaking things, throwing objects and threatening to kill everyone who owed him money. After that night, Ruditsky concluded that Siegel was way over his head with the Flamingo deal and decided to stay away from him because he was acting crazy.

Siegel was desperate for cash. Almost as soon as he arrived in the city, Al Greenberg and the McCadden Gang robbed the Mocambo nightclub on the Sunset Strip, making off with a small fortune in jewelry and more than

The Mocambo Nightclub

$6,000 from the past weekend's receipts. The jewelry had been placed on display at the Mocambo by Maurice Reingold, the fence that Siegel used and who had a history of frequent thefts of his heavily insured jewelry. The Mocambo accountant, Isabelle Koch, described the leader of the robbery as a man in a felt hat who held the staff at gunpoint, saying, "Let's nobody be no heroes now." As he kept his gun aimed at them, a younger man - at least six feet, four inches tall and walking with a limp - swept the jewelry out of the safe and into a bag. The leader in the felt hat was later identified as Al Greenberg.

According to FBI files, Siegel planned to stay in Los Angeles for several days and purchased a TWA ticket for a flight to New York, departing on January 14. He planned to spend a week there to visit his daughters. But on the morning of January 14, the FBI learned that Siegel had canceled the trip.

Author Donald Wolfe made the connections. On January 9, 1947, three days after the robbery at the Mocambo, Beth Short returned to Los Angeles from San Diego and was dropped off at the Biltmore Hotel by Robert Manley. On the morning of Tuesday, January 14, Siegel canceled his flight to New York. At some point on that same night, Beth Short was viciously murdered.

On January 15, the day that Beth's mutilated and bisected body was dumped in the vacant lot, Siegel made reservations at the Colonial House in Palm Springs, a known Syndicate retreat. FBI reports established that Siegel planned to stay in Palm Springs for ten days before returning to Las Vegas.

On January 16, the day after Beth's body was discovered, an article in the *Los Angeles Times* started that four suspects had been arrested on January 15 in connection with the robbery at the Mocambo. The article read, "Shuttled into a show-up on the ninth floor of the Hall of Justice were Al Greenberg, 42, operator of a café at 1735 N. McCadden Place, and Louis Abrams, 47, both ex-Sing-Sing convicts, along with Marty Abrams, 50, the latter's brother, and Harry Burnow, 31. Another younger thief, described by the Mocambo accountant as six feet, four inches tall, was not apprehended."

Even though Al Greenberg was positively identified as the Mocambo thief who held the staff at gunpoint, he was inexplicably released from custody for "lack of evidence." Greenberg was subsequently involved in another robbery - also connected with Maurice Reingold - on April 2, when he broke into a Beverly Hills apartment and beat the female occupant until she revealed the location of her valuable jewelry. All of it had been sold to her by Reingold. She was robbed of more than $150,000 in diamond and emerald jewelry. When she identified Greenberg's mug shot as the man who had robbed her, the Beverly Hills police discovered that he had suddenly left town.

Meanwhile, Siegel had returned to Las Vegas and injected a huge amount of cash into the Flamingo, which re-opened on March 1. Things began to change, but there was still a desperate cash crunch. Many of the people who worked for Siegel at the time later recalled that he became even more violent and out of control. When Siegel heard that Ray Kronsen, a desk clerk at the El Rancho Vegas, had referred to the Flamingo as "a place run by gangsters," Siegel exploded and pistol-whipped the man into unconsciousness. Despite his crazed behavior, the Flamingo seemed to be turning around. The idea of an "oasis in the desert" was catching on and people were flocking to Vegas and, by extension, to Siegel's casino and hotel. Lansky could finally show the other bosses that Siegel had been right about Las Vegas all along, but it still wasn't enough to save Siegel's life.

By the spring of 1947, Bugsy Siegel was doomed.

Back in Southern California, Beverly Hills Police Chief Clinton Anderson learned that Al Greenberg was in New York and flew there and arrested him on June 18 for the April 2 robbery. Greenberg denied that he had anything to do with it, claiming that he had been staying at the Flamingo in Las Vegas from March 30 to April 5. He told the police that Siegel would vouch for him - but it turned out to be too late for that. Both Maurice Reingold and Al Greenberg ended up being indicted for the robbery. Once again, Greenberg was mysteriously released.

On June 20, 1947, Siegel flew back to Los Angeles on another cash-raising trip. He was met at Mines Field by Al Smiley, who drove him to Virginia Hill's rented mansion in Beverly Hills. That afternoon, Smiley drove him to Drucker's barbershop for a haircut and manicure. After that, he walked to the nearby office of attorney Joe Ross on South Beverly Drive, where, according to Ross, they discussed the Flamingo's financial future. Ross said that Siegel planned to meet someone that night at a restaurant in Ocean Park to iron out some new arrangements.

Around 6:30 that evening, Smiley and Siegel departed for Santa Monica, where they dined at Jack's at the Beach, at the end of the Ocean Park Pier. Siegel ordered the trout. Jack's was a mob-connected hideaway that was popular with the Hollywood crowd. Managed by heavyweight wrestling champion Sonny Meyers, Jack's was owned by Barney Vandersteen, Mark Hansen's friend who bought Siegel out of the Florentine Gardens. Vandersteen also owned the Pig n' Whistle restaurant chain in LA and controlled several Syndicate gambling establishments in Redondo Beach. Others who were dining at Jack's that night later recalled seeing Siegel leave his table at one point and go to a rear corner booth, where he joined a group that included Barney Vandersteen. Smiley and Siegel left the restaurant around 9:45 p.m. and drove back to Beverly Hills, stopping at the Beverly Wilshire Hotel drugstore along the way.

After returning to Virginia Hill's house, Siegel sat down on the floral chintz sofa in the living room. Hill was away in Europe at the time. At around 10:30 p.m., he was reading a complimentary copy of the *Los Angeles Times* that he had picked up earlier at Jack's at the Beach when steel-jacketed slugs began tearing through the front window. Although the drapes were supposed to be kept drawn when Siegel was there, it was a hot night and someone had opened the windows and pulled back the drapes to let in some fresh air. Engaged in conversation, neither Siegel nor Smiley heard the car that pulled up outside or the gunman as he walked up to the window. Quietly placing a .30-calibre M1 carbine on a wooden trellis, the killer was only fifteen feet away when he squeezed the trigger and fired off an entire clip.

The first bullet smashed into the side of Siegel's head and tore out his left eye. Authorities later found it on the dining room floor, more than ten feet from his body. As his head snapped back against the sofa, a second bullet hit his face and blew out the back of his neck. Nine shots were fired. Four hit Siegel, breaking his ribs and shredding his lungs. One ripped through Smiley's coat and he dove to the floor. Siegel was dead before he slumped over on the sofa.

Siegel had been a marked man when he died and while he may not have known it everyone else did. Only five people --- all members of Siegel's

The end of the Hollywood gangster – and cold-blooded killer... Ben Siegel shot to death in his living room in Beverly Hills

family - attended his funeral as he was laid to rest in a $5,000 casket in the Beth Olam section of Hollywood Forever Cemetery. His friend Meyer Lansky was nowhere to be found and Virginia Hill was conveniently out of the country. His movie star pal, George Raft, was sick at home with asthma. All of Hollywood stayed away as their "golden boy" went to the grave at the age of forty-one.

After Siegel was assassinated, the mob continued to support the Flamingo Hotel and eventually saw it grow and prosper. They poured millions of dollars into Las Vegas and it became the gambling mecca that Siegel had envisioned in the early 1940s. Siegel had pioneered the luxury casino in Vegas and the popular performers that began playing at various resorts in town did much to make the city - and gambling - appear respectable. Meyer Lansky took over the running of the Flamingo and within a year, had made a profit of $4 million.

Rumors swirled, of course, about who had killed Ben Siegel. Some said that it was Meyer Lansky and the Syndicate, who knew that Siegel had been skimming from the Flamingo's construction fund. Others believed that it was Mickey Cohen, looking to take over Siegel's business. In the brief police investigation into the murder, though, there was one possible suspect whose name was never mentioned: Jack Dragna. He had both the means and the motive for carrying out the murder of his nemesis, but he was never questioned. Just like the murder of Beth Short, the Ben Siegel case was stamped "Open and Unsolved."

But author Donald Wolfe revealed a compelling motive for Siegel's murder - one that went beyond mere hatred over illicit business dealings and lost vice territories.

In 1973, while being interviewed by Martin Gosch, Charles Luciano revealed that Siegel had been murdered on orders from Jack Dragna. In 1987, Eddie Cannizzaro, Dragna's former driver and bodyguard, made a deathbed confession to federal agents that he had been the gunman who shot Siegel and he had done so on behalf of Dragna. Beverly Hills homicide detective Les Zoeller, who inherited the unsolved Siegel case in 1980, investigated Cannizzaro's claims and verified that he had indeed been Dragna's driver and bodyguard and the details in his confession were correct. Detective Zoeller was convinced that Dragna orchestrated the murder. He had the motive and the connections to get away with it. Increasingly violent and erratic, Siegel had become an alarming liability to the Syndicate - as well as to the mob's friends at City Hall.

Convinced that he would never be named as a suspect or even brought in for questioning, Jack Dragna had Ben Siegel murdered just five months after the Black Dahlia's body was discovered in the vacant lot near Dragna's home.

Was the location of the body just a coincidence? Donald Wolfe - who has put together the best theory (at least some parts of it) about the murder of the Black Dahlia that I've ever heard - doesn't think so. He asked the question: Was Ben Siegel the demented killer that slashed open Beth Short's face, pistol whipped her, carved the letter D into her flesh and then dumped her severed remains to be found almost in Dragna's backyard? FBI reports from the time, which refer to Siegel as "insane," indicate that he was exactly the kind of pathological killer who would be capable of committing such an act. He also had the means and opportunity. But what was the motive? Why kill a nobody like Beth Short? How did she become part of the war going on between Siegel and Dragna? Bad luck? Bad timing? Or worse?

In 1952, a reporter from the *Los Angeles Times* asked Detective Harry Hansen why the Black Dahlia killer had never struck again, and what the detective thought had happened to him. Hansen, always succinct when replying to reporters' questions, was even more concise than usual.

He gave a one-word response: "Dead."

14. UNRAVELING THREADS

The Black Dahlia case was stalled and placed on the back burner, but it was far from dead. Stories still swirled about Hollywood and while they were mostly rumors, they often connected various people to Beth Short's fate - some of them famous and some not.

An ex-con and artist named Arthur James, Jr. (alias Charles B. Smith) claimed that he had made some sketches of Beth Short and had painted her in oils. They met, he told reporters, at the City of Paris cocktail lounge in August of 1944. In November of the same year, James was arrested in Tucson, Arizona, for passing bad checks and violating the Mann Act. The fifty-six-year-old James was charged with bringing Geraldine Ann Gillig, age nineteen, across the California state border for "immoral purposes." At the time he was arrested, James told police he was "the son of one of the twelve richest men in the world." One of the bogus checks he signed was for $50,000. According to Tucson police, James also claimed to have been everything "from a switchman for the Southern Pacific to an FBI agent." James would later claim that the young woman he was arrested with was Beth Short, but Beth left California in September 1943 and did not return until the summer of 1946. James' "Black Dahlia" story turned out to be just another of his fantasies.

But perhaps the best-known man to be whispered about in connection with the Black Dahlia case was Norman Chandler, heir to the Chandler publishing dynasty. Rumor had it that Mark Hansen recruited pretty girls like Beth to work at the Florentine Gardens, making sure that his customers always had a good time. Hansen was said to have allowed some of the girls that he perceived to have "special qualities" to stay at his house, and he reserved those girls for special customers in the Hollywood crowd. Some "big shot" had taken a fancy to Beth and had gotten her pregnant. Hansen tried to set her up with an abortionist, but she got scared and fled to San Diego. According to the rumors, the "big shot" was Norman Chandler. But was he really?

According to officer Vince Carter of administrative vice, it was common knowledge among members of the LAPD that Norman Chandler was a womanizer, but one who carefully guarded his public life from public scrutiny. As publisher of the *Los Angeles Times*, Chandler insisted that his name be kept free from scandal. But Carter stated, "A lot of what was *not* printed about Chandler was common knowledge in administrative vice and the upper

Norman Chandler, newspaper publisher and heir to the Chandler empire after his father's death in 1944. According to LAPD sources, Chandler was a womanizer and some have linked him to Beth Short.

echelons of the Los Angeles Police Department - a department of the city government in which Chandler always had an intense and close, if usually covert, working relationship."

Chandler was powerful and wielded great authority in the city. His family picked mayors, political appointees, police officials and the men who truly ran the city of Los Angeles. But despite his position of power, he was a very private person. He placed barriers around his life that were seldom crossed by associates, friends and even members of his family. After he died in October 1973, his wife, Dorothy, remarked to a friend that, in all the years they were married, she had never really reached him. "Everyone loved him, but no one knew him," she said.

But according to Vince Carter, the intelligence units within the LAPD knew Norman Chandler very well indeed. They made it their business to discover everything they could about the man who was heir to the Chandler fortune and who wielded so much power in the city. It's often been said that there is no honor among thieves, and in this case, the corrupt officials wanted to know as much as they could about the man who kept them in check. They never knew when such information might be needed.

Ray Pinker, head of the LAPD crime lab, was ahead of his time when it came to devising new methods of police surveillance. He was indicted in 1942, along with Chief Horrall, for having the Gangster Squad place electronic listening devices in many of the key offices at City Hall - including the mayor's. Private detective Fred Otash, who was on Pinker's staff when he was an LAPD officer, later stated that Norman Chandler was one of the many city leaders that Pinker put under surveillance. Chief Horrall and Assistant Chief Joe Reed wanted to know everything they could about Chandler and Pinker's devices made them fully aware of Chandler's "womanizing and playboy lifestyle."

Chandler's marriage to Dorothy had been arranged by his father, Harry, who put his son together with the daughter of a wealthy and socially prominent Long Beach family. Dorothy was known to be an ambitious, strong-willed woman with plenty of drive and opinions of her own. However, her father-in-law believed that a woman's place was in the home. It wasn't until Harry Chandler died in 1944 that Dorothy saw a chance to bring her political and social ambitions to life. She assumed an active role in directing the editorial policy of the *Los Angeles Times* and had an apartment built on the top floor of the *Times* building at First Street and Broadway, where rumors swirled that she was having an affair with someone on the newspaper's staff.

The Chandlers had an estate in Los Feliz, but Dorothy spent most of her nights at the *Times* building penthouse, while Norman spent most of his time at his suite at the California Club. Harry Chandler had been one of the founders of the club, which counted among its members some of the most powerful businessmen in the city. Located downtown, it had a convenient rear entrance on Hope Street, just behind the Biltmore Hotel.

Before he retired from the LAPD and became a private detective, Fred Otash had been stationed at the California Club, conducting surveillance of the city's power brokers for Ray Pinker and the Gangster Squad. According to Otash, it was at the club where Norman Chandler rendezvoused with the women who were brought there by his friend, actor Arthur Lake, who was on Brenda Allen's "A" list. Lake was one of the few people that Chandler was close to. They had been friends for many years and Chandler had been the best man at Arthur Lake's wedding to Patricia Van Cleve, the alleged niece of actress Marion Davies. Patricia was long suspected of being the illegitimate daughter of Davies and William Randolph Hearst, which she herself publically claimed just before she died in 1993.

Arthur Lake, the actor who played Dagwood in the *Blondie* films, first met Beth Short in 1944 at the Hollywood Canteen. Both of their names were found in Georgette Bauerdorf's diary and Lake admitted that he knew Beth when he was brought in for questioning by the sheriff's department. Could it have been through Lake that Norman Chandler met Beth Short? If the rumor was true and Beth had been pregnant when she was murdered, and if the father of the unborn child was Chandler it might explain the extraordinary efforts made by the Chandler faction at City Hall to cover up many of the circumstances of the crime.

But didn't the autopsy report state that Beth was not pregnant? If so, then why did several people believe that she was? Her roommate, Lynn Martin, had implied that she might be, but no one else went on record.

Aggie Underwood, the hard-boiled reporter for the *Herald*, believed that Lake was somehow mixed up in the case, which might have made Chandler involved by extension. She thought the connection included something that linked the murders of Georgette Bauerdorf and Beth Short. She had been puzzled and angered about being ordered off both cases, and had intended to leave the paper when she was suddenly promoted to the city editor's desk. She later learned that dropping the story had to do with the Arthur Lake connection. Aggie learned from contacts in the sheriff's department that both Lake and Beth Short had been mentioned in Georgette's diary and that Lake had been brought in for questioning. She also learned that, after the contents of Beth's purse had been mailed to the *Examiner*, Arthur Lake's telephone number had been found in Beth's address book. She also later found out that Lake's wife was not Marion Davies' niece at all - she was actually Davies' daughter by her long-time lover, William Randolph Hearst. Hearst was determined to protect his daughter - and her husband - and he wanted no hint of scandal to touch Arthur Lake.

Even though Aggie was not allowed to write about the Bauerdorf or Short murders, she followed the Dahlia investigation for years and concluded that the case had been controlled and covered up by City Hall. From the beginning, she admitted, there were rumors that Beth Short had been pregnant, no matter what the official reports said. She also believed that this was the secret revealed by the autopsy - the so-called control question - that was privately guarded by Harry Hansen and a handful of others. Hansen would never admit it, but his replies led her to believe this was the case.

Another officer involved in the case told her that there was an underworld abortionist involved and Hansen brought him in several times for questioning, but Chief Horrall quashed the investigation. Aggie later told Donald Wolfe that the man died suddenly at his home in Pasadena. Suicide or murder? Aggie didn't want to say.

15. OFF THE RAILS

The murder of Beth Short is far from the only "Open and Unsolved" case in the files of the LAPD. In 1949, another young would-be movie star vanished in Los Angeles and her disappearance captured newspaper headlines. As detectives delved into the case, they discovered a number of parallels with the Black Dahlia case, although with one major difference: this time, they didn't find the body.

Jean Elizabeth Spangler was one of the hundreds of pretty, talented girls who come to Hollywood hoping for their big break in the movies. While she waited for it, Jean studied, worked hard, and did what she could to earn a living in show business. Jean had worked at the Earl Carroll Theatre and the Florentine Gardens as a dancer, earning money to support her mother and her daughter, Christine, who had been born during World War II. Jean's marriage broke up soon after the war ended.

At the Florentine Gardens, she met Ben Siegel's second-in-command, Mickey Cohen, and they began dating. Cohen escorted her Cohen to a number of Hollywood's hottest nightspots, including Slapsie Maxie's, La Rues, Ciro's and the Mocambo. She became a member of the Extras Guild, which Siegel controlled, and started getting bit parts in movies.

While waiting for their big break, both Beth and Jean seemed to travel down the same paths on their road to what would turn out to be infamy. Jean, too, hung around Brittingham's restaurant next to Columbia Studios. Hoping to become a Columbia starlet, she was promised a screen test by Maurice Clement's boss, Max Arnow, who introduced her to studio head Harry Cohn. Like Beth Short, Jean suddenly became famous - but not in the way she had dreamed. On Wednesday, October 7, 1949, Jean Spangler vanished and was never seen again.

When she disappeared, Jean was twenty-six years old, a tall brunette with an oval-shaped face, large dark eyes, and a wide, sensuous mouth. She had been raised in Los Angeles, attended Franklin High School, and got a job after graduation as a legal secretary, but gave that up to try and make it in the movie business. She was a beautiful young woman but, unfortunately, she had little to set her apart from scores of other beautiful young women who arrived in Hollywood every day - until the unthinkable happened.

On October 7, Jean left her home on Colgate Avenue in the Park La Brea apartment complex near Wiltshire Boulevard around 5:00 p.m. She left her daughter with her sister-in-law, Sophie Spangler, who lived with Jean, her mother, daughter, and her brother. She told Sophie that she was going to meet her former husband to talk about his child support payment that had

Hollywood starlet Jean Spangler vanished in 1949 – rumor had it that she had been pregnant, tried to blackmail the father of her child – and ended up dead.

been due a week before, then go on to work on a movie set. Jean had recently finished work on a small role in the romantic comedy *The Petty Girl* and had been in a good mood. She seemed nervous as she kissed her daughter goodbye and left the house. She was wearing a wool blouse, green slacks, and a white coat.

That was the last time that Jean's family ever saw her.

When Jean failed to return home that night, Sophie became worried. Jean had a number of friends and went out a great deal, but she had never before failed to telephone home, much less stay out all night. Jean's mother was visiting family in Kentucky at the time, so Sophie went to the Wilshire Division of the LAPD and filed a missing person report the next day. Believing that Jean would turn up, the Wilshire police did not bother to send a missing persons report on the teletype right away. Eventually, though, detectives began looking into the case.

Jean had told Sophie that she was going to work on a movie set after she met with her former husband, but the police checked and found that none of the studios had any work in progress or were even open on the evening of October 7. They next checked into her story about meeting her ex-husband. Jean had been through a long custody battle with him, and won custody of Christine in 1948. Dexter Benner, her former husband, had been awarded custody in 1946 at the time of the divorce. Police questioned Benner about her statement to her sister-in-law that she was going to meet him about the overdue child support payment. He said that he had not seen his former wife for several weeks. His new wife, Lynn Lasky Benner, stated that he was with her at the time of Jean's disappearance.

Two days after she vanished, on October 9, Jean's purse was found near the Fern Dell entrance to Griffith Park in Los Angeles with both of the straps on one side torn loose as if it had been ripped from her arm. There was no money inside (Sophie told the police that Jean had no money when she left the house, ruling out robbery as a motive in her disappearance), but it did contain her membership cards in the Screen Actors Guild, the Screen Extras Guild, her driver's license, and a curious note. The note read:

Kirk - can't wait any longer. Going to see Dr. Scott. It will work out best this way while mother is away,

The note ended with a comma and was apparently unfinished. A police handwriting expert was able to determine that the note was in Jean's handwriting.

More than sixty police officers and over one hundred volunteers searched the sprawling park, but no other clues were found. Detectives began working to track down any leads they could find about Jean's life and an all-points bulletin was issued. Photographs of the young woman were sent to newspapers and soon, witnesses began to come forward, disclosing the secrets of the aspiring actress' tangled and complicated life.

One of those witnesses was Hollywood attorney Albert Pearlson, who had employed Jean as a legal secretary for a short time. He told the police that Jean had met Dexter Benner in high school and the mismatched couple became romantically involved. Jean was outgoing and her boyfriend was an introvert. They were married in 1942, shortly after Jean started working at Pearlson's law firm. He told detectives that about six months after the wedding, Jean came to him looking for a divorce. Pearlson tried to talk her out of it, but Jean was insistent. A complaint was filed, but the couple reconciled and the divorce hearing was removed from the calendar. Benner went into the Army during the war and about six months after he left, Christine was born. Then, after she had broken into the movies as a bit player, Jean began to be seen around the Hollywood nightspots.

In 1944, Benner was discharged from the military and he sent word to Jean that he was coming home. Even though she no longer worked for him, Jean came to Pearlson and pleaded with him for help. She had apparently fallen in love with a first lieutenant in the Army Air Corps. Benner was under the impression that she had saved the money he had been sending to her, and that she owned a car. However, Jean had spent all of the money and had wrecked the car months before. Pearlson agreed to help her and when Benner returned to LA, Jean met him when he arrived and brought him straight to Pearlson's office to tell him that she wanted a divorce. Benner agreed and custody of Christine was given to him.

Four days later, Jean returned to Pearlson's office with a black eye and a bruised face. She said that her boyfriend had beaten her and threatened to kill her if she ever left him like she had her husband. The lawyer called him and issued him a warning, but didn't hear from Jean again until a year later. By that time, she had broken off the affair with the Air Corps officer and wanted Pearlson to help her file suit to regain custody of her daughter. She lost the initial suit, but sued again in May 1948 and won. Benner decided not to fight the second time after Pearlson convinced him that Jean was a troubled young woman and having Christine might help her.

Other witnesses came forward, including the owner of a store near where Jean lived. A cashier at the store, Lillian Marks, said that Jean had wandered around the place for a few minutes around 5:30 p.m. on October 7, as if waiting for someone. She saw no one approach her and she did not notice when Jean actually left.

On Wednesday evening, the night she disappeared, she was reported at the Cheese Box restaurant on Sunset Boulevard by Al "The Sheik" Lazaar, a Hollywood radio personality who knew Jean and did a nightly radio broadcast from the Cheese Box. Lazaar saw her sitting in a booth around midnight with two men he didn't recognize. When he approached the table, planning to put Jean on the air, he noted that she "appeared to be arguing with the two men," and one of them waved him away, signaling that they did not want to be interrupted. Terry Taylor, the proprietor of the Cheese Box, confirmed Lazaar's story and also recalled that Jean was there with two men and they had left together shortly after midnight. It was the last time that anyone saw Jean alive - or dead.

The only definite clue that the police had to work with was the mysterious note, but neither Jean's family nor her friends knew anyone named Kirk or Dr. Scott. Jean's mother returned to Los Angeles and told police that someone named "Kirk" had picked up Jean at her home twice, but he stayed in his car and didn't come in. Police searched for Kirk, and the only person in the Hollywood community that they could think of with that name was Kirk Douglas, who had starred in the recent film Young Man With a Horn, in which Jean had a small part. Douglas was vacationing in Palm Springs and heard about the disappearance. He called the police and told them he was not the Kirk mentioned in the note. Douglas was interviewed by the head of the investigating team and stated that he had heard of Jean Spangler, who had been an extra in his new film, but he didn't know her personally. He said that he didn't remember her at all until a friend reminded him that she had been in the film. He told the detectives, "If she's the one I'm thinking about, I remember talking to her. But I never saw her before or since and I never went out with her."

Exhausting their leads in the search for "Kirk," the police turned to finding "Dr. Scott." They questioned every doctor in LA with the last name Scott, but none of them had a patient named Spangler or Benner. Attorney Pearlson recalled that Jean had called her Air Corps officer boyfriend "Scotty," but the lawyer said that she not seen him since 1946.

Some of Jean's friends told the police that they suspected that she had been pregnant when she disappeared and that she had talked to one or two of them about getting an abortion, which was illegal at that time. The police talked with several people who frequented the same nightclubs and bars that Jean did who told them they had heard that there was a former medical student known as "Doc," who would perform abortions for money. Police searched for "Doc" with the idea that Jean had gone to him for an abortion and died as a result, but they not could locate him or anyone who would say that they had actually met him. The idea of Jean getting an abortion while her mother was out of town did seem to make sense in conjunction with the note that had been found in her purse, but nothing solid ever came from this line of investigation.

Over the years, two rumors have persisted about what happened to Jean Spangler - both of which involved Kirk Douglas, whom some of Jean's friends insisted she was dating at the time she disappeared. At one point, Douglas was pushed by the police about Jean and he admitted that he "might have asked her out on a date or two," but nothing else. One rumor claimed that Jean had a romance with Douglas and had gotten pregnant. She contacted a Hollywood abortionist, who botched the operation, and she died. Her remains were hidden and never found.

The other rumor claimed that when Mickey Cohen found out that Jean was pregnant, he sent Jean and one of his associates, David "Little Davy" Ogul, to shake down Douglas in Palm Springs. When Kirk's agent, Charlie Feldman, heard about the shakedown, he told Harry Cohn's pal, Johnny Rosselli. Rosselli talked it over with Jack Dragna and Jean Spangler and Davy Ogul never bothered anyone ever again.

As it turns out, there was a reliable sighting of Jean Spangler that occurred in Palm Springs about a week before she vanished - while Kirk Douglas was vacationing there. She was spotted with Davy Ogul - who disappeared two days after Jean did. This led the police to investigate the possibility that Jean had left California with him. In 1950, a customs agent in El Paso, Texas, reported seeing Ogul and a woman who looked like Jean in a local hotel. But neither Davy Ogul nor Jean Spangler's name appeared on the hotel register and neither of them were ever found.

As the investigation was running into dead ends in Los Angeles, tips began coming in from other places that kept the investigators busy. Each one of them was checked out over the weeks and months that followed, no matter how flimsy or strange. Rumors had her in Mexico City, the San Fernando Valley, Yuma, Arizona, San Francisco, and Fresno. A psychic contacted the police and offered her services and another man claimed that he could locate her body with a radar gadget.

All of the leads and angles in the case eventually reached a dead end. The police were never able to identify the secret boyfriend, or the mysterious doctor. It seemed likely that at some point, Jean had gotten mixed up in something that led to her death. The authorities continued the search and circulated Jean's picture for several years in an unsuccessful attempt to find her, but nothing turned up. Most veteran detectives came to believe that she was dead.

Following Jean's disappearance, a bitter custody battle for Christine began between Dexter Benner and Jean's mother, Florence Spangler. The courts awarded the child to her father, but Florence was given visitation rights, which Benner fought against. He claimed in his suit that Christine had been "abandoned" by her mother and that Florence was a negative influence on her. The case wore on until 1953, when Benner suddenly vanished with his wife and the child. He was never found.

Not every detective gave up on the idea of finding Jean Spangler alive. Nationwide bulletins were issued for years after she vanished, and Florence Spangler periodically appealed to the press for information about her daughter's fate. She even enlisted the aid of gossip columnist Louella Parsons, who appeared on television with photos of Jean and offered a $1,000 reward for information. But no information ever came and Florence, who hung onto the desperate hope that Jean might still be alive, eventually resigned herself to the fact that her daughter had been murdered.

To this day, Jean Spangler is still listed as a missing person with the Los Angeles Police Department and her case file remains open.

The disappearance of Jean Spangler - and her tenuous connections to some of the same people in the Black Dahlia case - came at an awkward time for Police Chief Horrall and the bosses of the LAPD. Solving the Spangler disappearance was not a huge priority for City Hall. She disappeared right in the middle of the 1949 grand jury investigation into unsolved crimes in Los Angeles - and payoffs by the underworld to police officials. Some of the payoffs had allegedly come from Syndicate abortion doctors, who ominously appear around the edges of both the Black Dahlia and Jean Spangler cases.

The Los Angeles Grand Jury Investigation of 1949 was spurred by a growing concern in the city about rampant crime and corruption. High-profile murders, shootings and robberies had created a buzz in the city's newspapers and among the people on the streets about what the police department was doing to bring crime under control.

Ben Siegel's murder had not ended the mob wars in LA. They had continued with a number of gangland killings and attempts to take out his successor, Mickey Cohen. The wisecracking little gangster - like Abe Reles, Cohen was short, although he boosted his height up to five-foot five by wearing elevator shoes -- always had a good quip for reporters. Cohen seemed to lead a charmed life. Bombs were set off under his house, his car was riddled with bullets, shotguns blasted at him on the Sunset Strip, but somehow, he always came through unscathed.

In 1948, Cohen took over a three-story building on the Sunset Strip and started calling it Michael's Exclusive Haberdashery, although in reality it was the headquarters for his bookmaking operation. On the night of August 19, 1948, Cohen was in the office with three of his men, Jimmy Rist, Albert "Slick" Snyder, and Harry "Hooky" Rothman until about 10:30 p.m. Hooky walked to the front door to leave and Cohen, a compulsive hand-washer, went to the washroom. As soon as Rothman opened the front door on Sunset Boulevard, two gunmen rushed toward him. One of them carried a shotgun and the other had a revolver. Without warning, the man with the shotgun aimed it at Rothman's head and pulled the trigger, blasting away his face and killing him where he stood.

Albert Snyder was sitting at Cohen's desk in the office, talking to Jimmy Rist, when he heard the blast. Suddenly, the man with the revolver burst through the door demanding, "Where is that S.O.B.?" He didn't wait for an answer. He shot Snyder in the chest.

Jimmy Rist told reporters, "When the guy with the pistol shot 'Slick' I was already up and in the air. I made a grab for him. I got my right hand on the barrel and my left hand on the butt of the gun, and we went to the floor. I was still twisting the pistol when the fellow with the shotgun fired at me. I could see this big thing coming... It looked like a cannonball. That's when he shot off my ear and everything went bleary."

In the meantime, Mickey Cohen - the "S.O.B." in question - was still in the bathroom, washing his hands. He later recalled, "When the shooting started, it sounded like a war broke out. I laid myself down on the floor of the washroom so my foot was holding the door shut, and my body was against the tile so I'd have some protection. After it quieted down and I looked out, Slick was laying by the desk screaming 'get me a doctor! Get me an ambulance!' Then I went to the front door and saw Hooky was laying there - I seen he was dead."

The shooting on the Sunset Strip led to further public outcry. Whether the men were gangsters or not, it simply meant to most people that the streets of LA weren't safe for anyone. Newspaper editorials called for a grand jury investigation into the gang wars, racketeering and the unsolved murders that tarnished the city's reputation. Not every newspaper agreed. The *Los Angeles Times*, for instance, stated that a grand jury wouldn't solve anything. The *Los Angeles Daily News* disagreed. In an editorial titled "The Jungles of LA," it stated:

The *Mickey Cohen* gangland shootings affair is another indication that the jungle is creeping up on Greater Los Angeles. There have been other signs over the past several years: The employers of violence, the vice promoters, the shakedown artists and gambling tycoons have moved into the Los Angeles area and made it a profitable stand for graft and robbery. What needs to be known is the relative responsibility of various local law-enforcement agencies for the Los Angeles area's unenviable reputation as a mobster's paradise.

As things were heating up for the police department, it all went from bad to worse with Sgt. Stoker's arrest of Brenda Allen. Although he had been warned by Gangster Squad officers Archie Case and James Ahern to put an end to his investigation of Allen, Stoker stubbornly refused. He was not just an honest cop, rare enough in those days; he was a crusader. When he received death threats and vows of retaliation if he did not remain silent and close down the investigation, he didn't quit. It had become painfully obvious to him that Allen's influence extended all of the way to City Hall. He defied his superiors and on September 11, 1948, brought along reporters from the *Daily News* when he raided Allen's Hollywood Hills hideaway and arrested the vice queen.

With mayoral elections scheduled for November 1949, Mayor Fletcher Bowron and Norman Chandler's *Los Angeles Times* tried to block the growing demand for an investigation into city corruption, but public outrage led to a grand jury being empaneled. Among the subjects proposed to be investigated were the mob wars, the scandal over the Brenda Allen prostitution ring and the unsolved murders of several young women, including the infamous Black Dahlia case.

Alarmed by the idea of someone looking into the murder of Beth Short, Chief Horrall, Assistant Chief Joe Reed and Gangster Squad Capt. Willy Burns made a concerted effort to send the impending investigation off the rails. Almost as soon as the grand jury was sworn in, and it was revealed that the Black Dahlia case would be among the unsolved crimes investigated,

Chief Horrall tried to get it removed from the jury's agenda by making the dramatic announcement that the LAPD had apprehended Beth's killer.

On January 10, 1949, Leslie Dillon, the former hotel bellhop, was arrested on suspicion of murdering Beth Short. Chief Horrall stated, "There is no doubt in my mind that Dillon is the hottest suspect there has ever been in this case." Police staff psychiatrist Dr. Paul de River proclaimed that Dillon was a psychopath who "knew more about the Dahlia murder than the police did, and more about abnormal sex psychopathia than most psychiatrists."

After he was booked and paraded in front of reporters and photographers at a chaotic press conference in which Dillon pleaded hysterically for help. It took five armed guards to drag the handcuffed suspect away. A spokesman for the district attorney told reporters, "We're not going to let anybody talk to him - except ourselves, until we've got a closed case." But, of course, the case against Dillon was never closed and it became one of the most bizarre chapters in the Black Dahlia case.

The case against Dillon was orchestrated by Dr. de River, one of the most unusual figures in LAPD history. Allegedly a psychiatrist, De River was a friend of Chief Horrall, who appointed him to be the department's psychiatric consultant and the chief of the so-called "Sex Offense Bureau." He was placed in charge of assembling files on sex crimes and keeping a cross reference of known sex offenders. Although he was not a civil servant or a police officer, he was a close friend of Horrall, which made him an enforcer in the department. De River was instrumental in bring the false charges against Leslie Dillon - a situation that became known as the "Dillon Catastrophe."

The entire fiasco began after Dillon wrote a letter to Dr. de River in October 1946, expressing his interest in the Black Dahlia case. At the time, Dillon was an aspiring crime writer living in Florida. He happened to pick up a pulp magazine that quoted de River in regards to the case and decided to write him a letter. Dillon stated that he had followed the case because he had been living in Los Angeles when it occurred. Expressing his belief in the pathological nature of the crime, Dillon said that a close friend of his, Jeff Connors, had once met Elizabeth Short in a Hollywood bar and he might be helpful to the police. After de River read the letter, he telephoned Dillon and told him that he was interested in talking with him further. Dillon was both surprised and flattered that the police psychiatrist found his opinion to be of value and happily offered more theories about the murder.

Sgt. Stephen Bailey, a homicide detective still attached to the Black Dahlia case more than two years later, later recalled that Dillon had written to de River at just about the same time that the grand jury was considering looking into the case. Bailey said that there was a lot of pressure within the department to deflect the grand jury's investigation - and that only an arrest could conceivably stop the grand jury from putting the case on its calendar.

LAPD crackpot, Dr. Paul de River – he tried to railroad Leslie Dillon into a confession and then it was discovered that he was a fraud.

It's for this reason that many believe that some elements of the LAPD attempted to pin the murder on Leslie Dillon.

When de River informed Chief Horrall about Dillon's letter from Dillon and their subsequent telephone conversation, Horrall, along with Assistant Chief Joe Reed and Willie Burns from the Gangster Squad, put together a plan to arrest Dillon. Unable to extradite him from Florida without evidence, they decided to lure him to California. Once they got him to LA, they could arrest him for the murder and convince him to sign a confession.

De River began making telephone calls to Dillon, manipulating him into talking about the nature of the crime, the site where the body was discovered, the finding of the autopsy report and the mindset of the killer. De River told him a number of things that Dillon didn't know about the crime, hoping that he would repeat them while in custody, making it seem as if he had come up with the information on his own. Claiming that he was impressed with Dillon's knowledge of a criminal's pathology, he told Dillon he would be interested in hiring him as an assistant in his Sex Offense Bureau at the LAPD. Perhaps they could even work on a book together about the Black Dahlia case. He asked Dillon to meet up with him to discuss things further and eventually, Dillon agreed to fly to Las Vegas, where he was met by de River in an unmarked police car. De River's "chauffeur" was Sgt. John J. O'Mara of the LAPD, dressed in plain clothes.

On the way back to California, Dillon and de River spoke in depth about Beth Short's murder and went over Dillon's theories about the pathology involved. De River asked how Dillon's friend, Jeff Connors, happened to meet Beth at a Hollywood bar and suggested that when Dillon was talking about Connors, he may have actually been talking about himself. The conversation then took a sharp turn and de River suggested that Dillon might be mentally unstable and that his underlying subconscious pathology may have led to him turning himself into the police. Before long, de River was coming right out and stating that Dillon had been the one who murdered Beth Short. Jeff Connors, he said, never existed at all.

Dillon was adamant about the fact that this was not true. If the police would take him to San Francisco, he could prove that Connors was real. This is where Connors lived and he could point him out. After reaching San Francisco, they searched for Connors, but could not locate him. After several days of searching, Connors was nowhere to be found - which is when de River began to say that he was convinced that Conners was a schizoid extension of Dillon's own mind.

Dillon was finally handcuffed by one of the officers and taken to the Strand Hotel in LA. Locked up in a hotel room, three or four other men arrived and began to question him. In the middle of it, de River began insisting that Dillon was "too knowledgeable and too intelligent to conceal the truth" from himself. He told him that the facts were just too painful for him to remember without "help" and began asking him intimate details about the mutilations and the things that had been done to Beth Short. But all that Dillon knew had been what he read in the newspapers and in the true crime magazine that had prompted him to write to de River in the first place. De River cleverly asked him questions - and then put the answers in his mouth.

The questioning went on for a week. Dillon wasn't allowed to talk to anyone, to call his wife, a lawyer, or anyone else who would help him. They questioned him day and night, refusing to let him rest. Dillon was stripped naked and photographs were taken of him. He was handcuffed to a radiator and beaten. Dillon later said, "They kept on with the questioning. They got really nasty."

Trying to force Dillon to confess, Archie Case and James Ahern of the Gangster Squad told Dillon that they had been tracking him for two years and could destroy any alibi that he came up with. De River told Dillon that he had no choice but to confess - that he had done something so horrible that he had hidden away the memory of it in his subconscious and that confession was the only thing that would keep him from going totally mad. He also told him that if he confessed and faced up to what he had done, he would not be treated as a criminal, but as a man who was mentally ill. He would not go to prison; he'd be sent to a sanitarium instead.

Dillon recalled, "He wanted me to confess that I'd killed the Dahlia, and I couldn't confess to it. But they had me just about convinced I was crazy or something, and that maybe I *did* kill the Dahlia, and then just forgot about it."

In a moment when he was left alone, Dillon managed to write a note on a postcard about what was happening to him and drop it from the hotel window to the street below. The card was address to Los Angeles attorney Jerry Geisler and read:

I am being held in room 219 and 21 Strand Hotel... in connection with the Black Dahlia murder - by Dr. J.P. de River, as far as I can tell. I would like legal counsel. - Leslie Dillon

Tucked into the corner of the card, he had scrawled the words, "Wife Georgia Stevens - Gulf Park Hotel or Wolfie's restaurant, Miami Beach, Fla." He also managed to write his mother's telephone number.

The next day, Dillon was taken to LAPD headquarters and ushered into the office of Chief Horrall by Burns, Ahern and de River. Horrall informed Dillon that he was being booked for the murder of Elizabeth Short and then he was taken away for more interrogation and demands that he confess. He was questioned for another ten hours, and during that time, Dillon began to lose track of what was happening. He kept insisting that he was not the murderer, but de River kept telling him that he was and that he was simply blocking out the truth. Confess, the psychiatrist urged, and he would be free of all of his troubles.

The day after Dillon was booked and paraded in front of reporters, someone found the postcard that he had dropped from the hotel window and forwarded it on to Geisler's office. One of Geisler's associates contacted Dillon's mother and helped her file a writ of habeas corpus so that he could be released. But it would soon prove to be unnecessary.

Almost as soon as Dillon was arrested, the case against him fell apart. Witnesses placed him in San Francisco at the time of the Black Dahlia murder and employment records indicated that he was working as a bellhop in a San Francisco hotel during the days in question. Geisler's investigators established that Dillon and his wife had not moved to Los Angeles until January 24, 1947, more than a week after Beth's body had been discovered. And Jeff Connors - the man that De River insisted was a product of Dillon's imagination - proved to be a real person, living in the Bay area. He verified to Geisler and the police that his story about meeting Beth Short in a Hollywood bar was true.

With the habeas corpus motion on the way and no evidence to defend against it, the D.A.'s office quietly issued a statement that the police had insufficient evidence to hold the "hottest suspect that there has ever been in this case." Avoiding reporters and refusing to make any further statements, Horrall and de River did their best to stay out of the public eye until the dust settled.

Accusing Horrall of "high-handed bungling and illegal methods in the re-opened Black Dahlia investigation," City Councilman Ernest Debs called for an investigation into Dillon's arrest and accused de River of being a con artist. It was discovered that de River was not a trained psychiatrist and that the institution where he claimed he had studied had no record of him as a student.

Leslie Dillon was released on January 22, 1949. He later filed a lawsuit against the City of Los Angeles, but dropped it when it came to light that he was wanted in connection with a robbery at a Santa Monica hotel where he had once worked. Dillon eventually faded into the history and became a bizarre footnote in the Black Dahlia case.

Even so, when the startling information about his false arrest was publicized, the Black Dahlia case was reconfirmed on the grand jury's agenda. It was scheduled to be the last investigation of the 1949 grand jury's term - after the mayoral election had already been concluded. The powers that wanted the case to remain dead may have lost the war, but they had at least achieved that one small victory.

16. GRAND JURY

As the grand jury moved forward, Harry Lawson, an independent man of great integrity, was appointed to the position of foreman. Frank B. Jemison, mentioned previously in this narrative, was a highly respected investigator for the district attorney's office. He had been assigned to re-open the investigation into the murder of Elizabeth Short. The problem was, no matter how upstanding and honest these men were, the politicians around them were swimming in a sea of corruption. Lawson, Jemison and the empaneled jury had to navigate such dark waters that there was little hope that they would ever make it to shore.

For those who don't know how a grand jury works, it is a sequestered legal procedure that is basically designed to avoid bias and collusion. In Los Angeles of the late 1940s, seventy-five Supreme Court judges each selected two prospective jurors that were known to be solid, upstanding citizens. The list of one hundred and fifty was then culled down to thirty names, which were placed in an election box. Nineteen of the names were then randomly drawn and those selected served for one year on the grand jury, which reviewed pressing criminal matters for possible indictment. The presiding judge of the state Supreme Court selected the foreman and the jury then worked with the district attorney's office and the police and sheriff's departments to review cases and then call witnesses to testify. All of the sessions were closed, and the records sealed, unless an investigation resulted in an indictment.

The selection system was meant to ensure the integrity of the jury. However, its integrity also depended on the honesty of the law enforcement agencies that rendered testimony and submitted evidence for review. The jury could only make its decisions based on what it was offered in evidence and testimony and if those things were corrupt or dishonest, the jury's decision-making ability would be hampered from the start.

In 1949, the powers in the district attorney's office, at City Hall, and in the upper echelons of the LAPD and the sheriff's department could not be trusted. Rumors swirled then, but it's since been presented as truth that the offices that ran the city were notoriously corrupt. Foreman Harry Lawson and investigator Frank Jemison may have been honest men, but there were soon drowning in the sea of corruption that had overtaken Los Angeles.

Jemison was assigned to the case in October 1949 and was assured by Chief Horrall and Assistant Chief Joe Reed that he would have their total cooperation in supplying the grand jury with anything that it needed from police files. Chief Horrall even went as far as to assign Finis Brown to assist

Investigator Frank Jemison

Jemison in his investigation. Of course, very few people knew at the time that Brown was an operative for the Gangster Squad, so unbeknownst to Jemison, there was little real help that he could count on - and anything he did would be reported back to Brown's bosses.

Brown himself was in a tough situation. His brother, Thad Brown, had become chief of the Detectives Division. He was an ally of Norman Chandler and was known to be Chandler's choice for the next police chief. In his Gangster Squad assignments, Finis had to be careful and avoid causing problems for his brother. Nearly two years before, Harry Hansen had discovered that Brown was a member of the Gangster Squad and concluded that Chief Horrall, Capt. Donahoe and the Gangster Squad were deliberately misdirecting the Black Dahlia investigation. He had vowed to continue investigating the case on his own. When he learned that Chief Horrall had assigned Brown as the department liaison to Frank Jemison, Hansen wanted little to do with what he feared would be a predictable outcome to the grand jury's inquiry.

In the early weeks of his investigation, Jemison, along with his assistant, Walter Morgan, prepared a history of the Black Dahlia case and a lengthy list of suspects, but it was not the first case on the grand jury's docket. They were also scheduled to hear a number of other inquiries into criminal matters that involved racketeering in the city. During their investigation into the mob wars and the attempts to wipe out Mickey Cohen, which led to the murders of six of his men, a secret conference was held with Cohen and his attorney, Sam Rummel. It was also attended by D.A. Simpson, Harry Lawson and Frank Jemison.

During the meeting, Cohen and his attorney agreed that Cohen would spill everything about the rackets in LA, payoffs to the police and sheriff's department and Jack Dragna's personal vendetta against him. He would also talk about an attempted shakedown by members of the LAPD to get him to pay $20,000 to avoid raids on his gambling operations and brothels. All that Sam Rummel wanted in return was for Cohen to get immunity from prosecution and a bodyguard assigned by the California Attorney General to protect his client from retaliation by Dragna and the Gangster Squad. Rummel had already informed the state's attorney general, Fred Howser, that he believed "certain officers within the LAPD" were motivated to murder Cohen.

At Howser's request, the LAPD and the sheriff's department agreed to withdraw their officers, who had been keeping Cohen under constant surveillance. The attorney general then assigned Special Agent Harry Cooper to protect Cohen until he gave his grand jury testimony, which was scheduled for July 28, 1949.

But on July 20, Cohen was exiting Sherry's nightclub on the Sunset Strip with his girlfriend Dee David, bodyguard Neddie Herbert and Harry Cooper when gunmen opened fire on them from behind a billboard across the street. One of the bullets wounded Cohen in the shoulder and Dee David was seriously wounded in the back. Three slugs shattered Neddie Herbert's spine and Harry Cooper was hit twice in the abdomen. Herbert died several hours later at the Queen of Angels Hospital and Cooper was given only a slim chance at surviving the ambush.

When the ambush was reported in the Los Angeles newspapers, people were confused about why the California attorney general had assigned Harry Cooper to protect a notorious gangster. Cooper managed to survive, but he refused to discuss what he was doing there. However, to those who knew what was going on, it was obvious that someone had leaked the information about Cohen's forthcoming testimony to the grand jury about

Mickey Cohen's Cadillac outside of Sherry's Nightclub

payoffs to the cops. And whoever was behind the latest assassination attempt was willing to open fire on a busy street while Cohen was standing outside of a club with a group of people and a state officer. It seemed like an act of desperation.

Interestingly, Florabel Muir, a writer for the *Mirror* and the *Daily News*, happened to be at Sherry's nightclub that evening and was standing outside when the gunshots rang out. In fact, she was slightly wounded in the buttocks by a ricochet. As the only press witness to the shooting, she scooped all of the competition and was one of the few to note that Gangster Squad Sgt. Darryl Murray was one of the patrons at the club that night. Murray was there with his wife, an attractive blonde who had been seen getting up from their table and leaving the club just as Mickey Cohen's party was getting ready to leave.

A witness who lived across the street from the nightclub, Lawrence Vaale, told the *Examiner* that he heard the gunfire, followed by shouts and the sound of running feet. Looking out his window, he saw a pretty blonde running to a gray Buick sedan that was parked on the street outside of his window. There was a man at the wheel and another in the back seat. The blonde and a third man hurriedly joined them in the car. The door slammed and the car roared away, heading west on Sunset.

According to his interview in the *Examiner*, Vaale stated that he believed "the blonde was inside Sherry's watching Cohen and came out just ahead of him as a signal to the two gunmen waiting across the street, while the third man waited at the wheel of the car." He described the woman as "about thirty-five, 120 pounds, shapely, with blonde hair combed straight back. She was wearing a dark suit and no hat." Although Vaale had no idea of this, it was a very close description of the wife of Sgt. Darryl Murray.

To anyone who knew about Cohen's scheduled appearance in front of the grand jury, it was painfully obvious who might have the motivation to see that he was silenced. When State Attorney General Fred Howser was asked by the *Examiner* why he had assigned Harry Cooper to be Cohen's bodyguard, he tersely replied that it was because Cohen's attorney, Sam Rummel, suspected that certain officers in the LAPD wanted his client dead.

While he was recovering in the hospital, Cohen missed the date he was supposed to testify before the grand jury. Not surprisingly, he chose not to reschedule when he got out. He believed that he'd live longer if he kept his mouth shut. As a postscript to this incident, attorney Sam Rummel was killed by a shotgun blast as he entered his Laurel Canyon home several weeks later. Needless to say, the crime was never solved.

There had been a concerted effort at City Hall to make sure that the inquiry into civic corruption went nowhere until after the November mayoral elections, but things spun out of control when the grand jury began looking into the scandal involving Brenda Allen's prostitution ring. Sgt. Charles Stoker, the honest vice cop who ignored all of the warnings to steer clear of trouble and arrested Allen, testified before the grand jury that he had discovered that Allen had been allowed to operate her exclusive Hollywood call-girl ring because she had been paying off top officials in administrative vice, including Stoker's superior, Sgt. Elmer Jackson, and the officer in charge of administrative vice, Lt. Rudy Wellpott. Stoker also testified to the fact that Brenda Allen had been in the car with Sgt. Jackson when Roy "Peewee" Lewis had been shot by Jackson on February 21, 1947. The newspapers had listed a different name for the woman in the car, but the shooting had occurred in front of Allen's former residence at Ninth Street and Fedora Avenue.

The *Daily News* leaked Stoker's testimony and also announced the fact that there were wire recordings - made by Stoker and electronic surveillance expert, Jim Vaus - of payoff meetings between Allen and top police officials, as well as "intimate" recordings involving some of Allen's girls and some of the top men at City Hall. It was rumored that one of the recordings concerned a conversation about the murder of Beth Short. The *Daily News* charged that Chief Horrall knew all about these recordings, but that he had suppressed them and took no actions against the officers that had been engaged in criminal activities. As a result, Horrall was called before the grand jury, along with Sgt. Elmer Jackson, Lt. Rudy Wellpott, and Assistant Chief Reed. Under oath, each of them denied the accusations made against them by Stoker, claiming that Stoker had perjured himself.

There was no question that Brenda Allen was shrewd and well-connected. After Stoker had arrested her in the presence of newspaper reporters and photographers, and her call-girl ring became public knowledge, the District Attorney's office had no choice but to file pandering charges against her and put her in jail. But Allen knew too much. She knew all about mob influence at City Hall, payoffs to LAPD officials, the private lives of the rich and famous - and about the murder of Beth Short. She had it all on tape. She held all of the cards and knew exactly how to play them. Allen publicly came forward and confirmed that Stoker had been telling the truth. She had obtained copies of the surveillance recordings that Jim Vaus had made and she kept them in a safe deposit box at a downtown bank.

When Allen was escorted to her bank to retrieve the incriminating tapes, a crowd showed up to witness her arrival. When the box was opened, her claim proved to be true. It was filled with tapes, photographs and documents, all set aside to ensure her wellbeing if trouble came along. Among the items was a mysterious photograph that had been taken of some lilies that were sent to her apartment shortly after the Black Dahlia murder. The photograph of the lilies was printed in the *Examiner*, and when asked about it, Allen explained that the flowers had been sent to her in 1947 by Sgt. Jackson. They were accompanied by a "revealing" note, but neither Allen nor the District Attorney's office would divulge its contents. Rumor had it that it somehow pertained to Beth Short.

After the grand jury listened to Allen's tapes, Chief Horrall, Assistant Chief Reed, Sgt. Jackson and Lt. Wellpott were indicted on perjury and bribery charges on August 16, 1949. Horrall resigned from the police department, but then - mysteriously, of course - the recordings and documents all vanished from the district attorney's safe. With this news, Brenda Allen declined to testify, which meant that Horrall, Reed, Jackson and Wellpott were acquitted for lack of evidence. After she was released, Allen went back to plying her trade.

Ironically - or not, depending on how you look at the state of affairs in the LAPD at the time - the only officer to be publicly punished as a result of the 1949 grand jury investigation was Sgt. Charles Stoker. He was reduced in rank and placed on the street as a traffic cop. He was subsequently framed on burglary charges and found guilty of "insubordination and conduct unbecoming an officer." Publicly humiliated and ridiculed in the *Los Angeles Times*, Stoker spent the next twenty-five years working as a brakeman in the Southern Pacific Railway yards of Los Angeles. He faded into history and died a forgotten man in March 10, 1975.

But he definitely left a mark on the history of the LAPD and his legacy opened many eyes to what was going on behind the scenes in the late 1940s. Part of his testimony before the grand jury revealed the existence of a mob abortion ring in Los Angeles, which he claimed was protected by Lt. Willie Burns and members of the Gangster Squad. The ring was operated by a group of medical doctors that paid protection money to the LAPD officers involved. Stoker told the grand jury that the ring was led by Dr. Leslie C. Audrain, whose office was in Room 417 at 1052 West Sixth Street in Los Angeles. Stoker said Audrain had a criminal record as an abortionist and worked under a number of aliases, including Dr. C.J. Morris and Dr. Scott. The designated police unit responsible for apprehending and arresting abortionists was the Gangster Squad, but Stoker discovered that they only arrested abortionists who were not members of Audrain's abortion ring and were not paying protection money to the police.

Audrain had come to Stoker's attention during his investigations with administrative vice. When it was discovered that he was looking into Audrain's activities, Stoker claimed he was paid a visit by two Gangster Squad detectives, Archie Case and James Ahern, who threatened him and warned him to shut down his investigation. These were the same detectives who worked the Black Dahlia case for Capt. Jack Donahoe and were involved in the arrest and interrogation of Leslie Dillon.

Stoker's revelations about Dr. Audrain and police payoffs came at the same time that Det. Harry Hansen was pushing for the arrest of an abortionist in connection with the murder of Beth Short. Aggie Underwood had stated that there was an abortionist whom Harry Hansen suspected was somehow involved in Beth's murder, but Chief Horrall had blocked the arrest. In an interview that appeared in the *Pasadena Star News* in 1987 - forty years after Beth was murdered - Finis Brown finally revealed a bit of the truth. In the article, it read:

Brown has an idea of who the Dahlia murderer was, a theory that he has never made public. "I didn't want the newspapers to get any of it," he explains. Now after 40 years he has decided to reveal it. He believes that Elizabeth Short was killed by a man who ran a Hollywood abortion clinic. "The girls were going to this doctor," he says. "We couldn't prove he was the killer, but some of the things I found out he was doing to the girls made me think he was the one."

The doctor committed suicide two years after the murder, just as Hansen and Brown were about to start asking questions.

Dr. Leslie Carl Audrain died at his home in the Hollywood Hills on May 20, 1949 at the age of seventy-three. His death certificate lists the cause of death as heart disease. There is no record of him ever being arrested for performing illegal abortions, as Stoker claimed.

Since Finis Brown was an operative of the Gangster Squad that had been positioned in the Homicide Division to spy on its activities - as Harry Hansen began to suspect - he knew a lot more about the Black Dahlia case than he ever admitted. It also appears that Brown was also used as a liaison with the grand jury, where he had been placed by Horrall, to mislead the investigation. In the district attorney's files that were opened it 2003, it can be seen that in the process of narrowing Frank Jemison's lists of suspects in the case to the "prime suspects" that would be investigated by the grand jury, Brown led Jemison to believe the main suspects that he should investigate were Leslie Dillon, Mark Hansen, Cleo Short and a relatively new suspect named Henry Huber Hoffman. The files make it clear that, during the term of the 1949 grand jury, the hearings centered on those four men as prime suspects. And yet, Brown knew from the start that all four of these so-called "prime suspects" had already been cleared. All of them had solid alibis, lacked advanced medical training and could not possibly have committed the crime. This was clearly the reason that Harry Hansen - knowing Brown was involved - wanted little to do with the grand jury.

Mark Hansen would not have been stupid enough to mail Beth Short's belongings to the *Examiner* if he had killed her. One of the items sent was an address book with his name embossed on the cover. On the night that Beth had been killed, a number of witnesses had placed Hansen at the opening of a movie theater in Long Beach and at a party that followed at the Long Beach Hilton. Barney Vandersteen, Hansen's associate who purchased Ben Siegel's share of the Florentine Gardens, testified in front of the grand jury that after the party that night, Hansen had been a guest in his home in Redondo Beach until well after 3:00 a.m. on the morning of January 15.

Besides that, as the grand jury would learn from Harry Hansen during his testimony, only someone with "advanced medical knowledge" could have bisected the body. Mark Hansen certainly didn't have that kind of knowledge.

Even though Brown had pushed Mark Hansen as an important suspect, it was obvious to Frank Jemison that Hansen had a strong alibi and that police investigators had known from the beginning where he had been on the night when Beth was killed.

Despite the so-called "Dillon Catastrophe," Brown also - ridiculously - pushed the hapless Leslie Dillon as a viable suspect. Jemison looked into this, traveling to San Francisco to check more thoroughly into the former bellhop's employment alibi. He discovered that Dillon, too, had a solid alibi and that it had also been confirmed in the course of the investigation. During his brief testimony, Harry Hansen also confirmed the alibis of Mark Hansen and Leslie Dillon. He also stated that, in 1947, he and Finis Brown had checked out the whereabouts of Cleo Short at the time of the murder and determined definitely that he could not have killed his daughter. When questioned by Jemison, though, Hansen admitted that he knew nothing about Brown's fourth suspect, Harry Hubert Hoffman.

Hoffman was placed in the Dahlia case shortly after the Leslie Dillon mess in January 1949. The police were desperate to present another viable murder suspect before the grand jury and Hoffman turned out to be a perfect scapegoat for Gangster Squad detectives Case and Ahern. An ex-convict who had been convicted of mail fraud, he had been the manager of the Astor Motel at 2101 South Flower Street. His ex-wife, Clara, who had divorced him in 1948, told the police that she believed he had been involved in the Black Dahlia's murder. She said that while cleaning up Unit 9 of the motel around the time of the murder, she found a bloody bundle of women's clothing in the room, along with a considerable amount of blood on the floor and mattress. Gangster Squad Chief Willie Burns assigned Case and Ahern to check out her story. The two detectives spent months trying to build a case against Hoffman for Beth's murder and to establish that her death had taken place in Unit 9 of the motel.

It just so happened that their investigation was leaked to the press - just before the grand jury began looking into the Black Dahlia case, of course - and reporters learned that the LAPD had discovered the murder site. On September 13, 1949, a *Herald-Express* article appeared under the headline "Black Dahlia Murder Site Found." The piece stated, "It was reported that the room where the murder took place was less than a 15-minute drive and in a bee-line from the vacant lot where the nude and bisected body of the girl was discovered... and the room was on one of Los Angeles's busiest streets."

Finis Brown got Hoffman added to the prime suspects list but, once again, the accusation lacked both plausibility and real evidence. Clara Hoffman's claims about her ex-husband kept changing, along with the alleged location where she found the bloody mattress and the clothing. Hoffman submitted to a lie detector test that was conducted under Jemison's supervision and he easily passed. Jemison became convinced that he had nothing to do with Beth Short's murder.

After thousands of hours were spent running down false leads, all four prime suspects that were put forward by Brown and presented by the district attorney and the LAPD to the grand jury proved to be innocent of the crime - and it was apparent that Brown knew that from the start. The testimony of Sgt. Conwell Keller of the Gangster Squad that Brown had been a secret operative during the initial investigation created suspicions that the grand jury had been deliberately misled.

And in the middle of the grand jury hearings, an event occurred involving Brown that confirmed the suspicions of the jury's foreman, Harry Lawson, and Frank Jemison. On July 14, 1949, Lola Titus, a twenty-five-year-old

Nightclub owner Mark Hansen had been mixed up in the Black Dahlia case from the beginning. When he was shot by one of his girls, he immediately sought out Finis Brown, who has been alleged to have been connected to Hansen's club.

blonde former dancer at the Florentine Gardens, entered Mark Hansen's home behind the club and shot Hansen twice while he was shaving in the bathroom. Titus, whom the press dubbed "The Lady in Gold," told reporters, "I made up my mind that he was either going to love me, marry me or take care of me or I was going to kill him."

Hansen was rushed to the hospital with a punctured lung and a wounded arm. He was conscious while in the ambulance and he continually pleaded for someone to get in touch with Finis Brown. As he was taken into the emergency room of the Hollywood Receiving Hospital, a reporter for the *Hollywood Citizen News* noted that Hansen was hysterically calling for the detective. Becoming curious, he did some digging. He quickly learned that Finis Brown was a regular at the Florentine Gardens. It had been rumored by several former employees that one of the assistant managers at the club was an undercover cop on the take - it turned out to be Finis Brown.

Lola Titus had once been a girlfriend of Hansen and when he dumped her, she tried to blackmail him over the shady mob operations that took place at the club. Shortly after Hansen told Brown about this problem, Titus was arrested for dealing drugs and posing for lewd photographs. Convinced that she had been set up by Mark Hansen, she shot him in revenge.

Although the LAPD tried to quash reports about Brown's connection to Hansen, rumors about the true nature of his "work" at the Florentine Gardens began circulating at the district attorney's office. Confused about Brown's involvement in the shooting, he was queried by Harry Lawson during his grand jury testimony. Brown skirted around the nature of his association with Mark Hansen, claiming that Lola Titus' arrest had been on the level and that he had only known Hansen through his undercover work at the nightclub, where he claimed to have been on the lookout for "bad characters and persons of ill-repute." He said he had no idea why Hansen had been so anxious to see him after he'd been shot.

Although the grand jury members felt that they had been misled and that police officials had withheld information from them, the Black Dahlia case had been (purposely) scheduled at the end of their term and they were left with no time to reexamine witnesses or redirect their questions to other suspects before their adjournment on December 29, 1949. Regardless, the grand jury did issue a scathing statement about the LAPD's cover-up of details of the Black Dahlia case and its protection of underworld elements who were involved in crime, murder and racketeering in the city. They stated quite clearly that the jury had seen evidence of payoffs for protection of vice and crime and gross misconduct on the part of some law enforcement officers.

An article that appeared in the *Herald-Express* on January 12, 1950 quoted the final report of the grand jury, stressing the jurors' findings that some LAPD officers were receiving payoffs from gangsters, gamblers, bookmakers and abortionists and that there had been a "cover-up" in the Black Dahlia investigation.

Grand Jury Foreman Harry Lawson called for a continuation of the Black Dahlia investigation by the next empaneled jury in 1950 - but it never happened. The jury's files, the transcripts of the testimony, and Frank Jemison's copious notes were taken away to an LAPD warehouse in West LA, where they would remain for more than five decades.

17. OPENING THE FILES

It's a matter of California law that, unless a grand jury investigation leads to an indictment, the files of the proceedings are sealed and are never made public. However, in the case of the Black Dahlia, some of the material from the 1949 grand jury proceedings was released in 2003 when the Los Angeles District Attorney's Office set up its archives and allowed researchers to delve into the files of some of the most infamous cases of the twentieth century. The Black Dahlia murder was among those cases, and when the files were sorted out, a portion of Frank Jemison's files on Beth's murder were included. The files that contained some of the grand jury proceedings and testimony were a small part of what was released, but they offered a wealth of new information that had not been seen for more than fifty years.

In the warehouse, clerks found sixty-five boxes of material about the Black Dahlia investigation, which included files from the LAPD, the sheriff's department and the district attorney's office. The boxes were culled through in early 2002 and the contents reduced to thirty-five boxes - most of which still remain locked away in the police warehouse. But a handful of boxes that included Jemison's 1949 grand jury investigation were among those placed in the archives of historical cases at the district attorney's office. They included Jemison's transcripts of testimony before the grand jury, as well his extensive notes on his investigation, which contain a lot of good information that hadn't seen the light of day in decades. In some cases, that information was known to only a handful of people involved in the case, which opened the door for new ideas and theories about the Black Dahlia mystery.

It becomes obvious in Jemison's notes that Finis Brown and the LAPD manipulated the grand jury and maneuvered the investigation down dead-end paths by forcing them to chase suspects that had already been cleared. Jemison had requested that the LAPD supply him with a list of key officers that were involved in the original Black Dahlia investigation. However, when he received the list, only Harry Hansen and a detective named Greeley were part of the homicide squad. The rest of the list contained names of Gangster Squad members, which made Jemison realize that the case had been much more secretive than what had been presented to the public. The fact that the Black Dahlia case had been handled by enforcers for the city's underworld was hidden from the public for more than fifty years, but when William Worton became the interim police chief after the resignation of Chief Horrall, he made the announcement that the office of assistant chief was being terminated. Reed was forced into retirement and the Gangster Squad's Willie Burns was transferred.

A new interim chief was appointed and charged with cleaning things up, but Frank Jemison still had to contend with a corrupt department during the grand jury hearings. In the closing weeks of the hearings, Jemison realized that he had been misled by Finis Brown into investigating suspects who had been already cleared. His notes indicate that he began a re-investigation into other suspects, believing that the Black Dahlia case would be placed on the 1950 grand jury agenda.

The notes and memos that Jemison left behind indicate that he had accepted the opinion of Harry Hansen, the medical examiner and the FBI, who all believed that an individual with advanced medical knowledge was involved with bisecting Beth Short's body. In the early months of 1950, Jemison began an investigation into suspected abortionists who may have been connected to the murder and mutilation of the Black Dahlia.

During her testimony, Ann Toth stated that in the days before Beth left for San Diego, she had driven Beth to a doctor's office on Hollywood Boulevard. She believed that Beth had met Maurice Clement there. One of the names that Jemison found in Beth's address book was Dr. Arthur M. Faught, an elderly physician from Nebraska who had once worked as a surgeon for the Union Pacific Railroad. Faught had an office in the Cherokee Building on Hollywood Boulevard. Jemison learned that Dr. Faught had died of a heart attack in September 1949 - right at the same time the new Black Dahlia investigation began. However, on February 1, 1950, Jemison questioned Dr. Melvin M. Schwartz, who shared Faught's office suite. Schwartz recalled seeing a young woman who resembled Beth Short in the office.

Schwartz told Jemison that the woman had come into the office approximately twelve or fourteen days before Christmas 1946, looking for Faught. He told her that Faught had left and would not return until 9:00 a.m. the next morning. He asked her what her trouble was, but when she seemed reluctant to talk in front of the other patients waiting in the reception area, he took her into Faught's office and allowed her to use the telephone. She pulled out an address book and had a conversation with someone. Schwartz said, "It was the type of conversation you couldn't tell who she was talking to, or what it was about, but it was on the shady side, I do recall that." He wasn't sure if the caller on the other end of the line was a man or a woman, but he believed that it was a man.

Jemison's notes included the names of suspected abortionists who worked out of the West Sixth Street professional building where Dr. Leslie Audrain's office had been located. He included many of them in his own lists of suspects, including Dr. A.E. Brix. On the list was a Dr. C.J. Morris, which

Sgt. Stoker claimed was an alias used by Dr. Audrain. After Brix's name and address, Jemison wrote "was written by Beth Short in her address book."

Stoker claimed to have first become aware of Dr. Audrain and the abortion ring as the result of an alert from the California State Medical Board. An inspector there had allegedly learned about the ring from an informant and requested that Stoker conduct an investigation. Stoker said he decided to do his investigating in secret because he didn't want anyone on the Gangster Squad to find out. He claimed squad members were receiving payoffs to protect Audrain's activities as head of the abortion ring. Stoker enlisted the help of a policewoman, Audrey Davis, who visited Dr. Audrain's office, posing as a "girl in trouble." Audrain was not there but Davis allegedly spoke to someone in the office who agreed to provide an abortion for $200. David made an appointment for the following week, when Stoker planned to make an arrest. But the day before the appointment, Stoker claimed he was told by the medical board inspector that Audrain had somehow found out about the investigation. When Officer Davis showed up for the appointment, Audrain's office was locked up and remained closed for the next week. Stoker said it was clear that Audrain had been tipped off. Soon after, Stoker said he was warned by Gangster Squad officers Case and Ahern to drop the case.

Jemison later learned that Dr. Audrain had died in May 1949 - a few months before the grand jury's Black Dahlia investigation was getting ready to start. Jemison never interviewed Audrain, but according to Finis Brown, Harry Hansen had questioned him several times and had tried to get Audrain indicted as an accomplice in Beth's murder. Unfortunately, though, Hansen's interviews with Dr. Audrain - if they indeed took place -- remain in the LAPD warehouse and were not included with the files that were released by the district attorney's office in 2003. There is no indication in what was released that the interviews were ever brought to the attention of Frank Jemison or the grand jury.

There are also notes that Jemison made stating that he re-examined Beth Short's address book in an effort to find new leads to suspects among the people she knew. One piece of paper found among his notes leads all of the way back to the short, swarthy man who drove the "1936 or 1937" black Ford sedan, Maurice Clement. Jemison had scrawled these notes on an invitation to District Attorney William Simpson's 1949 Christmas party, and they included the names and addresses of several suspects that he had gleaned from Beth's address book. At the top was "Red Morris (Bob)" with an address in Huntington Park. This turned out to be Robert "Red" Manley, whose middle name was Morris. Lower down, he had scribbled several aliases supposedly used by Dr. Leslie Audrain - "Dr. Morris," "Dr. Stott," and "Dr. Scott." The name of Dr. A.E. Brix was also found in the address book. Aage Emil Brix, a physician, played on the US national soccer team in the

1924 Summer Olympics. He wrote the words and music to a song called "Olympic Song of the USA," which was copyrighted in 1931. On the bottom of the invitation, Jemison wrote a question mark, followed by "Apt. 107-1616 No. Normandie Ave. Hollywood 27."

Opposite the names of Dr. Morris, Dr. Stott and Dr. Scott, he had written another question mark next to the number of an address on West Sixth Street - Room 417, which proved to be the office of Dr. Audrain. The address after the question mark on the bottom of the party invitation was discovered to be that of Brenda Allen's procurer, Maurice Clement. The question mark may have indicated that Jemison had trouble reading Beth's handwriting or that she had not written down the name connected with the address. However, a subsequent note regarding apartment 107 clearly established that Jemison discovered the address belonged to Maurice Clement and that Clement worked at Columbia Studios. Another notation with two names - Michael Anthony Otero and Maurice Clement - indicated that Clement "saw her about 6 times" and one of them was on December 1, 1946, in the week before she left the city. Otero was a Spanish teacher at Santa Monica High School who dated Beth about a dozen times, according to Ann Toth.

Oddly - or again, perhaps it's not odd considering his many connections - Maurice Clement was never named as a suspect in Beth's murder. Even though he was seen with Beth many times before she left for San Diego and drove a car resembling the one that had been seen on Norton Avenue during the early morning hours before her body was found, he stayed out of the investigation. Maurice Clement was identified by a clerk at the Hawthorn as man who visited Beth frequently and paid her rent. He was identified as the man who drove her to Hansen's house on Carlos Street, where Ann Toth testified that he was a frequent caller. He was identified by Beth's roommate at the Chancellor as someone who saw her frequently. He was identified as someone who had been seen with her at least four times at Brittingham's restaurant before she suddenly left Los Angeles. He lied to the police when he claimed that he only met Beth in early December 1946. Ann Toth said that she had driven Beth to the vicinity of the Biltmore Hotel in mid-November, where she thought Beth was meeting Clement.

And yet, Maurice Clement was never an official suspect.

It's believed that police officials went out of their way to avoid mentioning Clement or bringing him in as a suspect because he was a link to others responsible for the murder. As the procurer who drove around Brenda Allen's call girls for the Columbia Studios bosses, he was connected to one of the major mob prostitution rings in Ben Siegel's LA territory - a vice ring that was known to pay generously for police protection. It might prove perilous to the important men the LAPD wanted to protect if anyone started looking too closely into Maurice Clement. Corrupt elements in the department were receiving lucrative payoffs, and they had so far been

A postcard of Brittingham's Restaurant, where Maurice Clement was witnessed with Beth Short at least four times in the fall of 1946.

successful in covering up the motive and nature of the crime, as well as its links to the mob. Jemison had placed Clement at number seven on his suspect list, and it's possible that he believed that the man was somehow involved in the crime. He was sure that the Black Dahlia case would be added to the calendar for the grand jury in 1950, but that never happened. District Attorney William Simpson managed to stop it from happening, in spite of the conclusions of cover-up and corruption that had been found by the original grand jury.

Jemison's notes, along with the transcripts of the 1949 grand jury were locked away in an LAPD warehouse for more than fifty years, but when a few of those pieces were finally released, they provided some startling information about the crime.

Lynn Martin was the first of Beth's friends to come to the conclusion that she might be pregnant. Later, it was Ann Toth who drove Beth downtown and suggested that she was going to see a doctor, which may have been Dr. Faught. *Examiner* reporter Will Fowler, the first reporter on the scene at Norton Avenue, observed that there was an incision on the then-unknown victim's abdomen that appeared to be from a hysterectomy, and the uterus had been removed. Surgeons and medical experts who examined the photos of the body that were found in the Black Dahlia files later confirmed Fowler's observations. The addresses of at least four different suspected abortionists were found in Beth's address book and the grand jury transcripts state that in the last days before she fled the city, she tried to visit Dr. Faught.

The released district attorney's files finally revealed the secret information that had been closely guarded by Harry Hansen, Capt. Donahoe and a small handful of others: Beth Short had been pregnant and there was an abortionist involved in the crime. Public reports stated that she had not been pregnant, but this was the control information that had been kept secret so that detectives could determine a true confession from a false one. Or at least that's what was claimed. More likely, it was to protect the true motive behind her murder.

Tragically, it had not been the accidental death of a young woman who died while having an abortion. This was no mistake - Beth died from being beaten savagely in the head and from blood loss and shock from the knife cuts that sliced up her face, prior to any abdominal incision. The uterus - along with her unborn baby - were removed after her death.

The fact that Beth was pregnant and her baby was removed postmortem seems to offer a new view of the crime. It also provided the most important element in solving a murder: a motive. As depraved as her killer was, it explains the motive behind the madness and may offer some insight as to who was behind the Black Dahlia murder.

Harry Hansen was likely correct when he stated that he believed that Beth's killer was among her acquaintances. The name of the man who fathered her baby was probably among the names that were removed from her address book. According to some researchers and theorists, the man was Norman Chandler, one of the most powerful men in Los Angeles at the time. He was the man who literally picked the mayor, appointed the police chief, controlled the LAPD, ran the city council and published the *Los Angeles Times*. Unfortunately, the evidence of Chandler's involvement is pretty circumstantial. Former administrative vice officers Vince Carter and Ron Hardman believed Norman Chandler had a connection to the case. Fred Otash, the former LAPD officer who had placed Chandler under surveillance for Ray Pinker knew that Beth was among the young women that he and his friend, Arthur Lake, entertained at Chandler's California Club penthouse, located just behind the Biltmore Hotel.

But there's still a large gap between suspecting Chandler and proving that he impregnated Beth and then arranged for her murder. If Beth really was working for Brenda Allen's prostitution ring (and I believe that she was), her beauty would have made her popular among the city officials, wealthy businessmen and studio bosses in Hollywood - who had just as much power in those days as politicians and newspaper publishers did. I honestly believe that Beth got herself mixed up with one or more powerful men and ended up getting pregnant by one of them. It's also very likely - based on Beth's past behavior - that she somehow imagined that this was going to be her chance to get out of the disappointing life she was leading and live happily ever after with a wealthy man. As we know, Beth lived with the tragic delusion that happiness and marital bliss were waiting for her as soon as she found the perfect man. I think it's very possible that Beth approached this man when she discovered that she was pregnant, believing that he would be pleased - but he wasn't.

But Beth may have been terrorized before she ever tried to approach her baby's father.

If Brenda Allen's procurer, Maurice Clement, had arranged Beth's liaison with this man, and she had become pregnant, it explains many of the mysteries in the case. It was understood that the girls who worked for Allen should not get pregnant. If they did, they went to see a mob abortionist, who took care of things. Those who didn't cooperate ended up with serious problems. Allen's clients were among the wealthiest and most powerful men in the city. If Beth didn't proceed with the abortion, as Maurice Clement must have warned her, she would have reason to be afraid.

On December 6, 1946, the night before she left Hollywood for San Diego, Mark Hansen and Ann Toth found Beth in tears. She told them she was "scared." Her roommate at the Chancellor, Sherryl Maylond, said there had been a number of calls from Clement, after which Beth had become afraid and said that she "had to get out of there." Her landlady also noticed that something seemed wrong with her and that she was anxious to get out of LA. In fact, she was so frightened that she didn't want anyone to know where she was going. She told her roommates, as well as Hansen and Toth, that she was going to Oakland to visit her sister over the holidays. Of course, her sister later said that she hadn't heard from Beth and there had been no plans for her to visit. Instead, Beth went to San Diego, where she didn't know anyone and, more importantly, no one knew her.

While staying at the French home in Pacific Beach, both Elvera and Dorothy French noticed that Beth seemed anxious and bit her fingernails "down to the quick." They sensed that she was "hiding out." According to notes made by Frank Jemison, Beth made the mistake of calling Mark Hansen on January 4 and asking him for money. She told him where to send it, and two days later, three strangers appeared at the Frenchs' front door looking for Beth. She was terrified once more. After she turned to Robert Manley for help, he arrived in San Diego and assisted her in moving out of the French house. On January 9, he drove her to Los Angeles. On the drive north, Manley described Beth as anxious and said that she was frequently turning around to look at the passengers in nearby cars. He believed that she was worried they were being followed.

Evidently, Beth had no plans to stay in Los Angeles. She had written to Gordon Fickling on January 7, saying that she planned to go to Chicago, where she'd be modeling for "Jack."

But apparently, there was someone that she wanted to see in LA before she went to Chicago. They stopped for gas in Laguna Beach, where Manley said Beth made a call to someone. I feel confident in saying that the person she called was likely the father of her unborn child. It would have been too great of a temptation not to try and get some help from the man who had impregnated her. Perhaps she had approached him already, perhaps not. Perhaps it was simply a call for assistance, looking for enough money to get her to Chicago or home to Massachusetts or again - perhaps not. Depending on who this man was, perhaps Beth's desperate situation convinced her that blackmail might be in order. It's possible that she threatened this man - wealthy, powerful and probably married - with exposing his secret unless he paid her off. We'll never know for sure, but perhaps an arrangement was made for them to meet at the Biltmore Hotel.

But the man never planned to meet her at the Biltmore at all; he sent someone in his place.

Threatened, the man placed a call, which might have filtered through the LAPD and made its way to Jack Dragna, who did most of the dirty work for the people in charge in those days. He would be asked to solve the problem and as in the case of Jean Spangler, the problem might simply vanish. But Brenda Allen's operation was Ben Siegel and Mickey Cohen's business. That made it an awkward situation. Siegel was spending most of his time in Las Vegas and Dragna and Cohen hated each other. Although Dragna couldn't talk to Cohen, he could talk to Siegel, even if they didn't get along. Siegel was in town that week. He had arrived on January 6, the day of the robbery at the Mocambo, and it was one of his girls that was causing trouble for one of their benefactors. Siegel let Brenda Allen operate in his territory and that made it his responsibility - not Dragna's. Solving an embarrassing problem for a business mogul or studio boss would be a major marker for the mob. It was a debt that could be called in for repayment later.

When Beth and Manley arrived in Los Angeles, she checked her baggage at the Greyhound station and told Manley that she was meeting her sister Ginnie at the Biltmore. But after driving her to the hotel, Manley was unable to locate Beth's sister before he had to leave. He left Beth in the lobby at around 6:30 p.m. According to Ginnie, she had no plans to meet Beth that night, so we have to conclude that whoever it was that Beth was supposed to be meeting at the Biltmore was someone whose identity she did not want to reveal to Manley. Most likely, it was one of the people whose names were later removed from her address book.

The bell captain at the Biltmore said that Beth used the pay phone in the lobby to make several calls after Manley left. She was also seen in the restroom applying candle wax to her teeth, probably hoping to look her best for her baby's father. Beth was last seen in the hotel lobby at 10:00 p.m. We have no way of knowing if she met someone at the hotel, departed on her own, or was taken away against her will. We only know that the final sighting at 10:00 p.m. was the last time that Beth Short was seen alive.

There were various sightings of Beth that were reported in newspapers between January 9 and January 14, but all of them were discounted. When investigated, the witnesses spoke of her jet-black hair, but detectives knew that she had dyed her hair red before leaving San Diego.

Did Beth leave the hotel on her own? If she had, and she decided to stay in LA, she would have returned to the Greyhound station and picked up the luggage that contained her clothes and her makeup kit. She also would have, at some point during the week, contacted one of her friends - Ann Toth, Mark Hansen, or her former roommates at the Chancellor. Or she would have written to her mother, who was used to getting letters from her at least once a week.

I believe that Beth was taken from the Biltmore, or from someplace nearby, soon after she left - most likely by Maurice Clement. And I believe that she was abducted and held captive at a location not far from Pico and Crenshaw, where her shoes and handbag were found in the incinerator.

On the morning of January 14, Ben Siegel cancelled a planned trip to New York. That night, Beth Short was brutally murdered. Her face was slashed from ear to ear. She was repeatedly bludgeoned by a blunt metal instrument. Her uterus was removed. A tattoo was sliced from her left thigh. Strange cuts were made on her body. The letter D was carved into her flesh about her pubic area. Her corpse was severed and then the bisected remains were taken to a vacant lot on Norton Avenue, where it was displayed not far from Jack Dragna's home.

The horrific legend of the Black Dahlia was born.

18. THE KILLERS

After the grand jury's condemning statements about underworld payoffs to LAPD officers, Governor Earl Warren gave the job of investigating criminal elements in Los Angeles to the California Crime Commission. Soon, a bright light began shining on the darkest elements of the police department, the city government and the shadowy underworld of LA.

After Chief Horrall resigned in the wake of the Brenda Allen scandal, William Worton was temporarily appointed as interim chief. Worton was not a man to tangle with. He had been tasked with cleaning up the department and he meant to do so. Worton was a former Marine who saw combat in France during World War I. After the War, Worton remained in the Marine Corps, spending twelve years in China in the 1920s and 1930s, including two years as an undercover intelligence officer, conducting the first American espionage operations against Japan using agents recruited on the Chinese mainland. In 1935, Worton was assigned to the Far East Section of the Office of Naval Intelligence, where he continued spying on the Japanese. During World War II, he served as a Brigadier General in the Battle of Okinawa and headed the assault on the Tokyo Plain during an invasion of Japan. After the war's end, he was sent to China to accept the surrender of Japanese forces in the region.

Worton took over as chief of the LAPD, and almost immediately, he eliminated the position of assistant chief, which ended the career of Joe Reed. Worton was only supposed to be a temporary chief, but he was working to clean up the department as best he could. Powers at City Hall had planned for Thad Brown to be named as the next chief, but those plans were thwarted by the police commission. When Worton resigned less than a year after taking over the position, he was replaced by his chief of Internal Affairs, William H. Parker, whom he had groomed for the office. Parker went on to become a legendary chief in LAPD history.

Parker was an ambitious man and he set his sights on the chief's job early in his career. Having served as a lieutenant in the office of Chief James "Two Gun" Davis during the 1937 corruption scandals, he knew where the bodies were buried at City Hall. Corruption still existed under Parker's regime, but it went underground. Cooperating with the Crime Commission, Parker declared war on the criminal element in the city. Thanks to his strict policies, it became increasingly difficult for the mob to find the corrupt cops in the department. When it was discovered that Capt. Donahoe had become a major player in a mob narcotics ring, Parker pushed him into early retirement. He didn't arrest him because he didn't want the ugly story splashed all over the newspapers.

Donahoe died on June 18, 1966 and the *Los Angeles Times* gave him a glowing eulogy, calling him "One of the most noted detectives in the country." The articles stated that he had been found dead in his living room chair by his wife, but it didn't mention that he had died from a bullet through the heart. The coroner's report ruled it a suicide.

A number of Chief Horrall's former underworld enforcers were transferred or forced into retirement during Parker's years as LAPD's chief, but two of them, Archie Case and James Ahern from the notorious Gangster Squad, became Parker's golden boys and received plum jobs and special assignments. Both men had been closely associated with one of Parker's closest confidants, Lt. James E. Hamilton. He had worked with Parker in Army Intelligence during World War II and became a chief investigator for the police commission. While tied in with Norman Chandler, Joe Reed and other corrupt city officials, Hamilton's loyalty lay with Parker. When it looked like Thad Brown would be named as chief after William Worton, Hamilton used Case and Ahern to dig up dirt on police commission members so that the vote would swing in Parker's direction.

Once ensconced in the chief's office, Parker promoted Hamilton to captain and made him chief of the Gangster Squad, which became known as the Intelligence Division under Hamilton's command. Case and Ahern became his favored officers and over the course of the next decade, the squad gathered blackmail material on politicians, movie stars, studio bosses and the city's wealthiest power brokers. Not much had changed with the Gangster Squad, except for the name. According to Vince Carter, who wrote about the LAPD's dirtiest cops after he left the department, Case and Ahern's careers had truly started to rise one night in January 1947 - when they became inadvertently mixed up in the Black Dahlia case.

Keep in mind that the following scenario is based on the recollections of a retired detective, as well as a lot of supposition and little hard evidence. But in truth, it makes a lot of sense and is probably the only solution to the Black Dahlia case that I have ever seen that rings with authenticity. I don't claim to know for sure who killed Beth Short - but I have always believed that she was mixed up in prostitution, likely became pregnant, fled the city and returned to blackmail someone, only to end up dead. Putting that basic idea together with the theories of other writers like Donald Wolfe, John Gilmore and others, what follows seems the closest that I have ever seen to the truth.

Probably, anyway...

So, starting with Case and Ahern stumbling into a situation that they should never have seen, this is what *might* have happened to the Black Dahlia:

After World War II, Case and Ahern were two young detectives working out of the Wilshire Station on Pico Boulevard. They occasionally worked on stakeouts with Vince Carter and Sgt. Ron Hardman as they followed narcotics dealers. They were on a stakeout one night, passing the time, when Case and Ahern told Carter and Hardman about an incident that occurred on the night of January 14, 1947, when they were staking out Lucey's Bar and Grill on Melrose Avenue, near RKO and Paramount Studios. Lucey's was a mob nightclub, run by a front man named Nathan Sherry. It was popular with the film crowd as a late-night spot to buy drugs. Failing to spot the dealer they were looking for, Case and Ahern left Lucey's at closing time and drove down Western Avenue as they headed back to the Wilshire Station. When they crossed Wilshire and were approaching Eighth Street and Crenshaw, they saw a dark-colored sedan run a red light as it traveled east with its lights off. Ahern, who was driving, turned off his own headlights, did a U-turn, and followed the sedan. They saw the sedan's brake lights flash as it turned south off of Eighth Street onto Catalina near the Ambassador Hotel. Ahern followed and Case spotted the car as it pulled to the curb.

The detectives hurriedly parked about half a block down the street. Ahern turned off the engine and he and Case watched as three men got out of the sedan and walked toward a bungalow court at 836 Catalina Street. Case and Ahern silently got out of their car and quickly walked toward the bungalows, just as a fourth man - the driver - got out of the sedan and walked around the car to the sidewalk. The detectives followed him toward a rear bungalow, then darted forward and grabbed him before he opened the front door. Ahern shoved his badge in the man's face and barked, "Police!"

Startled by the two detectives as they came out of the darkness, the man panicked and rushed through the door into the bungalow. The detectives charged after him, pulled their guns and ordered the driver and the other three men inside to put up their hands. After they were searched for weapons, the men were ordered to provide identification. The man who seemed to be the leader of the group took a card out of his wallet and handed it to Ahern. It was a police courtesy card. He told Ahern to turn it over and the detective saw a handwritten notation on the back. It read: "The bearer is a friend of mine. Any courtesy you can show him will be appreciated." It was signed Capt. Jack Donahoe. Written below the signature was Donahoe's home telephone number. The man urged Case and Ahern to go ahead and give him a call.

Capt. Donahoe had been the detectives' boss when they were working robbery and as Ahern walked over to the telephone in the bungalow's hallway, he knew that the captain would not be happy to get a call in the middle of the night. As he reluctantly picked up the phone, he saw a smear of blood on the wall. Looking down the hall, he saw more blood. While Case

The bungalow court at 836 Catalina Street today – was this where the Black Dahlia was murdered in 1947?

held the four men at gunpoint, Ahern followed a trail of stains and smears to the bathroom - which looked like a slaughterhouse. Blood was splashed and spattered on the walls, the floor and even on the ceiling. The sides of the tub and the sink were covered in blood. Bloody towels were crumpled on the bathroom floor and in the hallway. Ahern staggered out of the room and stormed into the living room, demanding that the men tell him where the blood had come from. They refused to say. They weren't talking to anyone but Capt. Donahoe.

Convinced that they were in something way over their heads, the detectives had no choice but to make the call to Donahoe. Angry at being awakened, he demanded an explanation. Ahern detailed what had occurred, described the bloody scene inside the bungalow, and described the man with the courtesy card. There was silence on the other end of the line and then Donahoe blurted out that they should do nothing - he would be there in twenty minutes.

The two cops and the four occupants of the bungalow stood around awkwardly until Donahoe arrived. When he walked in and viewed the scene, he took the man who had produced the courtesy card into the kitchen and they talked in low voices for about ten minutes. When he returned to the living room, he told Case and Ahern that the men had thrown a poker party. There had been a lot of drinking and a brawl had broken out, which explained all the blood. Ahern spoke up and noted that there was no sign of a fight having taken place and none of the four men had blood on their clothes, or any signs of injury. Donahoe said that the injured participants had been taken home. That's where the men had been coming from when Case and Ahern spotted their car.

Donahoe would take responsibility for everything, he said, and ordered Case and Ahern to leave. He walked them out to the sidewalk and told them to forget about what they had seen. He explained that they had no idea what they were dealing with, and that the man with the courtesy card "could put all three of us in hell with one phone call."

The sun was coming up by the time that Case and Ahern made it back to Wilshire Division. The two exhausted men signed out and went home. Ahern later said that he slept fitfully and was up before noon. Going into the kitchen to get something to eat, he turned on the radio and heard a newscaster report the discovery of a young woman's nude body in a vacant lot on Norton Avenue in Leimert Park. The woman had been mutilated and cut in half.

Ahern grabbed the telephone and called his partner. They shared the terrible feeling that the body was connected with what they had seen at the bungalow court on Catalina Street. They decided to take a ride together to the lot where the body had been found. They found the area swarming with police, reporters and curiosity-seekers. When they heard from another cop that the coroner had not yet removed the body, they pushed their way to the front of the gruesome scene. It was evident to both men that the murder had not occurred where the body was discovered. There was little blood at the site because the remains had been drained somewhere - likely in a bathtub.

Capt. Donahoe had ordered more than fifty police officers to search the area around the lot where the body was found and to knock on doors to try and find someone who had seen something that could help them find the killer. He announced to the press that an exhaustive investigation would take place and that every lead, no matter how small, would be followed.

But Case and Ahern knew that none of the leads would take detectives to the bungalow court at 836 Catalina Street, and the four occupants of the dark-colored sedan would never be questioned. Donahoe had made it clear that the incident at the bungalow was never to be reported or discussed with anyone. According to Ahern, the man who had produced Donahoe's courtesy card was none other than Ben "Bugsy" Siegel.

The bungalow court, where Brenda Allen kept the girls that worked for her call-girl operation, was the logical location where Beth Short could be detained after she was picked up at the Biltmore Hotel. It was five blocks away from the professional building on West Sixth Street where Dr. Leslie Audrain had his office. If Audrain was the leader of the mob's abortion operation, as Sgt. Charles Stoker claimed he was, it would have not taken him long to drive from his office to the bungalow court. The incinerator where Beth's shoes and purse were found was roughly halfway between the bungalow on Catalina and the vacant lot where her body was found.

If whoever had bisected Beth's body was "a very fine surgeon," as Harry Hansen suspected he was, he had probably already left the blood-spattered bungalow by the time Case and Ahern arrived. So who were the three men who were present that night with Ben Siegel? Case and Ahern never revealed their identities, but it's likely that the driver of the sedan was the short, dark-skinned man who worked for Brenda Allen and who was known to drive Beth Short around - Maurice Clement. It's likely that one of the other men was Al Greenberg, owner of Al Green's Nightlife Bar and the boss of the McCadden Gang. Greenberg had worked with Siegel back in the days of the Siegel and Lansky operation. He was also involved in a number of jewel robberies with Siegel at the time of the murder. He knew Beth Short, who had worked for him as a B-Girl.

According to LAPD transcripts, as well as research conducted by author John Gilmore, the fourth man involved in the murder was almost undoubtedly Jack Anderson Wilson (a.k.a. Arnold Smith), who had been involved in the recent jewel robbery at the Mocambo. Wilson was a member of Greenberg's McCadden Gang. He was six feet, four inches tall and walked with a limp.

John Gilmore, who wrote a fascinating book on the Black Dahlia case, believed that Wilson was the lone killer of Beth Short. He based this on numerous interviews that he conducted with Wilson over a period of several years and discussions with LAPD detective John St. John, who had taken over the Black Dahlia case in 1968.

The Wilson interviews left little doubt that he was involved in Beth Short's murder. He knew far too many of the details of the crime - things that only someone who had been at the scene could have known. However, Wilson was certainly not the kind of person that upper levels of the LAPD would have tried to protect. In the 1940s, he was a little-known thug with a long rap sheet for burglary and assault who ended up in the McCadden Gang because he hung around Al Green's bar. It had been Siegel that the politicians and the LAPD brass had been trying to protect.

At the time he encountered Jack Wilson, John Gilmore had been working on the Black Dahlia case for several years. The district attorney's files were not released until 2003, and Gilmore was thrown off (like many writers were) by the planted stories about Beth's inability to have sex and was unaware that someone with advanced medical knowledge had been involved in her murder. Since he had no idea about the pregnancy, which created the motive behind the murder, he was convinced that the killer was a lone psychopath - which had been what Capt. Donahoe wanted the press and the public to believe.

In the early 1980s, there were a lot of people in the Hollywood community who knew Gilmore was working on the case. In October 1981, he was contacted by a man who referred to himself as "Eddie." He said that he was in touch with a "Mr. Smith" who had knowledge about the Black Dahlia murder. An arrangement was made for Gilmore to meet Mr. Smith at Eddie's home in the Silver Lake area, which Gilmore described as the stash spot for a small-time burglary ring. The garage was filled with electronics, golf clubs and a jumble of items that looked like they'd been gathered from many different households.

Eddie introduced him to two friends staying at the house - an Indian, whom Gilmore later learned was involved in neighborhood burglaries with Eddie, and a tall wiry man who was introduced as "Arnold Smith." Gilmore noticed that Smith was over six feet tall and walked with a limp.

After a few drinks and some small talk, Eddie started talking about some unsolved murders in Hollywood and said that Arnold Smith had known the Black Dahlia and even had a photograph of himself with her. Smith told Gilmore that he had met Beth at Al Greenberg's place through his friend, Henry Hassau, who had also been involved with the McCadden Gang. Smith told him that there had been a number of robberies that involved several men who hung around the bar, including Hassau and a man named Bobby Savarino. According to Smith, one of those robberies, at a nightclub on the Sunset Strip, had occurred around the time of the Black Dahlia murder and Hassau and Savarino had been arrested. Somehow, Smith had managed to elude the police.

Initially, Gilmore didn't realize that Smith was talking about the jewel robbery at the Mocambo, which had been carried out for Ben Siegel on January 6, 1947. Arnold Smith was the "tall, six-foot-four younger man with the limp" that was identified by the accountant as the thief who "scraped the jewelry from the tray removed from the safe." Although Smith was never arrested for the Mocambo job, Hassau and Savarino were picked up by sheriff's deputies on the afternoon of January 14, the day Beth Short was murdered. Al Greenberg was arrested several days later.

After the meeting at Eddie's house in Silver Lake, Gilmore met with Smith several more times in the fall of 1981. Smith would call Gilmore's office and arrange a time and a place to meet, which was usually a bar in downtown LA. Smith would not reveal his real name, where he lived or how Gilmore could get in touch with him. Smith was an alcoholic and his information about the murder of Beth Short spilled out a little at a time as Gilmore bought him drinks and gave him some occasional cash.

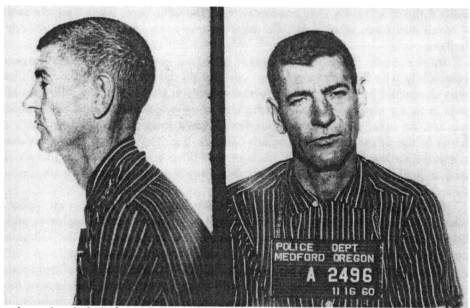

Mug shot of Jack Anderson Wilson (a.k.a. Arnold Smith) the fourth man involved in the Mocambo nightclub robbery and possibly, one of the men who killed and disposed of the Black Dahlia.

After weeks of meetings, it became obvious that Smith was teasing Gilmore with small amounts of information in return for drinks and cash. Usually drunk, Smith - or whatever his name was -- was often rambling, evasive and incoherent. He told Gilmore just enough to keep him hooked on the disjointed revelations. During one of the meetings, Smith produced a photograph that had been taken in a nightclub in 1946. It showed Beth Short seated at a table next to a much younger Smith and another couple. During another meeting, Smith told Gilmore that the person responsible for Beth's murder was someone named "Al Morrison." Gilmore tried to find out more about "Morrison" but Smith became cagey and evasive. He repeatedly placed Al Morrison at the scene of the murder, along with Al Greenberg.

Initially, Smith maintained the pretense that he had not been present when Beth was killed and had only been told about it afterwards by Al Greenberg, but as the meetings continued, it became apparent that Smith had been there and was involved in the disposal of the body.

According to Gilmore, Smith just knew too much. He described Beth being naked, with her hands tied up over her head. "They" had stabbed her with a knife a number of times, not deep, just slicing her open. Then she was cut

230

across the face because they didn't think she was dead. "But, oh yeah, she was dead," Smith added.

He described how two boards were placed across the bathtub and Beth was laid on top of them. Her hands were tied to the faucet handles with one board under her back and the other under her hips. A rope was then tied around each leg and the ropes were wrapped around the toilet bowl. The initial idea, Smith said, was to cut each leg off at the top, but since this would have to be done twice, it seemed too complicated. Instead, she was cut in half at the waist so that the two parts could be easily moved. The body was drained and washed in the tub, leaving bloodstains on the porcelain, and on the floor and walls. He said the blood sprayed so high that it spattered on the ceiling. The men used towels to try and soak up the blood on the floor.

After they were finished, the body was wrapped in a shower curtain and placed in the trunk of a dark-colored sedan. An empty paper sack that had held concrete was on the floor of the trunk and the body was placed on top of it. The sack was later found near the body in the vacant lot on Norton Avenue. Some of the bloody towels, Smith said, were thrown in an incinerator - likely the same one where her shoes and purse were later found. He said that the shower curtain was later thrown in a storm drain.

The text of Gilmore's interviews was chilling. Smith's statements had the eerie ring of truth. He knew many details that were consistent with the facts in the coroner's inquest. Smith had too much knowledge to be making it up. He knew where the body had been cut in half, and he described the marks left on the corpse and even how it was disposed of.

John Gilmore concluded that Smith was the only person involved in the murder and had made up the involvement of Al Greenberg to protect himself. In hindsight, it's easy for us to say that Gilmore missed a lot, but he did not have the luxury of the information that's available now. We can look at these interviews now and it becomes evident that Smith was Jack Anderson Wilson, the fourth man encountered by Case and Ahern at the bungalow court on Catalina Street.

I believe that when Beth returned to Los Angeles, she tried to contact the man who had fathered her child. Whoever this man was - whether or not it was Norman Chandler as some have claimed or some other influential person who had pull with the LAPD and the mob - Beth had become a dangerous liability for him. Ordered to handle the problem, Siegel was forced to make sure that she was silenced. He could have just killed her and made her disappear, but Siegel took things further. Violent and erratic under the best of circumstances, and under great personal and financial stress at the time due to the staggering cost of getting the Flamingo up and running, "Bugsy" was a ticking time bomb. He beat, savaged and literally butchered Beth

Short. He slashed her up, slicing her body and cutting the rose tattoo from her thigh. Siegel or one of the others washed the body in the bungalow's bathtub and then one of the mob doctors who provided abortions meticulously cut her apart to make it easier to move the body to the location where it was eventually found. Whoever the doctor was, he had little choice; he faced exposure or death at the hands of the mob if he didn't cooperate.

But murder wasn't enough for Siegel. The atrocity had been carried out on orders from the Syndicate because Jack Dragna, Siegel's nemesis, refused to take care of it himself. The display of Beth's body in Dragna's neighborhood had been a cold, calculated choice. Siegel wanted to make sure that Dragna received the message that he left for him. He slashed Beth's face from ear-to-ear and addressed the body with a letter "D" for Dragna.

Jack Dragna received the message loud and clear. And five months later, in the form of bullets, Dragna sent his response and ended Ben Siegel's life.

19. THE END OF THE LINE

Officially, the Black Dahlia murder remains one of the many unsolved mysteries of Los Angeles. As far as the official record goes, the case led to nothing but dead ends and the investigation eventually came to a halt. It's one of the most talked-about murders of the twentieth century, even though it involved a high school dropout from a small town whom no one really knew. Beth Short dreamed of making a name for herself in the movies, but like many others who had the same dream, she got lost on the dark side of Hollywood. She became infamous and infinitely more glamorous in death than she ever was in life. There's something about the fact that she was beautiful and died an unspeakably gruesome death at twenty-two that makes us still talk about her today. And of course, since her case was never solved -- and justice was never served - Beth Short becomes more intriguing than she would have ever have been if the murderers had been captured. Without the grisly aspects of the crime, her ethereal beauty, the links to the police, City Hall and organized crime, she would have been just another victim of the mean streets of LA.

Over the years, we have been unable to let her go.

And some of the detectives in the case were just as haunted. Harry Hansen never gave up on trying to find her killer, but then there's reason to believe that he figured out the clues and solved the case - off the record - before he retired in 1970. Hansen knew the secret that had been kept from the autopsy record - that she had been pregnant when the murder occurred and the baby was cut out of her body. In his grand jury testimony, he acknowledged that the bisection of the body had been performed by someone with surgical skills. He also knew the names and addresses of a number of doctors were in Beth's address book. He suspected at least one of them worked for the mob, providing clandestine abortions. According to Aggie Underwood and Finis Brown, Harry believed that an abortionist was involved in the crime and had been pushing for an indictment, but it was blocked by Chief Horrall.

On several occasions, Hansen also questioned Brenda Allen's procurer, Maurice Clement, and the grand jury files indicate that Clement was placed high on the suspect list. Like Sgt. Stoker, Hansen knew that Brenda Allen was working in Ben Siegel's vice territory and he also would have recognized the significance of Beth Short's body being dumped near Jack Dragna's house. The detectives who worked the streets at that time were well aware of the mob wars that were going on and the animosity between the various underworld factions. But there was only so far that Hansen could take it. Ben Siegel was murdered just five months after Beth was killed. Dr. Audrain died a few months before the grand jury was beginning its investigation and anything that he may have known about an abortion ring would never be discovered. By the time that Hansen was brought before the grand jury in November 1949, he undoubtedly had answers to a lot of questions that were never asked by the investigators. Although Hansen was an honest cop, he was no whistle-blower. He saw the corruption that was rampant in the LAPD, and while he stayed clear of it, he didn't go out of his way to fight it. It's more than likely that when he died in 1983, Harry Hansen took many of the Black Dahlia's secrets to the grave with him.

After Hansen retired and moved to Palm Springs, the unsolved Black Dahlia case was inherited by Det. John St. John, who was referred to as "Jigsaw John" due to his famous investigative talents. St. John carried the LAPD's Badge #1, given to him by Chief William Parker, and he was a one-man publicity campaign for the department. Although St. John had worked a number of famous robbery and homicide cases, his genius lay in making the LAPD look good. He became a public relations expert, devoted to restoring the department's tarnished image after the 1949 grand jury hearings. From his office at Warner Brothers Studios, he was involved in the creation of Jack Webb's *Dragnet* television series, for which he served as technical director. His reputation as a legendary homicide investigator was further enhanced by the short-lived 1976 television crime drama *Jigsaw John*, based on exploits that were invented by Chief Parker and the LAPD.

By the time that St. John took over the Black Dahlia case, it was so cold that it was more of a public relations gimmick than an actual investigation. He spent little time on it, except for dismissing the occasional theorist or researcher who came up with a new suspect in the case. However, he had a hard time dismissing John Gilmore when he presented Arnold Smith as a viable lead.

Following several meetings with Gilmore, where he read over the transcripts of the interviews that the writer had done, St. John found Smith to be a credible suspect. After re-examining the LAPD Black Dahlia files and conferring with Finis Brown, the crime lab and several detectives who had worked the case, St. John came to believe that Smith had may have been present at the murder scene and may have helped move Beth's body to the site on Norton Avenue. In addition, St. John suspected that Arnold Smith and Al Morrison were one in the same person.

Although St. John was quick to dismiss the possibility that Smith had told the truth about Al Greenberg being involved in the murder (remember, Gilmore was convinced that Smith acted alone), he must have known that Greenburg was the boss of the McCadden Gang, had known Beth Short and had worked for Ben Siegel. Faced with Gilmore's transcripts, however, St. John had to concede that Smith was a good suspect and that he needed to locate him and bring him in for questioning.

Smith had been careful about not revealing his real identity or where he lived. It was decided that if he called again, Gilmore would agree to meet him and then bring along a "friend" to the meeting, who would actually be an undercover detective. The cop would buy the drinks and try to engage Smith in the kind of conversations that Gilmore had been having with him. Gilmore warned St. John that the meeting would come with little notice because he never knew when Smith would call. Gilmore only heard from him when he was out broke and needed someone to buy him drinks.

The call came in late December 1981. A meeting was arranged at the 55 Club on Main Street. After several rounds of drinks, the undercover officer, Louise Sheffield, began asking Smith about Al Greenberg, the Mocambo robbery and the McCadden Gang's connections to Ben Siegel and Mickey Cohen. According to Sheffield, Smith became very uncomfortable and refused to talk to her anymore. He only mentioned "Al Morrison" one time.

Meanwhile, St. John had finally identified Arnold Smith. His mug shots were obtained from an arrest in Oregon, along with a long rap sheet for robbery, burglary and petty crimes. Smith proved to be Jack Anderson Wilson, who sometimes went by Grover Loving, Jr., Hanns Anderson Von Cannon and, of course, Arnold Smith. After the meeting with Gilmore and Sheffield at the 555 Club, Arnold Smith/Jack Wilson was put under surveillance and he was tailed to Room 202 of the Holland Hotel on Seventh Street in downtown Los Angeles.

St. John had come to believe that Gilmore was correct: Jack Wilson a.k.a. Arnold Smith was involved in the murder of Beth Short. But shortly after St. John acknowledged that Smith was a viable suspect, Gilmore made the mistake of going to the newly merged *Herald-Examiner* with the Smith interviews and the story of his discovery. Even after all of the years that had passed, interest in the Black Dahlia case was still strong and on January 17, 1982, the newspaper ran a front-page story that mentioned Arnold Smith and Al Morrison as "hot new suspects" in the murder.

At this point, St. John realized that it was imperative that he move quickly before Wilson/Smith became spooked. Gilmore left messages for him at the 555 Club but Smith never returned them, possibly because he found out that the police had the bar under surveillance. Finally, Gilmore received a reply and a meeting was set with Smith for late January 1982.

Unfortunately, just before the meeting was to take place, the case against Jack Wilson literally went up in flames. He was in bed in his room at the Holland Hotel when the room was engulfed in fire. Fireman had to break down the door to get inside, where they discovered Wilson's burning body. Although Room 202 was the only room in the hotel that burned, it took firefighters more than thirty-five minutes to put out the blaze. The fire captain stated that Wilson's body was lying on the left side of the bed, which had burned and collapsed onto the floor. The fire, he said, had been extraordinarily intense. All of the furniture in the room had been consumed by the flames. It was initially thought that Wilson had fallen asleep while smoking in bed, but the intensity of the fire suggested arson to the fire captain. He stated that the death of Jack Wilson was "possibly other than accidental."

Was the fourth killer of Beth Short murdered?

A short time after Wilson's body was released to the county for cremation, the Los Angeles District Attorney's office was presented with a file on the matter. It summed up by saying, "The case cannot be officially closed due to the death of the individual considered a suspect. While the documentation appears to link this individual with the homicide of Elizabeth Short, his death, however, precludes the opportunity of an interview to obtain from him the corroboration...Therefore, any conclusion as to his criminal involvement is circumstantial, and unfortunately, the suspect cannot be charged or tried, due to his demise. However, despite this inconclusiveness, the circumstantial evidence is of such a nature that were this suspect alive, an intensive inquiry would be recommended. And depending upon the outcome of such an inquiry, it is conceivable that Jack Wilson might have been charged as a suspect in the murder of Elizabeth Short - also known as the Black Dahlia."

But, of course, he never was and the "intensive inquiry" never took place.

Today, the Black Dahlia murder is a very cold case. What we can offer now is really only guesswork, based on the best available evidence that we have - but I think there is something to the theories that have emerged that explain why she was killed, who killed her and why her body was moved to the vacant lot where it was found.

Since the time of her death in 1947, many books have been written and many theories have been spun about who killed Elizabeth Short. But no matter how many theories, books and documentaries have come out of the case, to this date it remains officially unsolved. No one has ever been charged with her murder and her death has never been avenged. Of course, there is no statute of limitation for murder but it's doubtful that the LAPD or the district attorney's office will ever re-open the Black Dahlia case.

Beth Short will always remain an elusive mystery from the dark side of Hollywood - and the even darker side of the American landscape.

Perhaps this is why her ghost still walks at the Biltmore Hotel and her specter still looms over the shadowy streets of Hollywood. Even today, an occasional man who stays at the Biltmore encounters the spectral image of a woman in a black dress, sometimes in the lobby, sometimes waiting in one of the corridors or even riding to the sixth floor on the elevator. What is she trying to tell us? Are there still clues to the identity of her killer that have never been found?

Or does the Black Dahlia simply wish to continue the mystery that was created more than sixty years ago? For sadly, Elizabeth Short found the fame in death that she never managed to achieve in life.

BIBLIOGRAPHY

Anger, Kenneth - *Hollywood Babylon;* 1975
------------------ - *Hollywood Babylon II;* 1984
Arnold, William - *Shadowland;* 1978
Austen, John - *Hollywood's Unsolved Mysteries;* 1970
Blanche, Tony and Brad Schreiber - *Death in Paradise;* 1998
Carter, Vincent A. - *LAPD's Rogue Cops;* 1993
Cohen, Mickey - *In My Own Words;* 1975
Domanick, Joe - *To Protect and to Serve;* 1994
Douglas, John - *The Cases that Haunt Us;* 1995
Edmonds, Andy - *Bugsy's Baby: The Secret Life of Mob Queen Virginia Hill;* 1993
------------------ - *Hot Toddy;* 1989
Epstein, Edward Jay - *The Annals of Unsolved Crime;* 2012
Fowler, Will - *Reporters: Memoirs of a Young Newspaperman;* 1991
Freed, Donald and Raymond Briggs - *Killing Time;* 1996
Gilmore, John - *Severed: The True Story of the Black Dahlia Murder;* 1998
Global Book Publishing - *Cut! Hollywood Murders, Accidents & Other Tragedies;* 2005
Granlund, Nils T. - *Blondes, Brunettes and Bullets;* 1957
Halberstam, David - *The Powers That Be;* 1979
Hecht, Ben - *A Child of the Century;* 1954
Heimann, Jim - *Sins of the City: The Real LA Noir;* 1999
Henderson, Bruce and Sam Summerlin - *The Super Sleuths;* 1975
Henstell, Bruce - *Los Angeles: An Illustrated History;* 1980
Higham, Charles - *Murder in Hollywood;* 2004
Hodel, Steve - *Black Dahlia Avenger;* 2003
James, Bill - *Popular Crime;* 2011
Jennings, Dean - *We Only Kill Each Other: The Life and Bad Times of Bugsy Siegel;* 1967
Keppel, Robert D. - *Signature Killers;* 1997
Knowlton, Janice and Michael Newton - *Daddy was the Black Dahlia Killer;* 1995
Lacey, Robert - *Little Man: Meyer Lansky and the Gangster Life;* 1991
Lamparski, Richard - *Lamparski's Hidden Hollywood;* 1981
Leiberman, Paul - *Gangster Squad;* 2012
Lewis, Brad - *Hollywood's Celebrity Gangster: The Incredible Life and Times of Mickey Cohen;* 2007
Martinez, Al - *Jigsaw John;* 1975
Mordenn, Ethan - *The Hollywood Studios;* 1989
Muir, Florabel - *Headline Happy;* 1950
Munn, Michael - *The Hollywood Murder Case Book;* 1987
Nash, Jay Robert - *Bloodletters and Badmen;* 1995
Odell, Robin - *Mammoth Book of Bizarre Crimes;* 2010

Otash, Fred - *Investigation Hollywood;* 1976
Pacios, Mary - *Childhood Shadows: The Hidden Story of the Black Dahlia Murder;* 1999
Parrish, James Robert - *The Hollywood Book of Death;* 2002
Parrish, Michael - *For the People: Inside the Los Angeles County District Attorney's Office;* 2001
Reid, David - *Sex, Death and God in LA;* 1992
Richardson, James H. - *For the Life of Me: Memoirs of a City Editor;* 1954
Rothmiller, Mike and Ivan Goldman - *Secret Police: Inside the LAPD Elite Spy Network;* 1992
Rowan, David - *Famous American Crimes;* 1957
Russo, Gus - *The Outfit;* 2001
Sifakis, Carl - *Encyclopedia of American Crime;* 1982
Smith, Jack - *Jack Smith's LA;* 1980
Sterling, Hank - *Ten Perfect Crimes;* 1954
Taylor, Troy - *Bloody Hollywood;* 2008
Tejaratchi, Sean - *Death Scenes: A Homicide Detective's Scrapbook;* 1996
Thomas, Bob - *King Cohn;* 1967
Turkus, Burton B. and Sid Feder - *Murder, Inc.;* 1951
Underwood, Agnes - *Newspaperwoman;* 1949
Webb, Jack - *The Badge;* 1958
Wilkerson III, W.R. - *The Man Who Invented Las Vegas;* 2000
Wilson, Colin - *Murder in the 1940s;* 1993
Wolf, Marvin J. and Katherine Mader - *Fallen Angels: Chronicles of LA Crime & Mystery;* 1986
Wolfe, Donald H. - *The Black Dahlia Files;* 2005
Wride, Tim B. (Essay / Introduction by James Ellroy) - *Scene of the Crime;* 2004
Wright, John - *Unsolved Crimes;* 2010
Young, Paul - *LA Exposed;* 2002

NEWSPAPERS
Boston Globe
Chicago Tribune
Hollywood Citizen's News
Los Angeles Daily News
Los Angeles Examiner
Los Angeles Herald Express
Los Angeles Times
Oakland Tribune

ABOUT THE AUTHOR:
TROY TAYLOR

Troy Taylor is an occultist, crime buff, supernatural historian and the author of nearly 100 books on ghosts, hauntings, history, crime and the unexplained in America.

He is also the founder of the American Ghost Society and the owner of the American Hauntings Tour company.

Taylor shares a birthday with one of his favorite authors, F. Scott Fitzgerald, but instead of living in New York and Paris like Fitzgerald, Taylor grew up in Illinois. Raised on the prairies of the state, he developed an interest in "things that go bump in the night" at an early age and as a young man, began developing ghost tours and writing about hauntings and crime in Chicago and Central Illinois. His writings have now taken him all over the country and into some of the most far-flung corners of the world.

He began his first book in 1989, which delved into the history and hauntings of his hometown of Decatur, Illinois, and in 1994, it spawned the Haunted Decatur Tour -- and eventually led to the founding of his Illinois Hauntings Tours (with tours in Alton, Chicago, Decatur, Lebanon, Springfield & Jacksonville) and the American Hauntings Tours, which travel all over the country in search of haunted places.

Along with writing about the unusual and hosting tours, Taylor has also presented on the subjects of ghosts, hauntings and crime for public and private groups. He has also appeared in scores of newspaper and magazine articles about these subjects and in hundreds of radio and television broadcasts about the supernatural. Taylor has appeared in a number of documentary films, several television series and in one feature film about the paranormal.

When not traveling to the far-flung reaches of the country in search of the unusual, Troy resides part-time in Decatur, Illinois.

See Troy's other titles (including the rest of the *Dead Men Do Tell Tales* Series) at:
WWW.WHITECHAPELPRESS.COM